Critically Capitalist

# perspectives on CONTEMPORARY KOREA

SERIES EDITOR: YOUNGJU RYU

Perspectives on Contemporary Korea is devoted to scholarship that advances the understanding of critical issues in contemporary Korean society, culture, politics, and economy. The series is sponsored by The Nam Center for Korean Studies at the University of Michigan.

# CRITICALLY CAPITALIST

*The Spirit of Asset Capitalism
in South Korea*

Bohyeong Kim

University of Michigan Press
Ann Arbor

For questions or permissions, please contact um.press.perms@umich.edu

Published in the United States of America by the
University of Michigan Press
Manufactured in the United States of America
Printed on acid-free paper

First published January 2025

A CIP catalog record for this book is available from the British Library.

Library of Congress Cataloging-in-Publication data has been applied for.

ISBN 978-0-472-07726-7 (hardcover: alk. paper)
ISBN 978-0-472-05726-9 (paper: alk. paper)
ISBN 978-0-472-90487-7 (open access ebook)

DOI: https://doi.org/10.3998/mpub.14418165

The University of Michigan Press's open access publishing program is made possible thanks to additional funding from the University of Michigan Office of the Provost and the generous support of contributing libraries.

*To my parents*

# Contents

Digital materials related to this title can be found on the Fulcrum platform via the following citable URL: https://doi.org/10.3998/mpub.14418165

# Acknowledgments

Writing this book has been an extremely long process and I feel deeply indebted to many for their patience. I am grateful to my mentors at the University of Massachusetts Amherst, including Briankle Chang, Emily West, Mari Castañeda, and Shawn Shimpach. Special thanks to Briankle and Emily, who have always had my back. I learned tremendously what it means to be a scholar from them. I am also thankful to Lisa Henderson, Anne Ciecko, Sut Jhally, Henry Geddes, and Erica Scharrer for their intellectual support. My gratitude also goes to Jesook Song, who served as my outside dissertation committee member and invited me to present my research at the Center for the Study of Korea at the University of Toronto.

I would not be where I am now without the guidance of Myungkoo Kang, whose undergraduate class at Seoul National University hooked me on cultural studies. I am deeply grateful for the confidence he has shown in me over the past two decades. Misook Baek is another mentor I met at Seoul National University. I am forever thankful for her generosity and intellectual support.

I am also grateful to the faculty mentors I met at the SSRC Korean Studies Dissertation Workshop. Eleana Kim, Kyu Hyun Kim, Theodore Jun Yoo, and Kelly Chong provided invaluable support for my project, and fellow graduate students showed a great deal of enthusiasm about it: Jinwon Kim, Susan Hwang, Sung-Sook Lim, Jaran Shin, Hyo Kyung Woo, Anikó Varga, Myungho Hyun, Jin Su Joo, Chi-Hoon Kim, Joowon Park, and Stephen Suh. I have presented my research at various institutions, and I am deeply grateful for these opportunities. The Stuart Hall Foundation invited me to present my research, and I thank Michael Rustin for his enthusiastic response to my work. The Korean Studies Research Network at the University of Iowa invited me to present my project virtually. Special thanks to Hyaeweol Choi for the invitation and thoughtful comments. The OIKOS working group at New York University's Institute for Public Knowledge invited me to present my research. I thank Alex Campolo, Lily Chumley, and Gustav Peebles for thoughtful discussions at the event. I had the great fortune of meeting Paula Chakravartty at NYU and I thank her wholeheartedly for her intellectual support. The Nam Center for Korean Studies at the University of Michigan provided travel grants and accommodation for the NextGen Korean Studies Conference participants. Special thanks to Michael Robinson for commenting on my paper. I also express my sincere gratitude to the institutions that provided support for my research: Seoul National University Asia Center made my fieldwork possible, and the Academy of Korean Studies Fellowship (2021) allowed me to focus on writing in Seoul.

Two of this book's chapters draw from previous publications, and I extend thanks to those who gave permission to use that material here. An earlier version of some of chapter 2 appeared in "The Ecosystem of a 'Wealth-Tech' Culture: The Birth of Networked Financial Subjects in South Korea," *Media, Culture & Society* 42, no 2 (2020): 207–24. Permission to use this material is courtesy of Sage. An earlier version of portions of chapter 3 was published as "Think Rich, Feel Hurt: The Critique of Capitalism and the Production of Affect in the Making of Financial Subjects in South Korea," *Cultural Studies* 31, no 5 (2017): 611–33. Permission to use this material is courtesy of Taylor & Francis.

At Vanderbilt University, I am grateful to my colleagues including Jeff Bennett, Neil Butt, Bonnie Dow, Claire Cisco King, John Koch, ML Sandoz, John Sloop, Paul Stob, Courtney Travers, Isaac West, and Dustin Wood. I am especially thankful to Jeff, Claire, Sloop, and Isaac who read several chapters and spent all day discussing my book at a book manuscript workshop supported by the Dean's Research Studio grant. I was deeply touched by their generosity. I am grateful for the generous support my institution provides for junior faculty. Huge thanks to Jiyeon Kang and Roopali Mukherjee who traveled all the way to Nashville to discuss my manuscript. I am deeply grateful for their constructive feedback, mentorship, and encouragement. A faculty fellowship from the Robert Penn Warren Center for the Humanities allowed me to focus on writing. I am grateful to its faculty fellows who read my chapter draft and provided insightful feedback: Ashley Carse, Aimi Hamraie, Letizia Modena, Betsey Robinson, Steven Wernke, and Matthew Worsnick. Special thanks to Holly Tucker for her tremendous support. I also express my gratitude to Sarah Igo, Seok Bae Jang, Boyoung Chang, Ji You Whang, We Jung Yi, and Gerald Figal, as well as former colleagues Heeryoon Shin and Vanessa Beasley.

I owe a great deal to many academic friends, without whom this book would not have been possible. Seung Cheol Lee read my entire manuscript and offered me invaluable feedback. He also invited me to present an earlier version of chapter 5 at the "Global Korean Studies and Cultural Economy" conference in 2021. I am indebted to him for his friendship, generosity, and intellect. I also thank EuyRyung Jun, Joohee Kim, Seung Min O, and Dongjin Seo for the seminars and discussions we had about finance and affect. Several friends were generous enough to read earlier drafts and discuss them including Woori Han and Ju Oak Kim. I really appreciate their generosity and thoughtful comments. Special thanks to Ju Oak who kept me company virtually when I was often crying alone during the pandemic. I thank Hojin Song for our writing group and fun chats. I also extend my gratitude to the group of Korean Women Scholars in Media and Cultural Studies (한국 여성 미디어문화 연구자 모임) including Jungmin Kwon, Jinsook Kim, Haelim Suh, Chuyun Oh, Rachel Jong-in Chang Yoo, Hojeong Lee, Jennifer Minsoo Kang, and Kyung Sun Lee. Special thanks to Ji-Hyun Ahn for organizing and leading the group for multiple years. I am also deeply thankful to Myungji Yang for her support for my project and for her mentorship. I also thank Yisook Choi, Chang Hui Chew, Nimrod Shavit, Gwangseok Kim, Changwook Kim, Sungmin Kim, Jungyup Lee, Jung Hwan Koh, Seol Ki, Jungyoung Kim, and Alex Bilodeau.

Warm thanks to my manuscript editor, Christopher Ahn, who has always been the first person to read all chapter drafts. Beyond copyediting, he helped me sharpen my thinking and become a better writer. Chris, thank you for your patience, thoughtful comments, and strong work ethic. This book has become much better thanks to your labor. I also thank Katie LaPlant at the University of Michigan Press for showing confidence in my project. Deep gratitude goes to the two anonymous reviewers who showed strong support for my manuscript and provided incisive feedback.

Su Young Choi, Yangsook Park, Eunjin Cho, Misun Lim, and Joanne HyunJung Oh: thank you for our lasting friendship and care! I am lucky to have you all in my life and deeply grateful for the days and nights we spent together in Amherst, Seoul, and online. Misun and Su Young were long-time writing buddies and read my chapter drafts too, and I thank them for their tremendous intellectual and personal support. I also thank Minah Kim and Sunha Park for their longtime friendship and unwavering emotional support. A special shout-out to my favorite person, Jiwon Moon.

Of course, I owe a tremendous thanks to my research participants, who shared their personal stories and allowed me to blend into their worlds. I sincerely thank Bum Young and the many other participants who appear in this book under pseudonyms. She has not been part of this book, but I sincerely thank Geumsook Hwang.

I thank my sister and brother-in-law for all the pork belly and soju we shared. My dad, Myung Gil Kim, was one of the inspirations behind this project. Hyoran Lee has been the biggest cheerleader for me and for the book. Mom, you are the most incredible person I know, and I regret all the days I can't be physically with you. Every single day, my love and respect for you only grow. I dedicate this book to my parents.

# Introduction to Critical Capitalism

After the outbreak of COVID-19, South Korea witnessed extraordinary mass investing in the stock market by ordinary people. Their buying spree was in sharp contrast to the massive sell-off by foreign capital (*oegugin*) and domestic institutional investors (*gigwan*). When the two biggest players dumped shares based on fear of a recession, Korean lay investors immediately picked up those shares shed by the market giants. Many of these lay investors saw the market plunge as an opportunity to scoop up blue chip stocks at a margin that had been out of reach in the regular market dominated by the big players. Korean small investors, who had often been pitied and made the butt of jokes, seemed to be finding the momentum to overturn the status quo. During the first half of 2020, they purchased 29.4 trillion won (about US$24.9 billion)[1] worth of Korea Composite Stock Price Index (KOSPI)-listed shares as foreign investors sold shares worth 24.5 trillion won (about US$20.76 billion), while domestic institutional investors sold shares worth 2.9 trillion won (about US$2.45 billion) (Kim C 2020). At the end of 2020, KOSPI closed at a historic high of 2,873.47, more than 30 percent higher than the previous year (Kim, Kang, and Lee 2020).

This phenomenon was dubbed the "Donghak Ants Movement (동학개미 운동)." "Ants" is a tongue-in-cheek metaphor in Korea for retail investors and refers to their small capital yet tireless transactional efforts. The phrase also references a historical event of the late nineteenth century called the Donghak Peasant Revolution. Under the declining Joseon dynasty, Korean farmers suffered from growing threats of imperial intrusion, as well as from the tyranny of a corrupt ruling class. In 1894, peasants in the southeastern regions rebelled against greedy landlords and foreign invaders. It was a YouTuber who first coined the neologism Donghak Ants Movement. During his livestreaming, the lay investor and content creator declared that "the ants have begun a revolt" and presented a graph showing skyrocketing buy orders by retail investors. He pulled up an online encyclopedia page to look up the Donghak Peasant Revolution. As the cursor moved to highlight the search result, which described the revolution as an "anti-feudal, anti-foreign movement," the YouTuber excitedly pointed to the parallels. "It fits well, right? The feudal force is the institutional investors. The foreign force is the foreign investors. We [aim to] push them out. Let's occupy the stock market" (Sosohagekeuge 2020).

The Donghak Ants Movement—the name immediately went viral and hit the news headlines—illustrates how popular investing was touted as a form of protest for economic justice. In harkening back to the anti-feudal and anti-foreign rebels of the nineteenth century, contemporary Koreans saw their investing as a revolutionary uprising. Investing is not just about getting rich. It is about disrupting the monopoly of wealth. Change the market, change the world. Even before the Donghak Ants Movement, many talking heads likened popular investing to an expression of discontent: It is not just about acquiring a lot of money, it's a visceral call for resistance. It is about "wage slaves" becoming liberated in a world of economic polarization. Furthermore, the Donghak Ants Movement reveals how popular investing came to be mediated by networked culture. It is *not* about minding your own business. Investing is participatory. It is about building a "community" and mobilizing fellow citizens to revolt.

This book chronicles the cultural experiences of the predecessors of the Donghak Ants: lay investors, or "asset aspirants," in South Korea during the 2010s. It follows ordinary Koreans who aspired to become rich by routinely checking stock market charts, taking investing classes, or bidding on real estate. These practices are called "asset tech" (*jaetekeu*) in South Korea, defined as "a technique or method to grow assets."[2] *Jaetekeu* (재테크) combines the Sino-Korean word *jae* (meaning finances, assets, or wealth) and the Korean-English word *tekeu* (technique). A popular term that entered the everyday lexicon after the early 2000s, asset tech refers to a range of activities Koreans carry out, beyond saving their paychecks, in order to grow their wealth.[3]

*Critically Capitalist* is about a new spirit of capitalism, which I call "critical capitalism," that arose among those who practiced asset tech. They claimed that something was fundamentally wrong in the capitalist economy. To them, becoming an asset owner was a way to liberate oneself from the rotten world of capitalism, which they saw as full of exploitative labor, emotional wounds, and destroyed communities. Building assets was a way to challenge oneself to change the world. However, it is inherently contradictory to claim to transform the world by dedicating oneself to arguably one of the most dispossessive forms of profit seeking. Profit from trading financial assets is likely to be a "zero sum game" and the accrual process is not unlike "profit upon expropriation" (Lapavitsas 2013, 156). In addition, real estate investing is directly and undoubtedly linked to the dispossession of propertyless people. How then do asset aspirants justify their dedication to this form of profit seeking?

This spirit that I call "critical capitalism" is a culture in which people criticize capitalism in ways that legitimate their engagements in it. Critical capitalism is a historically distinctive form of Boltanski and Chiapello's "spirit of capitalism," or "the ideology that justifies engagement in capitalism" (2005a, 8). Critical capitalism valorizes the capitalist economy not through a triumphant narrative of capitalist modernity, but by highlighting the harms of modern and contemporary capitalism and by suggesting asset tech as an alternative.[4] This book demonstrates that *community*, *emotion*, and *critique* are central components of critical capitalism. The world of asset tech was inundated with community activities, emotional and therapeutic practices, as well as critiques of capitalism. In critical capitalism, people think critically about capitalism and try to recuperate what it has supposedly suppressed—including emotion and community—in ways that make rent-seeking appear unavoidable and pressing. By observing South Korea's broader community of asset tech, made up of amateur stock investors, aspiring rentiers, and money coaches, I probe how critical capitalism came to justify their devotion to financial and real estate speculation.

For many ordinary Koreans, generating cash flows and realizing capital gains were not seen as a lonely journey that one could embark on by oneself. Many quickly realized that they should help each other in order to survive in a market dominated by the rich and the powerful. Like the participants in the Donghak Ants Movement, many of those interested in accumulating assets during the 2010s turned to online communities as an entry point. Café Ten in Ten exemplifies the online asset tech communities, where asset tech adherents gathered to share interests with like-minded people.[5] Created in 2001, Café Ten in Ten made its slogan "Make Ten *eok* won (approximately US$775,193)[6] in Ten Years" popular across the country in just a couple of years. Café Ten in Ten (the Café hereafter) emphasized the importance for wage workers of securing investment income, and it made itself the epicenter of a nationwide phenomenon of aspiring asset owners. During the following two decades, the Café witnessed the creation of an entire ecosystem consisting of more than 800,000 users, celebrity authors and coaches, emerging gurus, online forum spin-offs, in-person seminars, study groups, and meetups. The asset tech participants explored in this book turned to Café Ten in Ten and other online forums in search of opportunities to learn about investing, find themselves, and achieve what they called "financial freedom" (경제적 자유).

Starting with Café Ten in Ten, this book shows that ruthlessly calculative and hyper-individualistic attitudes were shunned in critical capitalism. The ethnographic stories I will tell in the following chapters present individuals on the hunt for profit margins, rent, and dividends who were simultaneously active in community building. From novices to day traders to market professionals to real estate enthusiasts, asset tech participants gathered together to share, give, and socialize. The centrality of community means that asset tech was about much more than making money; it entailed a criticism of modern capitalism that severed social ties.

Thinking *critically* about capitalism was another practice shared widely among asset aspirants who were dedicated to speculative profits. In various communities of asset tech, participants articulated deep-seated discontent with the capitalist status quo, including economic polarization, structural inequality, *chaebol*-centered development, and the unchecked power of financial institutions. Dreaming of becoming rentiers who lived off investment income,[7] many considered this project to be a way of living that offered an alternative to oppressive labor. *Critically Capitalist* demonstrates that, by developing and sharing critiques of capitalism, asset tech participants have paradoxically become active conformists and contributors to one of the most dispossessive forms of capitalism in history.

If community and critique represented a distinct mode of being and thinking under critical capitalism, a very specific mode of feeling also appeared—namely, the mode of feeling wounded. Asset seekers were encouraged to feel more expressively vulnerable and, eventually, to incorporate therapeutic self-realization into financial projects. The growing presence of emotional wounds in the field of popular investing shatters the widely held imaginary of the model investor as a cool-headed, emotionally detached individual motivated by numbers only. More importantly, claims to emotional wounds allowed one to decry capitalism, i.e., to denounce the obstacles incurred by it, and to remoralize one's speculative pursuits at the same time. In this sense, critical capitalism overlaps with what Eva Illouz (2007, 5) calls *emotional capitalism* in which "emotional and economic discourses and practices shape each other" and emotional life "follows the logic of economic relations and exchange."

Ultimately, what this book reveals is the cultural and affective backbone of contemporary capitalism that allows for its reproduction. South Korea's mass investment culture occurred with the neoliberal financialization of the economy, but this does not explain why it is so closely tied to critique, community, and emotion. While recognizing the economic reality of the intensifying wealth gap between asset owners and non-owners, I will show that much more than a growing awareness of inequality compels people to live by a logic of asset capitalism that they might not actually agree with. Paying attention to both the economic representation and the engagement of people, *Critically Capitalist* is a work of cultural studies that emphasizes the discursive, affective production of economies (Berlant 2011; Deville and Seigworth 2015; Gibson-Graham 2006; Grossberg 2010; Hayward 2012; Martin 2002; Mitchell 1998; Ruccio 2008) and cautions against economic reductionism (Hall 1996; Thompson 1971). The aspiring asset owners discussed in this book are *critically* capitalist in two senses: (1) they are *critical of* capitalism while being deeply involved in the capitalist economy; (2) their practices (i.e., critique, emotion, and community) are very *critical to* the capitalist economy. Put differently, they practice capitalism and shape capitalist culture while nonetheless looking askance at the system they participate in shaping. At the same time, despite their wide-ranging practices of criticizing modern capitalism, their thinking and actions unequivocally and decisively contribute to reproducing dispossessive capitalism, thus they are critical to the maintenance of the capitalist economy.

## The Emergence of Critical Capitalism: Discontent with Neoliberal Financialization and Development

Critical capitalism gives a name to new meanings, practices, and relationships that cannot be grouped together under such rubrics as neoliberalism or financialization. Critical capitalism both debunks the violence of the capitalist economy and perpetuates it. Critical capitalism unites asset owners and non-owners to rebuke the capitalist economy in ways that enliven it. Critical capitalism is thus an inter-class phenomenon that mobilizes people across different economic backgrounds to participate in financial and asset markets. Wage workers and precariats, who grieved over growing inequality, responded passionately to the idea of asset building as a form of resistance. At the same time, a discussion of assets, conjoined with critique, emotion, and community, was appealing to rent collectors and rent seekers, a group of people who were financially secure but morally insecure.

In order to explain why critical capitalism resonated with many Koreans across class, I find Raymond Williams (1978) insightful, particularly, as noted by Berlant (2011, 7), in Williams' "incitement to think about the present as a process of emergence." A culture changes over time, Williams emphasizes, but it also bears historically varied and variable elements at every point in the process. Understanding the dynamic interrelations between *the dominant, the residual,* and *the emergent* is key to unpacking the complexity of the present. Critical capitalism emerged during the 2010s as a new attitude, orientation, and style of thinking.[8] It cropped up in tension with both *the dominant culture of financial neoliberalism* and *the residual culture of development.* The former, which took hold after the late 1990s, is related to a market-oriented way of thinking, which gives attention to the self in stark contrast to inattention about structural inequality, and a deep-seated embrace of individual accountability (Abelmann, Park, and Kim 2009). Financial neoliberalism normalized individual investing, generated a mass investment culture, and made the lives of wage workers and precariats extremely unlivable. To some degree, critical capitalism represents the assetless class's vehement dissatisfactions with the dominant. Critical capitalism promises that they can articulate their discontent with capitalism and regain hope in it, all at the same time.

While critical capitalism is not incorporated into the dominant culture, it is neither oppositional nor alternative to it.[9] A lot of the people I met who criticized existing capitalism most fiercely were those who were benefitting from swelling asset markets. In the course of my fieldwork, I discovered that many of those who expressed anxiety about insecure employment and defined their speculative project as a survival strategy were often already set for retirement. Nonetheless, they would lament about oppression, emotional distress, and impoverished social relations. What this shows us is the haunting specter of the past—the residual culture of development—that had censured unearned incomes in favor of hard work and thrift. Centered on national economic growth, the culture of development took off in the 1960s and 1970s when the developmental state controlled finance, jobs were abundant, and personal investing was disparaged. This gave way to the new dominant culture of financial neoliberalism after the late 1990s but remained "actively residual" throughout the new millennium.[10] Due to the active residues of developmentalist culture, the normativity of investing continued to feel indeterminate and fragile. While asset owners and aspirants vigorously pursued investment income, they lived with a felt sense of stigma. Critical capitalism enabled them to speculate on assets, lift the social stigma, and become comrades of the assetless all at the same time. In what follows, I offer a brief historical account of how critical capitalism emerged in relation to both the dominant and the residual.

## The Culture of Development

During South Korea's era of industrial expansion and high growth in the 1960s to the 1980s, the developmental state strictly controlled the flow of capital and finance, operating as an allocator of financial resources. While the state carried out planning for the advancement of the capitalist economy, it tried to mold its constituents into a unified, docile body that could be mobilized for state-led projects. When the culture of development dominated, each and every individual was expected to take on an assigned position dutifully within the giant assembly line that was manufacturing economic development. As part of the national body, an ideal Korean was to be hardworking, frugal, and loyal. The state and corporations compensated many individuals with stable jobs and middle-class lives, with male workers in large conglomerates benefitting the most. During these times, lifelong employment and seniority-based promotion operated as a normative ideal, based on plentiful employment opportunities (Lee SC 2018; Yang 2018).

Crucial to the state-led developmentalist mantra was the equation of national development with a social good (Chang 2019). While the developmental state promoted "a shared history of poverty and a shared future of prosperity" (Nelson 2006, 200), personal enrichment was not at all closely linked to the common good. Historian Carter Eckert (1991, 225) describes how early Korean capitalists had to express their *dislike* of money outright while underplaying the pursuit of wealth as their motivation. Likewise, anthropologist Laura Nelson (2000) indicates that the pursuit of enrichment was widely censured during the era of high growth, even though industrialists eagerly (and excessively) sought personal profits.

The emphasis on frugality and the de-emphasis on investing persisted in public discourses through the dissociation of individual fortune and the common good. Frugal modesty operated as a public moral standard, and the envy of wealth rarely found a place in public discourses. The Park Chung Hee regime (1961–1979) put a particular emphasis on extreme frugality and considered the *restraint* of consumption crucial to economic growth. The military government wanted to maximize household savings in order to mobilize and funnel capital to large conglomerates to achieve export-oriented development. To this end, the government implemented various campaigns such as establishing a National Day of Savings to recognize prudent citizens, encouraging housewives to do home accounting, and mobilizing students to collect scraps of metal and paper (Han 2017; Nelson 2000; Yi 2015). Luxurious lifestyles and the display of wealth were publicly condemned, and ordinary Koreans were pressed to live frugally as a way to contribute to the national project of capitalist development.

In a similar vein, individual interest in assets was shunned and expressing such a desire publicly was strongly condemned. This does not mean that individual investing in assets did not exist at that time. On the contrary, investing in real estate was already popular among the emerging middle class in the 1970s and 1980s (Choi S 2021; Choo 2021; Shin and Kim 2016; Sohn 2008; Yang 2018).[11] Nevertheless, it was associated with selfishness and impropriety, and investment income was identified as unearned income (Song 2014; Yang

2019).[12] Defined as "income from investments, assets, and income transfers from others" (Seoul YMCA 1990; quoted in Nelson 2000, 118), unearned income (*bullosodeuk*, 불로소득) was blamed as the root cause of corruption among the nouveau riche, especially those who came into wealth through the sale of land. The social condemnation of unearned income continued into the early and middle years of the 1990s. One anthropologist observed that Koreans during the time linked investing activities to "scandal, greed, and wealth gained at the expense of others" (Nelson 2006, 197). Another made a similar observation that those who made money from money were seen as acquiring wealth effortlessly by engaging in speculative, avaricious, and sordid activities (Abelmann 2003).

### Financial Neoliberalism

The socioeconomic atmosphere changed drastically in the late 1990s. A new economy was about to arrive that would change how South Korean people participated in the economy. The catalyst was the Asian financial crisis (1997), or what Koreans call the "IMF crisis." Faced with a national debt crisis, the Korean government received a bailout from the International Monetary Fund (IMF) and, in return, spearheaded extensive reforms to comply with its bailout packages—to liberalize and deregulate finance, privatize the public sector, and create a flexible labor market (Jang 2011; Ji 2013). Under this radical surgery, 14 of the largest industrial conglomerates collapsed; 12 of the 32 largest banks were closed or restructured; and 1.4 million workers, about 7 percent of the workforce, lost their jobs (Fackler 2011).

This economic restructuring marked a historical shift in the employment system. Firms increasingly hired workers as nonregular employees (*bijeonggyujik*, 비정규직), replacing full-time, secure employment with insecure, underpaid, and temporary positions. Nonregular workers had to work longer hours with lower wages, insecure contracts, and virtually no benefits.[13] Jesook Song (2009) defines this post-IMF transition as South Korea's entrance into the post-Fordist economy, and Chang Kyung-Sup (2019) describes the long-term effect of the neoliberal reforms as the disenfranchisement or "de-proletarization" of the working population.

Under neoliberal financialization of the economy, Koreans found themselves being made increasingly accountable for their own financial security and well-being. Instead of hard work and a puritan lifestyle, they were now called on to become the masters of their own lives, to cultivate individual capabilities and maximize market competitivity (Cho H 2015; Kim HM 2010; Park SJ 2011; Song 2011). In other words, financial neoliberalism interpellated Koreans as *independent*, *self-sufficient* individuals, or as "self-managing subjects" who would continue to improve themselves through their own freedom and responsibility (Seo D 2009, 2011). With the shifting imaginary of the model citizen, praise was given to new ideals such as flexibility, self-activation, entrepreneurship, creativity, and risk tolerance.

It was under this new dominant culture that chasing after personal speculative profits was normalized. In the immediate wake of the IMF crisis, the sudden economic uncertainty came with an explicit approval for popular investing. The Kim Dae-jung government (1998–2003) encouraged citizens to buy shares to help the economic recovery.[14] For instance, in 1998 when a financial services firm dubbed its stock fund the "Buy Stocks, Recover the Economy" fund (경제 살리기증권갖기 펀드), President Kim Dae-jung and other high-profile public figures openly invested in it. The fund reportedly turned a profit of more than 125 percent in 1.5 years (Im 1999).[15] Kim's successor, President Roh Moo-hyun (2003–2008), likewise strongly encouraged Koreans to invest in the stock market, announcing that he himself had put 80 million won (about US$78,215) into the market (Choi M 2011, 42). In this new era, Koreans were supposed to become active financial consumers, risk calculators, and informed investors. One had to become a manager of one's own economic life by sensitizing oneself to various financial products and asset markets.

## Discontent with the Dominant and the Residual

In 2014, one of my interlocutors, a 38-year-old woman and on-again, off-again kindergarten teacher, asserted that "no one my age would *not* be interested in asset tech." Another woman, Mina (age 41), a nurse and mother of three who was taking various asset tech classes, would lie to friends and colleagues and say that she was taking humanities classes at a local library. She said to me, "it makes me look unsophisticated if I say I take an asset tech class." These testimonies capture the contradictory situation in which many Koreans found themselves during the 2010s. On the one hand, neoliberal financialization seemed to do away with the culture of development. Personal investing was not just a normalized activity, it appeared to be an *obligation* for the self-managing citizen living through the new economy. Talk of money was pervasive to the extent that observers and scholars worried that Koreans had become infatuated with monetary gains and a speculative mania ever since the IMF crisis.

On the other hand, most asset tech participants I met believed that their practice was still seen negatively by society. Many of them said that people in their social circle rarely showed any interest in asset tech and that they had to keep their interest to themselves, except when they were with like-minded asset aspirants. It seemed that many felt uneasy about the residual culture and its ongoing disapproval of unearned income. To those with a felt sense of moral repugnance, the focus of the discourses of asset tech on community and emotion—the two domains that were commonly portrayed as having been ruined by modern capitalism—was conveniently engaging.

Discontent with the dominant was much more palpable in society. It was during the last year of Lee Myung-bak's presidency that I came to Seoul for preliminary fieldwork in 2012. Lee is a CEO-turned-politician who won the 2007 presidential election by promising high growth. Even though Lee's administration failed to implement his "747" plan (a promise to achieve 7 percent in annual gross domestic product (GDP) growth, raise per capita income to $40,000, and make South Korea the seventh largest economy in the world),[16] Park Geun-hye from the same conservative party won the next presidential election in 2012. Importantly, her presidential victory did not rely on pro-growth pledges but capitalized on an "economic democratization" (경제민주화) agenda. The fact that in 2012 the right-wing party stood up for a slogan about economic democratization while South Korean citizens were experiencing intensifying economic inequality is telling. During the span of five years from 2007 to 2012, the GDP per capita increased by 13.7 percent whereas real wages grew by only 2.5 percent, indicating that the fruits of economic growth were not distributed to workers (Jang H 2014). The Park Geun-hye government (2013–2017) retreated quickly from economic democratization shortly after her inauguration (see Doucette 2015; Kim BK 2012), setting the backdrop for most of my fieldwork.

More than a decade and half into neoliberal financialization, socioeconomic inequity was inflamed, and expressions of discontent were spreading widely in the 2010s. Emblematic of popular discontent was "Hell Joseon," South Korea's new nickname that gained currency during the time. Joseon refers to a dynasty that existed between the fourteenth and the nineteenth centuries. Outraged about social and economic polarization, many Koreans perceived their country as a hellish, feudal kingdom dominated by a rigid hierarchy (Koo 2015). The Hell Joseon discourse reflected the suffering of wage workers and precariats plagued with the lost promise of the good life. Above all, the labor market had ceased to be a space for social mobility as neoliberal financialization established the *structural* conditions for producing the precariat class. Wage workers and precariats suffered from low income and overwork, not to mention job insecurity.[17] For instance, almost two-thirds of the young people who found employment in 2015 were nonregular workers (Fifield 2016). South Koreans also worked the second longest number of hours among the 34 countries of the Organisation for Economic Co-operation and Development (OECD)—behind only Mexico—in the years of 2014 and 2015 (Kim Y-N 2016;

Ock 2015).[18] Neoliberal financialization made senior poverty a serious issue as well. It became common, after the IMF crisis, for corporate workers to be pushed out in their early 50s. Once laid off, these former workers had few options and many found themselves adrift in the informal economy, left with a fraction of their previous income (Klassen 2010). A 2016 report found South Korea's income inequality to be the most hideous in Asia, with the top 10 percent earning 45 percent of the nation's total income (*Korea Herald* 2016). It is surely not a coincidence that South Korea's suicide rate was the highest of the OECD countries, with suicide as the top cause of death for those aged 10 to 39 (Kirk 2016).

Against this backdrop, the Hell Joseon discourse emerged as an expression of dissatisfaction with social immobility, miserable work, lack of social welfare, and the hereditary privileges and corruption of the rich (Koo 2015). Epitomizing the Hell Joseon discourse, a popular novel titled *Because I Hate Korea* (Jang KM 2015) shot to the top of the 2015 bestseller lists. The novel centered on a 20-something woman who emigrated to Australia because she was sick and tired of her own country. To its many constituents in the 2010s, South Korea was a place where the present life was dire and future prospects were nowhere to be found. It was a place of despair that many wished to leave behind.[19]

Substantially echoing the Hell Joseon discourse, critical capitalism resonated deeply with those who found their waged, under-waged, or non-waged life unbearable. In its acceptance of individual accountability and emphasis on investing income, critical capitalism overlapped with the dominant culture, but it acknowledged and condemned the structural inequality aggravated by that culture. Critical capitalism represented the indignation of those who felt marginalized, including those who had worked arduously to become model neoliberal citizens only to find themselves stuck in endless precarity. When popular critiques about capitalist culprits became rampant, with a focus on themes such as inequality, exploitation, and alienation, the discourse of asset tech aligned itself with such critiques, promising frustrated people that they could grieve about inequality, articulate discontent, and take action all at the same time. Many enthused over the idea of asset tech as a rejection of oppressive labor and a hopeless life. It felt liberating to share emotional wounds with other like-minded people and to march together to take over entrenched wealth.

## Conceptualizing Critical Capitalism

More than particular investment techniques or portfolios, my interlocutors shared an ethos of critical thinking, community building, and emotional suffering. Critique, community, and emotion are the modes of thinking, being, and feeling nourished by critical capitalism. Critical capitalism finds the existing capitalist system and culture unbearable and suggests that finance and real estate offer an alternative way of life. In *The New Spirit of Capitalism*, Boltanski and Chiapello (2005a) define the "spirit of capitalism" as a set of shared beliefs that justifies people's engagement in capitalism and renders such a commitment attractive. Critical capitalism is *a* distinctive spirit of capitalism that emerged in South Korea's particular historical juncture. Boltanski and Chiapello specify that the spirit of capitalism sustains forms of action and predispositions that are compatible with the capitalist order it legitimizes. Asset tech participants understood the capitalist economy critically, connected with others, and expressed their inner wounds— all in conjunction with their interest in finance and/or real estate—which makes it possible for asset capitalism to reproduce itself.

## Critiques of Capitalism

Critiques of capitalism expressed in the world of asset tech are heterogenous, incoherent, and self-contradictory. Some might regard them as fallacious, hypocritical, or senseless, but we need to take seriously the emergence of what sounds like anti-capitalism at the heart of capitalism. Echoing Hirokazu Miyazaki (2013, 7), who viewed Japanese financial traders as "cotheorists and cocritics of capitalism," I maintain that critical capitalism becomes intelligible when we pay close attention to the vernacular, critical engagements of asset aspirants and their affective and communal articulations of anti-capitalism— however ambiguous and inconsistent they might be.[20]

Some of the most striking critiques of capitalism that emerged from the community of asset tech were critiques about *oppression* and *inauthenticity*. Asset seekers heavily denounced the oppression involved in wage work, slamming the undemocratic, authoritarian, and militaristic culture of corporations. Critiques about inauthenticity were also prevalent, especially regarding the dehumanization and impoverishment of social life caused by excessive commodification (see also Banet-Weiser 2012; Streeter 2015). Asset tech practitioners did not contend that they could solve all these problems by becoming asset owners, but critiques of capitalism's oppression and inauthenticity were effective in establishing the self-directed investor as a new model of wealth.

Due to their focus on oppression and inauthenticity, asset tech's critiques might appear to be tantamount to "artistic critique" or "ethical critique." Boltanski and Chiapello (2005a, 2005b) distinguish artistic critique from social critique, and identify oppression and inauthenticity as two major subjects of the former. Meanwhile, Fraser and Jaeggi (2018) divide the existing modes of the critique of capitalism into three different strands—functionalist critique, moral critique, and ethical critique—and define the key idea of ethical critique as positing that "a life shaped by capitalism is a bad, impoverished, meaningless, or alienated life" (116). Asset tech's critiques, however, included more than artistic or ethical critique and were surprisingly wide in scope. Not only did asset tech practitioners criticize corporations, but they also lambasted other capitalist institutions, including the state and even the financial market. For example, similar to poststructuralist critiques of financial capitalism (Bjerg 2014; Haiven 2014), asset tech practitioners developed an account of how financial markets rely on affective marketing and are sustained by beliefs shared by consumers. Rehashing the idea that assetless workers can't get ahead, they also pointed out that the South Korean state achieved rapid economic growth *at the expense of ordinary people*. Departing from the conventional narrative that identifies South Korea's compressed growth as the "Miracle on the Han River"—as will be specified in chapter 3—this view of woeful development instead rings like critical scholarly accounts of the state–banks–*chaebol* nexus (Chang 2019; Kim D 2018a; Shin and Chang 2003; Song 2014). In this sense, asset tech's critiques also contain elements of what Boltanski and Chiapello label as "social critique," which takes aim at inequality, exploitation, and misery.[21]

While asset tech's critiques were unexpectedly thought-provoking and effectively communicated many serious issues underlying capitalism, it is deeply problematic that such critiques were bound up with the notion of personal freedom. Critical capitalism acknowledged that capitalist problems were rooted in economic *structures* but the attention to systematic inequity was linked not to struggles for social justice but to struggles for personal freedom, i.e., "Build assets, achieve financial freedom. That's a revolution." In a world in which reading the contemporary capitalist economy *critically* became a primary mode of financial consumption, resistance was no longer a mode of collective dissent but a mode of self-making.

I use the term "critique" capaciously to include vernacular ways of thinking, generated outside of the scholarly or activist domains, by those who eventually embraced the capitalist system and considered private property sacrosanct, and who refused to go far enough to reject the system they lived in. In so doing, this book shows that much of the so-called critique, which has frequently been seen as exceptional and exclusive to a community of progressively oriented intellectuals, has been largely incorporated into the popular discourses of asset capitalism. In this regard, I concur with those who have called for a reappraisal of critique as an intellectual intervention (Boltanski 2011; Fassin and Harcourt 2019; Felski 2015). Rita Felski positions intellectual critique as "one form of suspicious reading among others" (40) in parallel with another form of suspicious reading: popular, vernacular critique exercised outside of the academy. She writes that "it seems misleading to claim that critique differs from criticism in being 'intellectually serious'—as if the realm of everyday interaction were entirely deprived of such seriousness" (Felski 2015, 135). For Felski, as a literary scholar, this is to recognize "the text's status as coactor" (12). For me as an ethnographer, acknowledging the partial, self-contradictory claims put forth by the asset enthusiasts as "critique" is to recognize them as cocritics, and, in the words of Felski, "to reject the premise of a radical asymmetry between academic and everyday thought" (139). Luc Boltanski's emphasis on "ordinary critiques" or "the critiques formulated by people in the course of everyday life" (2011, 6) brings our attention to the ordinariness of critique. Culture is ordinary (Williams [1958] 2014) and so is critique. In this regard, *Critically Capitalist* is an invitation to communicate with intellectual strangers who do not share our approaches and assumptions (Ang 2006).

To do so, I use the term "critique" in two ways, to refer to (1) vernacular critiques—the critical statements made about the capitalist economy (in a narrower sense of critique as one of the three aspects of critical capitalism), and (2) the performances of emotion and community, which comprise "critical capitalism" along with the narrower sense of critique. By including the latter as more indirect manifestations of the reprimanding of modern capitalism, this book comes to terms with ordinary critique's contradictory but productive nature, as will be discussed below. At the same time, I will also show how the narrower sense of critique became diluted as the other aspects of critical capitalism (i.e., community and emotion) were emboldened. Critiques of capitalism often imploded, demonstrating the internal incoherence of critical capitalism.

### Entrepreneurial Communitarianism

In addition to criticizing capitalism, community building was one of the most crucial daily practices of those whom I observed. Asset tech participants built communities to share investing experience, ask for advice, and make recommendations. They also sought to organize study groups and coordinate various other activities. At the end of the day, a vast number of their practices were about sharing knowledge, collective intelligence, hanging out, and giving informational gifts. Like fans, hobbyists, political discussants, and other *networked publics*, these get-rich wannabes were also participatory, collaborative, sociable, and even generous.[22] A more provocative comparison can be made between them and *networked counterpublics*. Often seen as part of a political, progressive commons, networked counterpublics celebrate marginalized identities and engage in self-advocacy (Jackson, Bailey, and Foucault Welles 2017; Renninger 2014). I find champions of popular investing carrying out similar activities, including the exchange of mutual support, building friendships, taking up marginalized identities, and advocating for their own practices. *Critically Capitalist* therefore is not a story of how financialization and asset capitalism destroy community. Instead, it highlights how the reproduction of financial capitalism depends on community performances (Allon 2015; Deville and Seigworth 2015; Gago 2017; Joseph 2002; Komporozos-Athanasiou 2022).

The point to be stressed here about the centrality of community to lay investors is that they practiced community in a specific way that I call *entrepreneurial communitarianism*. Entrepreneurial communitarianism blends community activities with entrepreneurship. I use "entrepreneurship" broadly to include practices of the entrepreneurial self, such as self-optimization (Bröckling 2015; Seo D 2011), self-appreciation (Feher 2009),[23] and what I call self-assetization. Asset tech participants pursued enterprise not just as an opportunity for profit-seeking but as a mode of activity and as a whole way of life. Compared to passive savers, investors are more closely tied to entrepreneurial selfhood in that they take responsibility for their own financial well-being and manage themselves in accordance with the norms of the market (French and Kneale 2009; Hall 2011; Langley 2008; Martin 2002; Mulcahy 2017; van der Zwan 2014). They also follow the logic of self-optimization by monitoring their own behaviors to evaluate and subject them to continuous improvement.

In entrepreneurial communitarianism, entrepreneurial interest and community are harnessed simultaneously. On the one hand, community facilitates the various entrepreneurial activities of asset tech practitioners. Community is where novices acquire financial literacy and the norms of calculation that are necessary to their entrepreneurial projects of buying stocks or flipping homes. Community is also where the tools for financial self-optimization are created, shared, and modified. On the other hand, shared resources are not the only driving force for the dynamic community practices of asset tech participants. Many of my interlocutors joined an online financial forum with entrepreneurial aspirations in mind but turned it into a space for gift giving, hanging out, and socializing. Experienced traders were willing to teach novices without monetary compensation, and many participants took their asset tech forum as their primary space for hanging out online. Many believed that they could become affluent together and that it would be beneficial to themselves to help each other acquire assets. Taken together, entrepreneurial self-interest and sociality reinforced each other, and participants often experienced a strong sense of comradeship in the spaces created by rent seekers for personal enrichment.

Entrepreneurial communitarianism also refers, on a more complex level, to how *self-assetization* and *community building* are entangled with each other. Many asset tech practitioners wanted to turn themselves into an asset from which to generate cash flow by speaking at conferences, publishing tutorials, and holding lectures (see Lukács 2020). To do so, they chose to build convivial, non-commercial communities. In a field dominated by dubious pep talkers, self-claimed experts, and scammers, creating an authentic knowledge community became a crucial way to distinguish oneself from others. Many successful "gurus" and "experts" in asset tech were able to launch paid lectures and other forms of pedagogic products by, paradoxically, providing an affectionate and generous community that even resisted the force of commodification.[24] In entrepreneurial communitarianism, community was taken to be a path to self-assetization, and creating a convivial community of giving became indispensable to the entrepreneurial project of expanding one's assets.[25] In tandem with stocks and real estate, community became a crucial part of one's asset portfolio. In this case, communitarianism and entrepreneurialism became inseparable from each other, not just mutually supportive of each other.

Entrepreneurial communitarianism allows one to juxtapose community and the entrepreneurial self. By making self-interest compatible with communitarianism, entrepreneurial communitarianism makes economic calculation and cooperation inseparable (Davies 2012; Gago 2017). At the same time, in creating a community of sharing, giving, and socializing, asset tech comes to be about much more than making money. Importantly, entrepreneurial communitarianism has included, implicitly and explicitly, criticisms of crass self-interest and commodification. In other words, entrepreneurial communitarianism promises that one can both criticize capitalism and participate in it in communitarian ways.

### Emotional Wounds

When I say that critical capitalism is *emotional* as much as it is critical and communal, I am alluding to the widespread claims made by asset seekers about emotional wounds. Existing capitalism is bad, they feel, not just due to exploitation and individualistic isolation but because it *wounds* ordinary people. Rather than making themselves into homo economicus who dwell on mere calculative habits, asset aspirants are eager to recuperate emotion. In many studies on how affective practices are entwined with popular finance, financial consumers appear to be given the task of cultivating *positive* feelings (Binkley 2014; Maman and Rosenhek 2023; Zaloom 2016) or "an upbeat spiritual attitude" (Konings 2014, 47). In contrast, my interlocutors saw themselves as deeply violated by economic polarization, foreign capital, skyrocketing real estate, or exploitative labor. The claims to emotional wounds were not limited to those caused by the capitalist economy. In a distinctively therapeutic language, various kinds of personal pain and psychic misery (e.g., abusive parents, wrecked marriage, low self-esteem) were narrated on many social sites for asset tech. As chapter 4 will illustrate, instructions for asset tech often purposefully incorporated therapeutic practices into its pedagogy, turning seminars in asset tech into quasi-therapy sessions full of memories of suffering and confessions.

Asset tech participants actively *expressed* and *performed* emotional suffering in the various sites created to discuss finances. From investing lectures to advice literature to online financial communities, claims to emotional wounds were endemic. Given that critical capitalism is simultaneously a critique of capitalism and its legitimation, the focus on emotional wounds in the broader community of asset tech is not incidental to it. Narratives of emotional injury lend themselves to suspicions about capitalism and help the narrators justify their speculative projects. As Chouliaraki (2021) acutely notes, victimhood is an *affective act of communicating* vulnerability and it morally valorizes those who communicate it.[26] Anxious about unearned income, asset enthusiasts found themselves continuously needing to defend their desire to gain income from the possession of assets rather than hard work. Making claims to emotional wounds provided an effective shield from their imaginary judging public. As Jodi Dean (2009) puts it, a victim is always "morally correct" because who can deny the suffering of a victim? A quest for speculative benefits became morally justificatory and socially accepted if the pursuer had suffered and been wounded. The project of achieving financial freedom by accumulating wealth was now identified as a project to recover the injury caused by, among others, capitalism. Therapeutic culture rose in tandem with neoliberalism in South Korea (Joung 2010; Ryu 2012; Shim 2013)[27] but I find that its prominence in the realm of popular finance testifies to the specter of the culture of development.

Claims to emotional wounds not only provided moral valorization for asset seekers but also neutralized the critique of structural inequality they had articulated. By embracing therapeutic discourses, asset tech practitioners juxtaposed various forms of psychic pains and economic suffering—not in a way that explained their complex relationships but in a way that collapsed all manner of hardships into inner wounds treated as "democratic" ills that everyone suffered regardless of class membership. While the structural and systemic problems of existing capitalism were acknowledged, therapeutic discourses provided the vocabulary and tools with which to translate such problems into personal, emotional wounds that anyone could have. As Illouz (2007, 42) elaborates, psychic misery "has now become a feature of the identity shared by both laborers and

well-to-do people" in contemporary therapeutic discourses. In critical capitalism, the harms that corporations, the state, and global finance cause are transposed into a psychic misery, as a shared and democratized identity across class
and gender. Drawing on scripted therapeutic practices that combine narratives of
suffering and narratives of self-realization, asset tech discourse described financial self-realization as a route to repair. Emotional wounds made a perfect hinge,
linking critiques of capitalism and dedication to the financial and asset markets.

## The Social Reproduction of Asset Capitalism

As a new spirit of capitalism and as an emergent culture, critical capitalism
enables the contemporary asset economy to be sustained. As will be shown
in later chapters, the practices of critical capitalism have outcomes that are
essential to the *social reproduction* of the capitalist economy. Feminist scholars
originally used the notion of social reproduction to encompass "the activities
associated with the maintenance and reproduction of peoples' lives on a daily
and intergenerational basis" (Ferguson et al. 2016, 27–8). Some of the most
common examples include domestic housework—such as cooking, cleaning,
and caretaking—that reproduces the physical bodies of workers. Drawing on
its recent theoretical resurgence with a broader definition, in this book social
reproduction refers to "the reproduction of less tangible entities, like values,
norms, and forms of common sense" (Parish 2020, 265) that allow the economy
to be maintained. Underpinning this expansive view is that producing shared
meanings, interpretive frameworks, affective dispositions, and subjectivity is
essential to reproducing the capitalist economy—just as domestic housework is
essential to capitalist accumulation (Bhattacharya 2017; Fortunati 2007; Fraser
2016; Fraser and Jaeggi 2018; Jarrett 2014, 2016).[28]

In order for financial and asset capitalism to be sustained, it is necessary to
establish an understanding that pursuing capital gains is a legitimate way of
earning a living. Various forms of practices and transactions (e.g., speculating
on shares, hoarding or flipping homes, and amassing other forms of assets)
must also be established as socially acceptable, worthy of one's consideration,
or, at the very least, not despicable (Banner 2017; de Goede 2005; Ho 2017;
Preda 2009). Likewise, cultivating affective dispositions that lend themselves
to such practices is also an essential part of social reproduction. Critical capitalism is the very process of—and in itself a product of—forming the shared
understandings, horizons of value, and cultural habitus that are crucial to the
reproduction of the financialized asset economy.

Social reproduction theory highlights unrecognized and often unwaged
forms of work that carry out the essential task of reproducing the labor force.

The separation of social reproduction from economic production, and defining the former as irrelevant to economic value, are key to oppression and inequality. For example, housewives perform domestic work, child-rearing, and various forms of care work. Their work is essential to capitalist accumulation but their role in the production of economic value is ignored; this operates as a key mechanism of women's oppression. This perspective prompts us to ask if the practices of asset tech adherents—building communities, articulating particular forms of critique, producing shared meanings and emotional dispositions—are forms of uncompensated, reproductive labor that the contemporary economy depends on for the circulation of financial capital. Much of the work that had been provided by the financial services industry in the past, i.e., socializing citizens into the new economy,[29] has now been taken up voluntarily by ordinary people. They have cultivated and practiced a new spirit of capitalism that allows for the maintenance and sustenance of the capitalist economy. More importantly, however, while their practices are uncompensated consumer labor that serves the interests of the financial services industry, what I stress throughout the book is that the practices of critical capitalism reinforce the inequality and oppression of the assetless by creating shared understandings that privilege accumulation, and by turning a blind eye to politics and to the displacement of propertyless people.

Last, but not least, positing critical capitalism in relation to social reproduction brings out the question of gender. It is well known that conventional norms for the household economy were highly gendered during South Korea's rapid industrialization: a wife was expected to manage finances while a husband was expected to bring paychecks to her. This explains why traditional forms of rotating credit in Korea, known as *"kye"* (계), were controlled by women (Janelli and Yim 1988) and the work of real estate speculation was merged with women's domestic work (Choo 2021). Importantly, while women across class lines engaged in various methods of investment, such as lending money, *kye* participation, and real estate investing, their contribution to the family's enrichment was easily dismissed and often disparaged as harmful to society (Choi S 2021; Choo 2021; Nelson 2000; Yang 2019). In a sense, critical capitalism illustrates how this gender expectation has been dismantled to some degree as neoliberal financialization has normalized speculative activities for *both* men and women. On the other hand, critical capitalism signals abiding gender norms in capitalist culture; after all, when investing was considered the job of housewives, it was defamed ruthlessly in public moral discourses. It was not until men became openly involved in the "dirty work" of investing (Choi S 2021, 211) that the practice began to be reframed from a positive angle. Critical capitalism illustrates this complexly gendered dynamic. Critical capitalism's embrace of emotion rather than its exclusion is indicative of the shifting gender dynamic in the reproduction of the capitalist economy (see chapter 4), but the practices of community are highly gendered (see chapter 6) while the critique of capitalism articulated within the asset tech community is inattentive to gender (see chapter 3).

## Sites and Methods

*Critically Capitalist* draws on years of multi-sited, connective fieldwork. I followed the broader community of asset tech, both on and offline, for a decade: observing online communities; attending lectures and exhibitions; participating in study meetings, gatherings, and meetups; and interviewing and hanging out with those who are interested in asset tech. Whereas much work on the culture of financial capitalism has examined textual materials such as advice books, campaigns, and business papers (Davidson 2012; Greenfield and Williams 2007; Joseph 2013; Langley 2008; Lee M 2014; Martin 2002) or historical archival records (Edwards 2022), ethnographic fieldwork is suitable for understanding the cultural logic of financial capitalism *in action* (Fridman 2016). In observing how Koreans get together to develop strategies to manage money and grow wealth, I focused on their shared practices, and the narratives and meanings they created about their projects, rather than looking at investing behaviors and outcomes. The capstone of the research that informs this book is 11 months of fieldwork carried out in the greater Seoul area between 2014 and 2015, and three more periods of fieldwork conducted in the summers between 2012 and 2016.

Like many anthropologists and media studies scholars, I consider field sites as *constituted*, not as existing somewhere "out there" (boyd 2015; Burrell 2009; Lingel 2017a; Marcus 1998). Rather than discovering a preexisting field, constituting a field site requires the researcher to "follow the people" or "follow the thing" (Marcus 1998, 90–2). From the moment when asset tech was normalized, those who were interested in it turned most commonly to online communities to find out what others were saying and where to begin. They not only joined multiple online forums, but many also hopped into one conference after another and mobilized study groups. Beginning with Café Ten in Ten, I followed people who were interested in asset tech, the materials they produced and consumed (e.g., postings, books, influencers), the groups they created, and the events they attended. Three more field sites in addition to Café Ten in Ten emerged during my journey, all derived from Café Ten in Ten and loosely connected to one another: an in-person seminar on the subject of asset tech ("Ten in Ten Academy"), one of the seminar's many alumni groups, and a group of unmarried asset followers who met through Café Ten in Ten.

The Ten in Ten Academy, which will be discussed in chapters 3 and 4, was launched in 2009 by the creator of Café Ten in Ten. A former salaried employee in the consumer credit sector, Bum Young (44, M) turned himself into a self-made investor and asset tech lecturer. Participants in this for-pay program met once a week for five consecutive weeks for a lecture followed by an afterparty. By the time I embarked on my research, it had already become a lucrative self-help program that had been taken by several thousands of participants. The program included how to become rich and why asset tech is necessary for wage earners who do not have an inheritance, as well as information on financial literacy and "investment 101."

After the five-day program ended, many participants went on to form their own subgroups to continue networking. The group that I call the "Alumnigroup," which is the focus of chapter 5, was one of the countless subgroups created by Ten in Ten Academy's attendees. Made up of 18 participants (ranging in age from their 30s to their 50s) who attended the seminar in the fall of 2014, Alumnigroup met once a month to discuss financial and real estate investing, and members were connected 24/7 through an online group. Several of them also often met for drinks and casual conversation.

Another group I observed shared some distinct identities in addition to their attention to the matter of money (chapter 6). They were all unmarried 30- or 40-somethings—thus I call them "Singlesgroup." This was an interest-based, age-based, and marital status-based subgroup for those who were in search of a socially intense discussion group. Singlesgroup was created by two active regulars of Café Ten in Ten who wanted to foster a more tightly knit space for singles interested in the subject of asset tech. When they ventured into holding a face-to-face gathering, dozens of users showed up, leading to the creation of their own online group and subsequent regular study meetings. Like the Alumnigroup, Singlesgroup met once a month to discuss asset tech, maintained active online chats, and routinized various practices including team research, spontaneous gatherings, and collective leisure activities. For these urban singles, their projects of asset making were inseparable from the pursuit of intimacy.

Following the threads and connections of asset owners and aspirants, I was able to better understand the larger ecosystem they inhabited. The social worlds that asset seekers created were multi-sited and increasingly connected. For my project, multi-sitedness was more about the "connective" and "networked" aspects of sites (Hine 2015; Lingel 2017b) and less about transnationalism or a higher-level *system* manifested locally (Falzon 2009; Marcus 1998). While lay investors found an online community like Café Ten in Ten helpful, many wanted to meet face-to-face to carve out a more personable, congenial space that was socially engaging as well as informative. The field of asset tech, therefore, was rife with smaller groups, like Alumnigroup and Singlesgroup, with vibrant *offline* interactions.[30] The four field sites this book examines are part of the larger ecosystem that participants navigated through and formed provisional alliances within. The asset tech adherents I observed were the builders shaping this ecosystem, and I also consider them my research collaborators in drawing the contours of my field sites, whose scope was itself emergent (Boellstorff et al. 2012; Marcus 2009; Pink et al. 2016).

Conducting multi-sited fieldwork is not about how many sites of observation one accumulates, but about deepening one's understanding of the broader culture under study. It involves "working across multiple sociotechnical assemblages within a particular community and also looking across these communities to see shared practices" (Lingel 2017b, 15). Moving across different yet connected field sites, I was able to better understand seemingly contradictory practices of aspiring asset owners and capture the complexity of critical capitalism. Critique, emotion, and community were shared themes and practices that emerged from across my field sites to reveal a somewhat holistic picture of critical capitalism.

## Outline of Chapters

Following this introductory chapter, the book is divided into two parts. Part I cuts across different themes of critical capitalism within two field sites. Focused on the on and offline worlds of Ten in Ten, each chapter of Part I elaborates on one of the three themes introduced earlier—community, critique, and emotion. Part II highlights critical capitalism's link with social reproduction. Through the lenses of Alumnigroup and Singlesgroup, each chapter of Part II traces the ways that critical capitalism socially reproduces the asset economy.

Chapter 2 introduces Café Ten in Ten in detail, focusing on how it fixated on the culture of entrepreneurial communitarianism in various ways. The chapter begins with a description of how an ordinary salaried worker, Bum Young, created an online asset tech community that would rampantly grow over the following decades. After situating the rise of Café Ten in Ten within the expanding financial services industry and financial media, I show that the symbolic number 10 *eok* won came to represent the practice of financial self-optimization to be achieved through community. This section demonstrates how various tools of financial self-optimization were circulated, reused, and modified within the online community. The next section turns its attention to the relationship between *self-assetization* and community building. Highlighting the way that Bum Young moderated Café Ten in Ten, I illustrate how building an authentic, affective community—as opposed to commodifying it—became a crucial part of his asset portfolios. The chapter concludes by contending that Café Ten in Ten created a communitarian network of enterprising individuals that included lay experts, asset enthusiasts, and playful investors.

The next two chapters offer ethnographic accounts of Ten in Ten Academy. Chapter 3 analyzes the critiques of capitalism produced in the Ten in Ten Academy. Identifying four different themes of its critique—oppression, inauthenticity, development, and finance—I juxtapose each theme with other forms of critique articulated in different venues. The first two sections position the material of Ten in Ten Academy as a translation of the work of global financial self-help guru Robert Kiyosaki. The Academy followed Kiyosaki's approach to present the notion of financial freedom as a primary goal of asset tech. However, while Kiyosaki viewed inner dependence as freedom's biggest foe, the Academy criticized the *oppression* of corporate Korea as an obstacle to freedom. Likewise, the Academy offered a critique of *inauthenticity* that was absent in Kiyosaki's original instructions. The remainder of this chapter examines critiques of finance and national development. By juxtaposing them with academic discourses, I demonstrate how Ten in Ten Academy provided quasi-sociological critiques of development and quasi-postcolonial and quasi-poststructuralist critiques of finance. This chapter argues that a *critical* reading of capitalism as a mode of interpretation, with a focus on power, structure, and history, lends itself to defining the self-directed stock investor as a new model of the rich.

By examining various narratives of suffering made by asset tech instructors and participants, chapter 4 traces how asset tech became a site for the performance of emotional wounds. I begin by reviewing Eva Illouz's discussion of the centrality of emotional wounds in therapeutic practices and, more broadly, in emotional capitalism. My first analytical focus is on the incorporation of therapeutic practices by Ten in Ten Academy. I first show that its afterparty became a ritualized space for expressing emotional wounds. The next section provides additional examples of how the narrative of psychic injury structured the ways in which asset seekers articulated their aspirations. I close the chapter by circling back to the lectures of the Ten in Ten Academy and argue that claims to emotional wounds neutralized critiques of structural inequality.

Part II links critical capitalism to the social reproduction of the capitalist economy, illustrating how community and emotion were invigorated while critique was eroded away in the afterlives of Ten in Ten. Chapter 5 turns its attention to the way in which Alumnigroup discussed real estate, demonstrating how the group's practices of critical capitalism generated a shared meaning about foreclosure investing. The argument put forth here is that Alumnigroup socially reproduced investing subjects who treated homes as things to speculate on and flip around for rent and profit margins, while marginalizing the idea of the home as a place to live and, more importantly, rendering invisible the dispossession of propertyless people. I begin by foregrounding the historical backdrop against which the foreclosure auction emerged as one of *the dominant* strategies for asset aspirants after the IMF crisis. However, the moral dilemma foreclosure investors felt appeared *actively residual*, due to the vulnerability of tenants intensified by South Korea's unique rental system. In parallel with historical accounts, this chapter also closely reads a scene from one of Alumnigroup's study meetings. In doing so, I describe how its participants developed the art of seeing like an investor, including the intentional obfuscation of what was dominant and what was residual. By positioning their interest as one that was *oppressed by* the dominant, and by aligning their practice with a common good for the national economy, they claimed victimhood and acquired moral capital. I show how this reversal of victimhood was crucial to the social reproduction of foreclosure investors.

Chapter 6 delves into the link between critical capitalism and the social reproduction of investor subjectivity within the context of urban singles. I begin by contextualizing Singlesgroup against the backdrop of South Korea's long-held marriage normativity, showing how the pursuit of sociality and intimacy was entangled with the pursuit of assets for singles in their 30s through their 40s. The chapter unpacks how spontaneous meetups, group study, and information sharing socially reproduced a particular type of heterosexual singlehood and, simultaneously, investor subjects. The investing subject was a gendered one, since heterosexual singlehood was linked not only with mobile, flexible, and connected lifestyles but also with male financial virility. The next sections delineate the multiple ways in which social activities spurred participants toward asset tech, including financial socialization, risk management, and self-entrepreneurship. Taken together, chapters 5 and 6 demonstrate the dilution of critique in its narrow sense, in contrast to the ongoing significance of community and emotion.

The epilogue shows that the distinction between critical capitalism and financial neoliberalism has become increasingly fuzzy in the 2020s. After describing a culturally significant moment for neoliberal financialization and some troubling accounts of it, I provide a brief afterword about Ten in Ten in the post-COVID 19 context and revisit the broader movement of popular investing called the Donghak Ants Movement. In situating critical capitalism within a global context and discussing its pitfalls—the double marginalization of poor people in the labor market and in the asset market—I also reflect on recent popular investing movements such as FIRE (Financial Independence, Retire Early) and the GameStop short squeeze, as well as some scholarly discussions of them. I conclude the book by highlighting the importance of understanding critical capitalism in ordinary contexts and by arguing that critical capitalism is the cultural and affective backbone that sustains the contemporary capitalist economy. Finally, the methodological appendix provides more detail about the fieldwork and interviews with the goal of helping the readers understand the conditions of production for my ethnographic account.

# PART I

Community, Critique, and Emotion

TWO

# The Entrepreneurial Communitarianism
## of Aspiring Millionaires

It was in June 2001 when Bum Young jumped on the participatory bandwagon and created Café Ten in Ten. A 30-year-old wage worker in a credit card company, he spent most of his workday struggling with spreadsheets in a corporate cubicle. Bum Young was born in 1971 to working-class parents in a rural village and ended up as a business major in one of Seoul's top-tier colleges in the early 1990s. He was fortunate enough to secure a regular, stable position (*jeonggyujik*) in a *chaebol*-affiliate firm during the height of the IMF crisis. His passion was elsewhere though. Heavily influenced by global self-help discourses, Bum Young wanted to build assets and retire early. He took his job as a mere stepping-stone that could be leveraged to build capital for investment. Reluctant to socialize with any of his colleagues who, he thought, were buried under their meaningless jobs, he turned to online communities "out of loneliness." When he created Café Ten in Ten, Bum Young couldn't predict how wildly the community would expand and how long it would be sustained. Two decades later, he found himself as the admin of a 20-year-old online community, esteemed by its almost 800,000 users.

This chapter traces the development of Café Ten in Ten, with a focus on different ways in which it nurtured entrepreneurial communitarianism. Although the quick expansion of Café Ten in Ten was indebted to the growing financial media, it attracted users by creating a communitarian space where they pooled resources to march toward each individual's financial self-optimization. Bum Young and other participants provided various tools to help each other establish financial goals, log expenditures, make plans for saving and investing, and evaluate their own finances. In addition, looking at the ways Bum Young moderated Café Ten in Ten reveals how building an authentic, affective community—as opposed to commodifying it—became a crucial part of his asset portfolios in tandem with stocks and real estate. What I witnessed here was a communitarian way of assetizing the self and investing in one's human capital. In this way, Café Ten in Ten created communitarian networks of individuals who were enterprising to varying degrees, including lay experts, asset enthusiasts, and playful investors.

## Getting Ready to Be a Millionaire with the Financial Services Industry and the Financial Media

"If you have ten *eok* won, you can live an affluent and more valuable life from interest income only, without labor. It is a symbol of economic independence," Bum Young wrote in 2001 in his first posting to the online forum he had just set up. He considered ten *eok* won (about US$775,193 in 2001; see note 6 of chapter 1) as the minimum amount of money necessary to liberate ordinary people from economic insecurity, particularly those without an inheritance. Not only was this sum emblematic of wealth, but Bum Young also took it as an enabler of freedom. Making ten *eok* won was the one and only path, he asserted, through which a person could find and enjoy personal freedom.

Why was it ten *eok* won though? How did he come up with this specific number as a symbol of freedom?[1] "It's simple. It's the Excel spreadsheet," he explained to me. Bum Young wanted to retire in ten years. To do so, he wanted to secure a monthly investing income of ten million won (about US$77,519 in 2001). He estimated that having assets of ten *eok* won would generate the monthly income needed after leaving the labor market.[2] On a spreadsheet, he entered his monthly household income and expenses, and calculated how much his family could make each year by factoring in estimated salary raises for himself and his wife, average interest, and expected investment returns.[3] All the calculations were predicated on the idea that his family would live far below their means by saving 70 percent of the family income and that his stock investing would continue to bring positive returns. According to the spreadsheet, his assets were expected to rocket to ten *eok* won by 2011.[4]

The numerical representation of affluence, however, was more likely an instance of how the global financial services industry had influenced South Korea's mass investment culture. The financial industry of the global superpowers during the 1990s was increasingly investing in the new market of private wealth management. Beginning in 1996, Merrill Lynch—in collaboration with a multinational consulting firm—began publishing an annual *World Wealth Report* in which "high-net-worth-individuals" (HNWIs) were defined as those who had at least US$1 million in assets (see Santos 2021). Each year, the report estimated the number of HNWIs by country. When it began to include information on South Korea for the first time in 2002, Korean financial services firms—which were likewise trying to expand their private banking services—adopted the same numerical standard as a measure of what it means to be rich in Korea (see Jeon, Gwon, and Kim 2003; Lee S 2002). US$1 million, which was equal to about 12.5 *eok* won in 2002, was translated roughly into "ten *eok* won." Using the language of prestige and exclusivity, Korean financial services firms targeted those who had ten *eok* won or more in their bank accounts to promote their new services. At the same time, the financial media reproduced the rich-equals-ten-*eok*-won discourse, recklessly quoting the *World Wealth Report* (Yu 2002). Making ten *eok* won in ten years was clearly beyond the reach of most wage workers, let alone the increasing number of precariats, no matter how financially intelligent they were. One report estimated that it would take 19 years for a median-income earner to make ten *eok* won, even if she were to invest *all* of her paychecks at an annual compound interest rate of 5 percent (Cha 2002).

Nevertheless, the number of Café Ten in Ten users ballooned and a diverse group of people joined—wage earners, small investors, penny-pinchers, students, housewives, day traders, professional dealers, real estate brokers, and so on. Café Ten in Ten became a community of 52,000 in just two years and 200,000 by the end of 2003. It was a hub for a broader, nationwide fad at the time, which the media dubbed the "ten *eok* won mania (*yeolpung*)." During 2003 and 2004, in particular, Koreans seemed to be obsessed with the idea of becoming millionaires. The number of publications dedicated to the topic of ten *eok* won exploded, with titles such as *My Dream, Making Ten Eok Won* (나의 꿈 10억 만들기, Daejung Kim 2003)—one of the bestselling books of the year—and *Just Live Cheap: Techniques for Salarymen in Their Twenties and Thirties to Make Ten Eok Won* (그냥 구질구질하게 살아라: 2030 샐러리맨의 10억 모으기, Yeongcheol Shim 2003). A TV network (SBS) created a prime-time series called *Miss Kim's Million Dollar Quest* (its original Korean title was *Miss Kim's Saga of Making Ten Eok Won*; 파란만장 미스김 10억 만들기). The Café served as the switchboard for this nationwide phenomenon, and its slogan "ten in ten (텐인텐)" was selected as one of "the new words of the year" in 2004 by the National Institute of the Korean Language. Fast forward a decade and a half, Café Ten in Ten had more than 822,000 users and over 302 million hits, 2.4 million posts, and 10.4 million comments, as well as more than 100,000 daily visitors in 2016.

One important context that enabled Café Ten in Ten to rapidly create buzz was the evolution of the financial media. The financial media began to proliferate in the early 2000s in the forms of literature, television programs, cable channels, and online websites. Whereas sales of the top ten general newspapers dropped by 22.1 percent between 1997 and 2008, sales of the top four financial papers rose by 62.7 percent (Park D 2014, 101). The growing financial media companies went multimedia, launching 24/7 cable channels, while the owner of South Korea's oldest business paper *Maeil Business Newspaper* (매일경제) launched a cable channel in 1995, and another prominent financial paper, *The Korea Economic Daily* (한국경제), began its own cable TV channel in 2000. As a result, television viewers came to be saturated with glowing stock tickers, constantly moving images representing the market, and video clips featuring investment talking heads 24/7 (see Clark, Thrift, and Tickell 2004). These emerging financial media turned to online forums to seek news stories and expand their audience bases. Filled with personal narratives and threshold knowledge, not to mention its catchy slogan, the story of Café Ten in Ten was a perfect scoop for financial reporters and media producers who did not just depict the phenomenon of lay investors gathering online, but actively capitalized on and collaborated with Café Ten in Ten in various ways. When the ten *eok* won slogan spread with fervor in 2003, a number of casting calls were posted in the Café for ordinary people willing to appear on talk shows or reality TV. In another instance, *Maeil Business Newspaper* embarked on a "Get Rich Campaign (부자되기 캠페인)" in 2004 in collaboration with Café Ten in Ten (Maeil Business Newspaper 2004). As part of this campaign, the financial media company invited users of Café Ten in Ten to its investing conference, which in turn became a feature story for the paper.[5] The ample media attention that Café Ten in Ten grabbed led to a further surge in its membership. When Bum Young appeared on television in the summer of 2003, for example, Café Ten in Ten saw more than 10,000 new users in just two days (Oh 2003).

## Optimizing the Financial Self through Community

It is misleading to assume that participants were delusional believers in get-rich-quick scams. Café Ten in Ten might have created buzz around the idea of making a million dollars, but not everyone took this as their goal. Whereas some financial self-help communities had a profound faith in specific accumulation strategies—such as Robert Kiyosaki's followers who participated in multilevel marketing (Fridman 2016) or the FIRE (Financial Independence, Retire Early) community who invested in index funds (Taylor and Davies

2021)—users of Café Ten in Ten were disparate in their asset-tech strategies and did not have a shared belief in one particular technique. Some advocated for stock investing. Others believed ordinary people could never beat the market but could find hope in real estate.[6] Bum Young retained a laissez-faire way of moderating, letting people discuss what they would like. He created a couple dozen topical discussion boards and assigned funds, stocks, real estate, and many other subjects to their own discussion boards. Café Ten in Ten ended up with 36 discussion boards in total. Each one operated as a sort of independent online forum. Due to the sheer number of discussion boards, users tended to participate in a couple of their favorites while being oblivious to what was going on in other parts of Café Ten in Ten.

In the absence of a shared investing strategy, Bum Young promoted frugality, financial planning, the acquisition of financial literacy, and self-directed investing. More specifically, he put the greatest emphasis on *financial self-optimization*. A bookworm who read across a wide range of genres, Bum Young was influenced heavily by self-management literature, with American self-help books and New Age spirituality impacting him most strongly during his time in college.[7] Underpinning his practices was the tenet commonly shared in such literature: the idea that working on the self and conducting one's life as a series of projects is key to individual success in a rapidly changing world. During the infancy of the Café, he offered various tools for optimizing one's financial behavior and lifestyle. Focusing on refashioning the self in a financially desirable way, the tools he provided included a personal account book, a "Ten Year Financial Plan," and a "Life Master Plan." These were all tools for self-monitoring and self-examination that led practitioners to hatch plans, set targets, and seize control of their own activities. For example, Bum Young firmly upheld the utility of a personal account book (*gagyebu*, 가계부) and demonstrated how to create one's own. By means of the account book, he suggested that participants keep records of income and expenses, track purchases and payments, and create a personal financial profile. Like the broader discourse of self-optimization that emphasized the need to make the self "knowable, calculable, evaluable, and correctable" (Seo D 2011, 84), the account book was a tool that made one's financial status legible, changes in assets calculable, and spending habits evaluable.

Bum Young also created a spreadsheet template for what he called a "Ten Year Financial Plan." He provided his own example and added that he always carried his Ten Year Financial Plan in his wallet, like Benjamin Franklin who always carried with him a little book for moral optimization (see Schaupp 2016, 251). This long-term plan was complemented by annual financial plans, which he evaluated and reflected upon every year—all of which were shared with other participants so that they could replicate such planning. He reflected at the end of 2001 that his finances did not reach the goal for that year. The next year, he confessed again that he fell short of his desired numbers due to an inaccurate prediction about the stock market. Apart from accomplishing such goals, however, it seemed that the self-optimizing practices of planning, sharing, and evaluating took on a greater significance. Although his financial goals had not been realized in those years, Bum Young claimed that his assets still swelled by almost 65 million won (about US$50,387) because of savings, the increased value of his condo, and gains from stocks. Through his focus on planning, accurate bookkeeping, and constant reflection, Bum Young continued to stress that the key to getting rich is not just the masterful art of investing, but self-optimization.[8] Providing templates and reserving a discussion board for each tool, he encouraged other users to do the same exercises.

Over time, ten *eok* won came to represent a set of specific practices: quantifying a personal goal, breaking it down into measurable numbers and, more broadly, making oneself accountable to one's financial future. To the users of Café Ten in Ten, these self-optimizing, entrepreneurial practices were to be acquired through community. Participants without knowledge of complex mathematical formulas were able to use the templates to make concrete yearly plans for the span of a decade, with inflation and interest rates reflected. Importantly, the tools and templates Bum Young provided continued to be reproduced, modified, and updated by other users as they worked to revise their own practices and exchange feedback about each other's practices. Skillful users created a number of templates for different tools, making them available for free sharing. Other participants felt grateful as they filled in the ready-made accounting tables. Through these processes, many learned how to practice community as well as how to financially optimize the self, all at the same time. In this respect, Café Ten in Ten exemplified what participatory culture looked like under asset capitalism. It functioned as a knowledge community where participants could learn financial self-optimization in a generous, supportive environment.

## Self-Assetization through Community Building

Bum Young described himself as "a community (*keomyuniti*) CEO" (Han 2004). Little can illustrate better the conjunction of entrepreneurialism and communitarianism than the pairing of these two words. Establishing community spirit as the most important norm of Café Ten in Ten signified Bum Young's belief that communal, humanist practices, and affective relationships were as important as making money. To him, seeing himself as a corporate executive was not at odds with putting enormous time and energy into this free-to-use online community. He had a day job (until he retired at the end of 2008) but spent every single night, hours upon hours, moderating the Café that was growing at an exponential rate. His practice might be seen as "free labor" (Andrejevic 2012; Terranova 2000) that made the platform owner Daum massively rich, but I want to highlight that it was equally essential to Bum Young's assetization of himself (see Jarrett 2022). An authentic, convivial community that was far from the market exchanges became a crucial component of his asset portfolio, in addition to conventional forms of assets such as stocks and real estate. Bum Young contributed his free labor to developing a space that offered numerous users a vibrant community experience. He also largely rejected the force of commodification, judging that it would erode the authenticity of Café Ten in Ten. Like a corporate executive concerned more about "capital growth or appreciation rather than income, stock value rather than commercial profit" (Feher 2009, 27), to Bum Young commodification was something that would likely *depreciate* Café Ten in Ten and, by extension, himself. Therefore, communitarian management of Café Ten in Ten often involved resisting immediate commercial profits to avoid its devaluation. In doing so, Bum Young came to garner media attention and expertise, ultimately making himself an asset from which to generate income. His trajectory inspired many others to pursue assets and self-assetization simultaneously through community practices, as will be shown in the next section. Café Ten in Ten enriched the culture of entrepreneurial communitarianism by demonstrating an innovative way to work out the relationship between community building and asset building.

It is hard to deny that Bum Young put considerable effort into making Café Ten in Ten a convivial space, not a space of crass self-interest. One instance demonstrating his concern for community was the makeup of various discussion boards. To be specific, from the outset he included a socially oriented board in the list of discussion boards,[9] which was not focused on asset tech but on life (thus I use "social board" and "life forum" interchangeably). The board had no central topic, and participants shared anything related to everyday life and interacted with others in dynamic ways. They schmoozed about work, family, marriage, celebrity, and politics. It was a space for venting, confessing, gossiping, and goofing around, although money talk was a big part of these conversations. This life forum became one of the most popular and "sticky" (Ahmed 2004; Jenkins, Ford, and Green 2013) spaces within Café Ten in Ten. Many of the users I met in the course of fieldwork said that they tended to go straight to the life forum whenever they logged into Café Ten in Ten and enjoyed the random posts that came up daily.

Sharing everyday bits and pieces of their lives helped participants develop an emotional attachment to Café Ten in Ten and a shared sense of community. It was not uncommon to see users describe Café Ten in Ten as their "family and friends." For example, a user nicknamed 1,500sqft, reflecting on a decade of experience using the Café, wrote: "I'm a hillbilly with no relatives or hometown friends in the greater Seoul area. People at Café Ten in Ten, especially this life board, became friends, sisters, and parents to me. I'm celebrating a ten-year anniversary of my Ten in Ten membership and confessing my love of Ten in Ten" (February 3, 2015). In one of the many replies to this post, ShakeIt wrote:

> I also sometimes read my past postings here, which feels like browsing my past. [...] Looking back, I have grown up with Ten in Ten since my late twenties (I was maybe 27 or 29 when I joined here). I am now 40. So our friendship is lasting at least ten years. It's pretty special like my offline friends, or like my parents and childhood home (*chinjeong*, 친정).

To many participants, Café Ten in Ten was more than a knowledge community for financial self-optimization. Within the social forum, they turned a space created for aspiring millionaires into a community of mutual understanding, emotional uplift, and social bonding.

In addition to the purposeful composition of its discussion boards, Café Ten in Ten eschewed the force of commodification in order to articulate a community principle. Bum Young was highly concerned about keeping Café Ten in Ten non-commercial. Whereas participants shared chitchat and discussed a variety of accumulation strategies without heavy moderation, postings by commercial stakeholders were closely monitored. Those who were tied to financial services (e.g., insurance salespeople, realtors, financial consultants, self-promoting money bloggers) were allowed to use the Café like any other users, but any promotion of their own financial products or services was strictly banned, with the exception of one designated board. Bum Young and other admins tenaciously tracked and identified anyone trying to mobilize users for her or his own profit. Committed to keeping the Café as an authentic, non-commercial community, many regular users also participated in boundary policing and reported suspicious solicitations. Commercial users were quickly removed if they were confirmed to have tried in any possible way to lure other users into their services or products.

Crucially, Bum Young applied the non-commodification rule to his own practice. Most notable was his refusal to accept advertising, which could have brought him substantial revenues. Over the past two decades, countless commercial pitches have come his way from financial services firms, among many others, wanting to advertise to the users of Café Ten in Ten. There were even takeover bids made by those who wanted to acquire Café Ten in Ten. "If I had accepted all these commercial suggestions," Bum Young said in a media interview, "I would have earned tens of millions of dollars" (Jang HJ 2020). His numbers might be overblown here, but it is nonetheless remarkable that his course of action was in stark contrast to the widespread practice of commodification that occurred in other popular online communities.

To contextualize this, it is worth mentioning that developing an online community became a lucrative enterprise in South Korea. Due to the readily available community platforms provided by the large portals since the early 2000s, Korean Internet users have been able to create online communities in just a few minutes. It was the portal site Daum that made the term "café" (*kape*, 카페) South Korea's generic term for an online community. Beginning with an email service, Daum offered an array of services including blogs, a search engine, news curation, e-commerce, and so on. It launched an online community service, which it called "Café," in 1999, leaving the platform entirely free to use. The latecomer Naver followed suit by developing its own online community service in 2003 and calling it "Café" as well. Since then, these Café platforms have provided a home for many hobbyists, alumni groups, fans, gamers, political discussants, and others who flock online. For 20 years between 1999 and 2019, 8.8 million online cafés were created within Daum alone (Kim JM 2019).

As digital culture bloomed, many of those who incubated a popular online café came up with different ways to profit from the community they developed. Placing banner ads was at the top of the list. The emergence of popular online cafés became a powerful draw to advertisers and various sponsors who sought the cafés for marketing schemes. To moderators of cafés, advertising was particularly lucrative because the portal sites providing the Café platforms neither pulled revenues from their Café services nor interfered in individual cafés. Once a café admin decided to place paid advertising, they reaped all the profits without having to pay commissions to Daum or Naver. The same went for other sponsored activities, such as paid postings or brokering group buying (*gongdong gumae*, 공동 구매). One café admin who managed a community of 4,000 users revealed that they pulled in about US$52,000 every year through advertising (Jo Y 2016). A larger online café of more than 100,000 users, the same source estimated, could bring its admin 1 *eok* won (US$86,240) or more every year from paid advertising.

Bum Young took a different path. Running banner ads was off the table and so were other commercial proposals. It was precisely this no-ads policy that helped Bum Young assetize himself. While he might have relinquished numerous money-making chances for the sake of community, the community principle enabled Café Ten in Ten to gain a reputation as authentic and communitarian, which in turn was crucial for Bum Young in increasing his asset value. Bum Young himself identified the rejection of commodification as key to Café Ten in Ten's sustained success. Users likewise spoke highly of the no-ads policy. Many people I met were happy to describe Café Ten in Ten as "one of a kind." They were grateful for it being "innocent," "pure," and "full of affection." Among such people was Sunwoo (49, M), a retired fund manager who was exploring a number of online asset-tech communities. He described Café Ten in Ten as the least commodified among its tens of thousands of counterparts. According to him, Café Ten in Ten carried forward "a sense of fellowship (*dongnyu uisik*; 동류 의식)" and boosted morale for participants by asserting that "We can really become rich together. Let's do it together." The rejection of paid advertising, Sunwoo thought, was what made Café Ten in Ten stand out among many similar others. Sunwoo spoke highly of Bum Young's faith in communitarianism.

By virtue of the sustained success of Café Ten in Ten, Bum Young garnered media attention and expertise. He was frequently interviewed by the mainstream media, invited to speak at conferences, and cast in a reality TV show as a money coach. While I was in Seoul in 2014–2015, for instance, he spoke multiple times at a series of conferences called the "Wealth Tour," organized by a financial media firm, on such topics as "How a Wage Earner Can Become a Financial Freeman" and "Start with Stocks and Invest in Real Estate Later." Bum Young began to appear in the media in the early 2000s, and the focus of his media representations changed over time—from his individual practice of extreme frugality and financial planning to his expertise. A reality TV show called *Homo Economicus* (EBS 2018–2019) on a public network exemplifies the latter. Bum Young appeared as one of its several coaches who mentored young, money-tight participants. Describing the group of coaches as the nation's "top economic *experts* and finest asset tech mentors," the program dubbed Bum Young "a living legend who made a million dollars in ten years" and "a straightforward talking head in asset tech" who "shared his know-how with eight hundred thousand people" (Kim B 2022). It was the number of Café Ten in Ten users and Bum Young's supposed generosity here that credentialed his expertise.

He reaped more than expertise and media attention with his community-centered entrepreneurialism. Bum Young launched a fee-based seminar, which he called "Ten in Ten Academy." The five-day program began in 2009 after Bum Young declared that he had accomplished financial freedom and quit his salaried job. Ten in Ten Academy quickly grew as a lucrative business, with almost every session completely filled. Its tuition was affordable (120,000 won or about US$113 in 2014),[10] compared to overpriced workshops found in abundance in the shadowy field of asset tech instructions. The running of its offline program was largely independent from Café Ten in Ten, although one discussion board in the Café was used as a primary channel to promote the Academy. Because of the limited exposure, it was possible for one to *not* know at all about Bum Young's offline program while using the online space of Café Ten in Ten. Those who were aware of, and willing to try, the fee-based seminar did not see it as excessive commodification, given Bum Young's long-term dedication to the community they loved.

In a 2018 media interview, Bum Young revealed that he was earning five to six million won (about US$4,500–5,400) each month from the Ten in Ten Academy only. When asked about his asset portfolio, he described the revenue he pulled from the program as labor income, juxtaposing it with three other income pipelines of pension, real estate, and stocks (Kang A 2018). Although he gained more from real estate and stocks (ten million won or about US$9,090 from monthly rental income and more from stock holdings), he emphasized that creating a portfolio that generates regular cash flow is as important as accumulating assets. To this end, he explained, it is helpful to have regular income. "For me," he said, "that is teaching."

By following Bum Young's trajectory, we learn how communitarianism was packaged into one's asset portfolio. If placing paid advertising is a way of acquiring monetary gain through market exchange, choosing communitarian aspirations over immediate commercial profits was, to Bum Young, the way to "constantly value or appreciate" (Feher 2009, 27) himself. By dedicating himself to the free labor of cultivating community, and by rejecting the force of commodification, Bum Young grew his own asset value and eventually came to generate cash flow from himself without hurting the authenticity of his persona.[11] Café Ten in Ten demonstrates how one can become the entrepreneur of oneself through community—a pivotal way in which the Café cultivated the culture of entrepreneurial communitarianism.

## Communitarian Networks of Enterprising Individuals: Lay Experts, Enthusiasts, and Playful Investors

Moving from the individual moderator to other users, I see a similar amalgam of communitarianism and entrepreneurship thriving in the widespread practices of information giving and online socializing. The argument I am developing here is that Café Ten in Ten created communitarian networks of entrepreneurial selves, producing different types of lay investors simultaneously.

Similar to Bum Young, those who gifted valuable information to other users emerged as layperson-turned-experts ("lay experts"), followed by enthusiastic asset seekers ("enthusiasts") who were "geeking out" (Ito et al. 2010) in real estate and/or stocks. If lay experts leveraged fame and status to become another Bum Young, enthusiasts paid close attention to these lay experts, perusing their tips and advice books, attending lectures, and investing arduously. Unlike enthusiasts, "playful investors" were akin to "socializers"[12] and were more deeply into the on and offline mingling experience offered by Café Ten in Ten than into developing investing skills. By hanging out in a community saturated with asset tech information, however, many socializers found themselves in a position conducive to a transition into enthusiasts. By building a communitarian network for these individuals who were enterprising to varying degrees, Café Ten in Ten created a community of sharing, giving, and socializing, making asset tech about much more than making money.

### Emerging as Lay Experts through Gifting Calculative Information

Not unlike Bum Young, numerous ordinary users emerged as "experts" by providing informational gifts. Many of them were alleged self-made investors without professional ties to the financial services industry. They continued to generously provide what other users found helpful and inspirational. What they offered took various forms. Most of all, they provided all manner of calculative tools and accounting logics (such as formulas, models, statements, techniques, and experiments) that other users could apply to their own practices. Scholars in social studies of finance indicate that such calculative tools turn human beings into self-interested economic actors (Callon 2007; Chen 2013; Miyazaki 2013; Wosnitzer 2014). In the words of Fridman (2016), therefore, popular financial "gurus"—mostly positioned outside of the academic field of economics—are "economists in their own way" (11). They operate as "a vehicle by which economic concepts, language, and techniques reach mass audiences unlikely to have direct contact with more legitimate forms of economic expertise" (12).[13]

Rather than the impacts that popular experts and gurus have on others, my emphasis here lies on the ways in which certain information givers are made into "experts"[14] while helping ordinary users become calculative, skilled, and self-directed investors. It was through the *communitarian* practice of giving information—which involved the free labor of reflecting upon one's own experience, processing information, and presenting that information in digestible forms—that these information givers came to garner expertise (see Hartelius 2020). As they gained popularity and followers, many information givers began to be treated like *credentialed experts*: invited to publish advice books, hold lectures, and make comments in the media. In this regard, while they described their practice of information sharing as "giving back" to the community, it was also a process of investing in themselves so that they could earn fame and status, and eventually, increase their own asset value. The way they made themselves into business enterprises followed the path Bum Young had carved out: creating an online community like Café Ten in Ten, boosting community spirit, and developing for-pay instructional programs.

We can look at Expert Seo (a pseudonym) to understand how lay experts emerged through information giving and became important nodes in the entrepreneurially communitarian networks of enthusiasts and socializers. Expert Seo's prime focus was on real estate, flipping foreclosures in particular. A few years after he joined Café Ten in Ten, he began to share firsthand accounts of his investing experience. He first told a story of how he made a fortune through real estate, using the narrative form of what Chris Martin (2018) calls "the hero's journey" as a template for property investment promoters: "Starting from the mundane world of work and deprivation, the hero—the property investor—overcomes (with the help of their property investment mentor) obstacles internal and external, to achieve self-realization and 'financial freedom' in property ownership" (1067). Expert Seo's recounting of his speculative quests likewise began with a mediocre college degree, parents unable to support his study abroad, and landing his first job at a night club. He allegedly saved up about 1.2 *eok* won (approximately US$104,895 as of 2004) over the span of four years by living extremely frugally, "resisting even a can of soda that costs a couple dimes," and investing most of his paychecks in funds.

The next stage involved extensive self-learning. He "didn't know how to research and where to begin" and thus "joined every asset tech café and looked up gurus and read their writings." "Probably," he continued, "I read Café Ten in Ten most zealously at this point." After deciding to focus on foreclosures as an investing item, he claimed, he read 25 books on the subject, each one three times. He also went on field trips to see actual homes and neighborhoods, by means of which, he explained, he developed a real estate investor's sensibility. Networking was an essential part of such field trips. He vividly described how he formed a rapport with realtors in each town he visited. In 2005, the word spread that one of Seoul's districts would soon be redeveloped by the city government, which led real estate investors to busily speculate on its whereabouts.[15] It was at this point that Expert Seo's networking paid off. One of his contacts tipped him off about a condo in the neighborhood that was a strong candidate for the upcoming redevelopment plan. He purchased the condo, judging that it would be a good deal regardless of the government's plan. This investment ended up being massively lucrative, turning a profit of almost 2 *eok* won (US$195,253). This narrative form of the hero's journey, as Martin (2018, 1067) points out, was "an attractive, legible narrative" that allowed the storyteller to connect with readers.

Expert Seo's post received overwhelming praise from other users. Café Ten in Ten confers the rank of "Expert" or "Leader" to active advice givers who are supported by other users, and Expert Seo quickly acquired the "Expert" status and began to write regularly about how to buy real estate at court auctions.

In comparison to lifestyle gurus who rely merely on narratives of self-transformation, anecdotal evidence, or folklore testimonies (Baker and Rojek 2020), Expert Seo offered specialist information in the forms of practical tips from A to Z about his topic—such as how to look up foreclosed homes, take out loans for leveraged investing, find good tenants, and calculate return on investment—all based on his own experience and lay language. Through a series of postings, he offered investing vocabulary and norms of calculation that helped others establish the knowledge necessary for participating in the property market. For instance, his post titled "Buying a condo with 2.62 million won (US$2,558)"[16] (March 13, 2008; the transaction was made in 2005) demonstrated a leverage effect—which was still new to many Koreans in the 2000s because of the tight restriction of credit and the absence of mortgage loans before the IMF crisis (see chapter 5)—by taking account of how average people with small capital could buy real estate by taking out loans. After narrating another long story from his investing journey, Expert Seo added a detailed investing statement that included how much the property cost, how he made payments, how much he pulled in every month by renting out the property, and how much he was expecting to turn by flipping it:

## Cost

Price: 28.77 million won (US$28,095)
Taxes: 1.2 million won (US$1,171)
Bills: 150,000 won (US$146)
Cleaning: 200,000 won (US$195)
Other costs: 300,000 won (US$292)
Total: 30.62 million won (US$29,902)

## Payment Methods

Loan: 18 million won (US$17,578) (with monthly interest of 100,000 won or US$97 to pay)

A security deposit from a new tenant: 10 million won (US$9,765)[17]
Out-of-pocket: 2.62 million won (US$2,558)

## Monthly Earnings

Rent: 400,000 won (US$390)
(-) Loan interest: 100,000 won (US$97)
Total (rent minus loan interest): 300,000 won (US$292)

I am still holding this property. By investing 2.62 million won (US$2,558), I earned 300,000 won (US$292) every month. It took less than a year to recover my out-of-pocket expenses. Fortunately, the neighborhood was later selected for the New Town development plan so the condo's market price is currently 120 million won (US$117,187) and I will sell it this year because the transfer tax is exempted when you hold it for three years or more.

## Returns

Rent: 8.7 million won (US$7,830), i.e., 300,000 won (US$292)
  multiplied by 29 months
Profit margin: 91.23 million won (US$ 89,092), i.e., 120 million won
  (US$117,187) minus 28.77 million won (US$28,095)
Total: 99.93 million won (US$97,587)

His investing statement taught readers a number of norms of calculation: return is calculated by dividing the sum of earnings by one's out-of-pocket expenses, not by the sales price; buying a foreclosure can bring the investor two different revenue sources including monthly cash flow and profit margin. Readers took away that one's out-of-pocket expenses can be surprisingly low when combining the cost of a leveraged purchase and the earnings from renting it out. Asserting that one has to establish his or her own rules, Expert Seo slammed both academic theories and media pundits, noting that "expert theories and prospects never help your investment in practice." While rejecting traditional forms of expertise explicitly, he made himself an expert by providing informational gifts. As he gained popularity, he came to publish several advice books, create his own online café (which has attracted more than 400,000 users), launch for-pay seminars, and train other would-be investors. In observing the popularity of health and wellness lay experts online, Baker and Rojek (2020) note that "deference to expertise has been replaced by deference to the celebrity lifestyle guru." In contrast, Expert Seo and other lay experts who emerged from Café Ten in Ten were highly respected for their experience-based expertise, not just their celebrity.

## Enthusiasts Who Follow Lay Experts

In 2015, I attended a one-day seminar that was promoted in the online café created by Expert Seo. While he was holding multi-day investing lectures himself on a regular basis, his online café also promoted investing classes taught by a pool of other instructors, most of whom were up-and-coming lay experts. The seminar I attended was titled "Investing secrets of a 35-year-old investor who has bought 200 apartments." In the beginning, the lecturer recognized some faces in the front row. "You guys look familiar," he said. "You all must have good computer skills." The lecturer was making a joke about how competitive it was to enroll for his seminar. Indeed, I had to act sharply to get in this seminar. Having marked in my calendar its enrollment starting date and time, I made myself ready at a laptop right before the clock hit the starting time. I clicked my mouse as quickly as possible, just like K-pop fans do when they buy popular concert tickets. The seminar was sold out in three minutes, but I was in.

In this program that encouraged an explicitly speculative ethos, a lot of participants seemed to know each other. I too saw someone I knew in the lecture hall. Yoo was a 38-year-old woman I had interviewed the previous year after we had taken the Ten in Ten Academy together. In that interview, she said it was more than ten years ago that she joined Café Ten in Ten and she was currently "betting everything on asset tech" after quitting her designer job. Fed up with her busy work and meaningless life, she enjoyed learning new things, had participated in the famous self-help program "Landmark Forum" (see chapter 4) and had come to believe that real estate suited her better than stock investing. She was therefore taking several classes taught by Expert Seo and was volunteering to be a peer leader (반장) for her classmates. Since I had already learned how highly she spoke of Expert Seo, more highly than she did of Bum Young, and knew how enthusiastic she was about his instruction, it came as no surprise that I ran into her in the "200 apartments" seminar.

Some months later, I had an opportunity to talk about this program with another Café Ten in Ten user. Jisu, a 37-year-old man working for a medium-size tech company, was "quite pessimistic about being a wage worker for life" because he could see no bright future in it. Just one year into his current position, his firm carried out a downsizing and let one-third of its workers go. Jisu survived. But he could not stop dreading that he might be laid off in the near future while his children were still in school. Hoping that real estate could bring him an alternative source of income, he joined several online asset tech forums, including Café Ten in Ten. Jisu was a man who had a shy smile, spoke softly, and remained reserved in social settings most of the time, but he got carried away when we talked about the ecosystem of online asset tech communities and the offline classes they offered. He quickly became curious when he discovered that I managed to enroll for the "200 apartments" seminar. He was one of many who had been unable to sign up. Jisu seemed disappointed, but at the same time he was hopeful about a different opportunity. At the end of the day, he was a big fan of another lay expert who had become famous by contributing lay knowledge to Café Ten in Ten. Like other lay experts, this expert had made himself known to the public as an asset tech blogger, author, and lecturer. Shyly smiling, Jisu confessed that he once wrote "a fan letter" to this real estate star. Jisu was excitedly waiting for the opening of his upcoming investing lecture, determined to hit the mouse frantically as soon as enrollment began.

Like Jisu and Yoo, Café Ten in Ten gave birth to many enthusiastic investors who worshiped lay experts, passionate not just about investing but about any activities involved in it. They closely followed lay experts and what these experts offered, tracked a variety of events in the field of asset tech, and invested arduously.

### Playful Investors (Socializers): Hanging Out in a Financial Community

Unlike enthusiasts, playful investors in the Café had only a casual interest in asset tech. They did not want to bother with optimizing themselves financially, making a ten-year financial plan, or logging their expenses in detail. They did not "geek out" like Yoo or Jisu who were constantly in search of asset tech classes, write fan letters, or bet everything on the asset market. Instead, they found the socializing aspect of Café Ten in Ten fun and developed strong attachments to the community. To many of them, Café Ten in Ten was a space for hanging out where they could meet new people and engage in ongoing social contact that moved across on and offline spaces. As they hung out with other users, however, many of them came to experiment, or "mess around" (Ito et al. 2010), with some of the investing pathways that they found manageable and potentially profitable. I observed that some of these playful investors ended up becoming much more serious, enthusiastic, and/or principled about asset building. To them, socializing with others was the way in which they were socialized into the asset market.

A 35-year-old retail worker, Jinwook was a health-conscious, confident, and frugal man. He had moved around several online financial communities before calling Café Ten in Ten home. When he first became interested in asset tech, he joined another famous online community that was heavily focused on frugality. Although Jinwook acquired many tips from it for a thrifty life-style, he was more fascinated with the dynamic hanging-out opportunities that community provided. Similar to Café Ten in Ten, Jinwook's previous favorite community had a socially oriented discussion board where numerous social opportunities emerged, such as meetups and gatherings. Jinwook enjoyed such Internet-enabled socializing but, for some reason, the social forum was elim-inated. He wanted to find an alternative and discovered that Café Ten in Ten was still offering ample social opportunities.

It goes without saying that the life forum in Café Ten in Ten played a cru-cial role in turning participants like Jinwook into playful investors. Being an online playground for participants, this socially oriented forum helped many users with an ephemeral interest in asset tech stick around. When Bum Young first created the life discussion board, it was named "Life of Married Couples with Two Paychecks (맞벌이 부부의 삶)" (commonly abbreviated by users into something like "the Married Life Board"). Its focus on marriage and double incomes was reflective of Bum Young's initial target audience. He imagined Café Ten in Ten would resonate with those whose financial and marital status was like his own. However, the Café was joined by a whirlwind of users who went beyond such specific demographics, and the original focus on married, working couples was quickly diluted. Per user requests, one more life forum was added later, which was to be used by unmarried users. As an online social mixer for singles, the new life board was named "Beautiful Singles (아름다운 미혼)."[18] Thanks to these socially oriented discussion boards where lively chats took place, many regulars of Café Ten in Ten perceived it as a comforting, go-to space for casual conversations and ongoing interactions.

Jinwook also took Beautiful Singles as his primary online social forum. As a particularly active socializer, he became one of the founding members of Singlesgroup (see chapter 6), where he socialized with a group of enthusiasts and aspiring lay experts. Jinwook was especially close to one of the enthusiasts ("Mr Seven") who was financially savvy, friendly, and generous. Inspired by him, Jinwook began to invest in real estate funds. In our interview, Jinwook said that he was not a good student and researching the asset market on his own was too challenging. He had tried to read business papers, which ultimately proved to be unsuccessful. Instead, Jinwook found it much more helpful to utilize personal networks and to hear from experienced traders in person. He was confident when saying to me that "I believe it's right to learn from those who make money well rather than those who have a PhD in Economics."

I met Jinwook again about one and a half years after I first interviewed him and a few months after he had married. Jinwook told me he had recently closed his investing accounts because his risk-intolerant wife wanted to put the money back into a savings account. Jinwook's story demonstrates how asset tech becomes entangled with the social aspects of one's life, especially for some of the Café Ten in Ten users who were unwilling and/or unable to practice self-directed investing. As Jinwook's case illustrates, however, many of them were made into playful investors who experimented with small capital in the asset market. It was not until Jinwook joined Café Ten in Ten that he learned that money could make more money. All he knew previously was to work hard and reduce expenses. He came to "mess around" with the asset market while hanging out with more "geeked-out" enthusiasts.

## Conclusion

This chapter has shown how entrepreneurial practices of financial self-optimization and self-assetization took place in communitarian ways in Café Ten in Ten. As the epicenter of the Ten in Ten movement and as a push button for an ecosystem much larger than itself, Café Ten in Ten promoted a frugal lifestyle and self-directed investing, among other things, as pathways to financial freedom. But it was much more than that. Not just the provision of thrift hacks or "Investing 101," Café Ten in Ten gave rise to a particular spirit of asset tech. It created a space where individual projects for asset accumulation were closely intertwined with community building. Asset tech became an act of sharing one's experience and giving one's knowledge and expertise without monetary compensation, and a coming together with like-minded people. By creating a community of sharing, giving, and socializing, Café Ten in Ten provided a new way to conceptualize asset tech as more than turning profits.

By pointing to the centrality of community within Café Ten in Ten, I do not mean to reproduce "a romantic discourse of community" that positions community as the defining other of capitalism (Joseph 2002, vii). Rather, I make the case that communitarian aspirations are increasingly mobilized for financialized asset capitalism. With the explicit promotion of mutual support, convivial interactions, and non-commodification in a space created for discussing finance and real estate, Café Ten in Ten demonstrates how such communitarian practices can become pathways for increasing one's asset value with a strong potential for cash flow. Just as it was suggested that financial self-optimization is to be acquired through community, sustaining an authentic, affectionate, and non-commodifying community is to be juxtaposed with speculative activities. The slogan "Ten in Ten" may no longer be popular in the larger Korean society, but the ongoing legacy of Café Ten in Ten is widespread and enduring.

THREE

# Anti-Capitalist Investing

What I want to tell you guys is "Hey, don't live like a slave. Don't live for others. Make a *system*."

### The Anti-Capitalist Rant

One fall night, I was sitting in a classroom waiting for the first session of the Ten in Ten Academy to begin. Participants arrived, some alone and others in pairs. Free copies of a popular finance magazine were displayed in the entryway and most participants picked one up upon arrival. When the clock struck seven, the awkward silence in the seminar hall was quickly replaced with Bum Young's forceful opening statements. The audience appeared puzzled by his unwavering anti-capitalist speech just a few seconds into the program. "You guys should learn how brutal capitalism is […] Fucking capitalists exploit you and rip you off!" As he talked about exploitation and inequality, Bum Young asserted that capitalism was designed to widen the gap between the haves and the have-nots. I had not expected an asset tech seminar to begin with a critique of capitalism. Neither, I suspect, did most of other participants who had likely been inculcated with the superiority of South Korea's capitalism over the communism of the North.

Whereas Bum Young retained a laissez-faire approach to what people discussed in Café Ten in Ten and focused his time on administrative roles that he called "housekeeping," especially after the Café became established, he was an unreserved rhetor in the Ten in Ten Academy. He was not afraid of taking a side or "talking shit." The first lecture was meant to be three hours, but it went on much longer. Cooped up for such a long time without even a bathroom break, many in the audience had to fan themselves with their copies of the finance magazine. The room was hot, not just because of how many

49

participants were crowded into the room but because of the unexpectedly tense ambience. Bum Young had been running this program for five years now and had become a charismatic speaker with an authoritative persona. He was able to talk ceaselessly about the global economy, financial terms, the history of the Korean economy, and what he called "the principle of capitalism." He was funny, self-deprecating, and assertive all at once.

This chapter takes a close look at the critiques of capitalism developed in the Ten in Ten Academy. The snapshot of capitalism painted over the span of five weeks was far from a prosperity gospel advocating that capitalism would enrich the poor and solve social problems (see Comaroff and Comaroff 2000; Han J 2011). On the contrary, the capitalist system was described as fundamentally unequal and polarizing: Capitalism was in essence predatory and would make the rich richer and the poor poorer. Ordinary people would likely be ripped off, live as capitalism's slaves (*noye*, 노예),[1] and face a miserable retirement unless they protected themselves against the brutality of capitalism. In hindsight, this sort of motivational speech was vital to the Ten in Ten Academy—even more so than instruction about investing techniques—and the critiques of capitalism were a key element of such speeches. On the one hand, such speeches can be seen as a form of populism, in the sense that they were based on a firm division between "us and them," with "us" describing the wounded wage workers versus "them" described as a giant evil that included the state, corporations, entrenched wealth, and global capital. On the other hand, Ten in Ten Academy's anti-capitalist statements might be seen as a vernacular critique (Ono and Sloop 1995) that put into words "underarticulated, yet intense feelings of vulnerability" as it unveiled structural inequality (Kang J 2017, 756).[2] Rather than choosing between condemnatory and commendatory positions, I do a close reading of the critiques of capitalism articulated in the program in comparison with other related discourses produced in and outside of academia. The Ten in Ten Academy adopted a *critical* reading as a mode of interpretation, with a focus on power, structure, and history (see Holm 2020), which ultimately served to justify speculative pursuits. This critical reading needs to be taken seriously if we are to understand the crucial role critique plays in providing capitalism with the "moral foundation it lacks" (Boltanski and Chiapello 2005b, 163).

## The Critique of Oppression: Wage Slavery vs Financial Freedom

Bum Young characterized himself as an authentic, freedom-loving individual. If he had to choose a single word to define himself, it was always *jayuin* (자유인, "freeman" or "person of freedom") rather than *tujaja* (투자자, investor) or *buja* (부자, rich person). Freedom was one of the most used words in the Ten in Ten Academy. As its antithesis, *noye* ("slave") was used to refer to ordinary people who were seen as brainwashed and unaware of how the capitalist system oppressed them. On the first day of the program, Bum Young called the participants, most of whom were 30- and 40-something wage workers, "slaves" to their faces. Given that "freedom" is one of the most beloved words in the vocabulary of neoliberalism, it comes as no surprise that it became a keyword for asset seekers. The centrality of freedom in asset tech discourses evinces the influence of a Western notion of financial freedom and the broader discourses of neoliberal self-help. However, as I will show in the following pages, the meanings of freedom articulated by asset tech practitioners were significantly different from those of Western self-help discourses and reveal the force of critique in South Korea's community of asset tech.

American financial self-help guru Robert Kiyosaki and his *Rich Dad* series had the strongest impact on the material of Ten in Ten Academy.[3] According to sociologist Daniel Fridman, Kiyosaki's Rich Dad "has been the most successful brand of financial self-help in the last decade" (2016, 15). In 2000, a Korean translation of *Rich Dad, Poor Dad: What the Rich Teach Their Kids about Money That the Poor and Middle Class Do Not!* (1997) was published, selling more than 170,000 copies in the first three months (Go D 2000). Worshipped by Korean asset seekers, this book depicts two contrasting attitudes toward money, personified by a "poor dad" and a "rich dad." The poor dad is a highly educated, salaried employee who teaches his son to follow the traditional forms of the good life such as studying hard, getting good grades, and finding a good job. In contrast, the rich dad is a businessman who pursues entrepreneurship and individual autonomy. If the former represents "a social path of conformity to welfare society, someone who values security over freedom" (Fridman 2016, 64), the latter signifies "the exuberance and vitality of market agency" (Binkley 2009, 61). Describing the former as a failure, Kiyosaki promotes the rich dad's way of living. Encouraging readers to become entrepreneurs or investors rather than workers, Kiyosaki describes financial self-help as a quest for freedom that is not just about getting rich. In the popular theory he provides, Fridman writes, "freedom has a higher value than riches. Thus, money does not appear as an end in itself, but rather as a means to attain freedom" (2016, 54). Likewise, the stated goal of Ten in Ten Academy was to motivate "slaves" to learn about capitalism, and becoming a freeman was presented as the ultimate and utmost goal to pursue. Bum Young urged participants to consider money as instrumental to freedom, rather than to follow wealth itself.

For both Kiyosaki and Bum Young, the meaning of freedom had to do with the state of "not having to work for one's income" (Fridman 2016, 5), i.e., freedom was one's ability to cover all of her or his expenses via investment revenue.[4] On a deeper level, however, what Kiyosaki and Bum Young purported to debunk differed significantly. The notion of freedom in the Ten in Ten Academy played an important role in revealing and criticizing the *oppression* involved in wage work, whereas Kiyosaki's notion of financial freedom condemned the so-called "dependent disposition" of individuals. In other words, Kiyosaki defined freedom as a rejection of dependence, while freedom was seen in the Ten in Ten Academy as, above all, liberation from oppression. The former presupposes the existence of free human beings, based on which freedom is no longer defined as an escape from institutions of oppression (see Rose 2004). Therefore, Kiyosaki advised individuals to exercise already existing conditions of freedom. Distinctively rooted in American libertarianism, Kiyosaki's discourse of financial freedom therefore problematized the "conformist self" (Fridman 2016, 21) and urged readers to reject their own tendency to depend on external institutions (e.g., employers, the state, social security) and combat their inner dependence on fear and anxiety (Fridman 2016, chapter 2).

In contrast, freedom as liberation from oppression presupposes unfreedom and oppression. It is predicated upon the belief that individuals are yet to be free and that authority is a tyrant. Contrary to Kiyosaki's freedom, which pointed at allegedly dependent individuals, Bum Young's talk of freedom targeted the oppression that wage workers experience due to the undemocratic, authoritarian, and militaristic culture of corporate Korea. Bum Young had managed to land a stable job in 1998 but found the work neither satisfying nor fulfilling. He had been disheartened most by the corporate culture of hierarchy and collectivism. He had felt "imprisoned while earning money" and came to realize that "corporate work is slavery." He believed that corporate discipline was killing human dignity and individual autonomy:

> My life as a married salaryman was very typical. The daily commute took three hours. [At work] we were supposed to leave the office at seven p.m. according to HR guidelines. But no one went home at seven. You can't leave until your boss heads out, so we usually stuck around until eight or nine o'clock. The work they gave me also had a totalitarian character. Although I considered myself autonomous (주체적) and awakened (깨어 있다), I still felt I was subservient.

To him, work was something that suppressed his desires, inner passion, and individuality, and was far from a means of self-realization. Looking around at his colleagues and superiors, he came to the conclusion that seniority, experience, and promotion would not bring him any satisfaction. He continued to describe his disappointment with the disciplinary and collective culture of corporations:

> [I thought,] "Ah, everything will remain the same ten years from now." [...] No one would want this kind of life. At the end of the day, however, you are gradually drawn in, like the way you become addicted to drugs. [After work] they [colleagues and superiors] always get wasted and complain [about the company], and the next day they apologize.[5] Looking at things like that, this was not the life I wanted and [I felt] I was raised only as a slave without knowing it. [...] There was an invisible taming. I call it being a "slave."

The most striking story of oppression Bum Young referenced in lectures came not from the daily grind of the precariats but from those working for a highly paid financial firm: one of South Korea's major banks. In a leaked video of its 2011 orientation for new employees, which Bum Young liked to play the first day, row after row of new hires in white-collared shirts—many of whom were certainly recent graduates from elite colleges—were lined up, shoulder-to-shoulder. "You must serve the corporation as if it were your own business!" shouted the drill sergeant, probably an HR manager or the like. In unison, the young, new hires were squatting, extending both arms and holding up a sheet of paper in front of them, chanting their allegiance (figure 1). The YouTube video went viral in early 2014. It was just one horror story illustrating what Hell

Figure 1. A screen capture of a major bank's new employee orientation (Image Credit: https://www.youtube.com/watch?v=NBWvV81i3OQ&t=68s.)

Joseon was like. As one news outlet put it, the orientation, which apparently lasted for half a day, should be seen as "physical abuse (가혹행위)" sanctioned by the firm (KBS News, February 26, 2014).

This video was perfect instructional material for promoting freedom over "slavery." Oppression in corporate Korea existed not just in the forms of long work hours, tedious tasks, and hierarchical chain of commands; it threatened human dignity. Furthermore, wage slavery was not just limited to factory labor but was very much about prestigious jobs with fat paychecks and good benefits. The torturous training by the bank proved the point of wage slavery precisely because such major financial services firms were highly sought after by top-tier college graduates. Before playing the video, Bum Young said, "Those working for this bank are top-rated slaves." The audience broke into laughter while he continued:

> They are very loyal to their firm because they are paid really well. [...] When parents raise children and send them to Seoul National University or the business school of Yonsei or Korea University,[6] then they feel really proud. Look at what those smart kids are doing now.

He was apparently scoffing—like Kiyosaki—at a traditional notion of the good life linked to good education, good jobs, and loyalty to work. For wage workers who found themselves in an onerous environment, however, such derision came off as a powerful critique.

While watching the video in which young workers were in pain, sweating, crying, and even vomiting, the audience exhaled sighs of shock and sympathy. The sounds of yelling, shouting, and chanting from the video echoed in the lecture hall, mixed with Bum Young's speech. Mentioning how competitive it was to get into the firm, Bum Young lamented, "Do we really need to be this servile?" He called on the male participants in the audience: "Men, you guys must recall. What does this remind you of?" Some of male participants whispered, "The military." In South Korea, military service is required of all male citizens between 18 and 35 who do not have a disability. Bum Young raised his voice, "What was the military like? Was there human dignity? Did you have freedom there?" He played the outrageous clip repeatedly week after week. While posing like one of the young trainees squatting in the video, he mentioned another time that even those who go to a top school will "end up like this [...]. Their role is being a tool for the system. There's no self-realization for them." One could not find a better example of the oppression inherent in wage work; the video, or the reality mirrored in it, became a compelling wake-up call for the urgency of freedom, demonstrating how financial freedom was defined as an escape from oppressive work.

Bum Young often concluded his lectures—in the Ten in Ten Academy and elsewhere—by presenting a movie poster of *The Shawshank Redemption*. In this 1994 Hollywood film about a man incarcerated and sentenced to two life sentences for a crime he did not commit, the protagonist ends up escaping prison after 16 years of nearly impossible effort. In the movie poster, which many 30- and 40-something Koreans would recognize, the main actor, Tim Robbins, is looking up at a sky full of rain with both arms wide open. Breathing the fresh air outside of the prison walls for the first time in one and a half decades, Robbins' character became an iconic image of liberation after long, unjust suffering. This still image brought into relief an affinity between the unfairly imprisoned protagonist and the newly hired bankers and, more broadly, the Korean wage workers at large who were ground down by various mental and physical oppressions at work. They were all shackled by unfreedom. The film poster, with its tagline "Fear can hold you prisoner. Hope can set you free," brought the audience back to the idea of freedom as liberation from oppression.[7]

## The Critique of Inauthenticity

If freedom's biggest foe was oppression, another foe was inauthenticity. Ten in Ten Academy provided a forceful critique of inauthenticity, particularly in relation to the loss of meaning and the dehumanization of the world caused by the excessive pursuit of monetary gain. Such a critique was directed at inauthentic riches—including inherited wealth, the capitalist class, speculators, and "business owners"—and this ultimately worked to crown only the self-directed stock investor as authentically rich.

Above all, Bum Young's critique of inauthenticity was best exemplified in the way he reappropriated Kiyosaki's notion of "business owner." The term "business owner" was crucial to Kiyosaki's series, particularly in *The Cashflow Quadrant* (1998), where the guru offers a popular theory about the capitalist class structure (see Fridman 2016, 46–52). Divided according to one's source of income, not by one's occupation or by one's level of income, his class structure is composed of four different positions: Employee (E), Self-Employed (S), Business Owner (B), and Investor (I) (see figure 2). Whereas Kiyosaki encourages readers to pursue the position of the business owner, Bum Young harshly criticized them for inauthenticity.

Specifically, Kiyosaki recommends that readers move from the positions of employee and self-employed to the position of business owner and then, ultimately, to the position of Investor. For him, the vertical line dividing the left side (E and S) and the right side (B and I) is the most decisive one: those

Figure 2. Robert Kiyosaki's Cashflow Quadrant (Image Credit: https://www.rich dad.com/cashflow-quadrant.)

on the left represent the pursuit of security while those on the right represent freedom (Fridman 2016). The former put their labor and time to use in order to earn income, but the latter use money or other people's time or work to generate their income. Kiyosaki argues that, however prestigious their jobs are, employees and the self-employed remain stuck in "a rat race" because they work for money. In contrast, however low one's initial income might be, the person who can command autonomy will likely achieve financial freedom if she has other people work for her (B) or has money work for her (I).

The Korean edition of *The Cashflow Quadrant*—titled (in Korean) *Rich Dad Poor Dad 2* (2000)—translated the B as *saeopga* (사업가), a Korean term equivalent to "business owner."[8] Adopting Kiyosaki's class theory, Bum Young referred to the four class positions in Ten in Ten Academy, which many participants were already familiar with. However, Bum Young's revision of the theory placed the greatest emphasis on authenticity. To him, the horizontal line dividing B and I was as crucial as the vertical line; those above the horizontal line (business owners) turn profits by taking advantage of other people while those below the line (investors) do not have to exploit other workers to make money. However inaccurate and dichotomizing, Bum Young's argument was that even though business owners are likely to make more money than investors, the wealth acquired by investors is more real and genuine, because it is earned the hard way at no one's expense. To him, the I represented authenticity while the B was all about inauthenticity.

In Ten in Ten Academy, the Korean term *saeopga* did not refer just to business-owning individuals. Instead, it was used as an emblem for greed and crass self-interest; it was a metaphor for inauthentic wealth or, more broadly, the inauthenticity inherent to the capitalist system. Whether individuals or institutions, the perpetrators who destroy authentic communities and dehumanize the world were dubbed *saeopga*, e.g., the capitalist class who exploit workers; the canny entrepreneurs who put money before human beings; and the *chaebol* corporations that wipe out street vendors, small shops, and local businesses.

Take the following two contrasting cases, for instance, that Bum Young frequently mentioned in his lectures. One case was about the founder and CEO of what was then Korea's largest coffee shop brand. He was quoted in the media as saying that he aspired to develop his coffee shops into the world's largest chain. It was known that his coffee shop brand pushed PR aggressively and planned to open stores across the country. The other was the chef-owner of a small ramen restaurant in Japan. This famous ramen chef was an artisan, ran only one store, and cooked the noodle dishes on his own. Asked why he was not franchising out, he said that what made him happy was just making soup stocks every morning by himself and watching customers enjoy his food. Kiyosaki would have commended the coffeeshop founder as an entrepreneurial, independent business owner and put down the ramen chef as one of the self-employed who pursued security over freedom. Bum Young, on the contrary, accused the former of being a *saeopga*, calling him "a grabby wingman (앞잡이)" of capitalism, while speaking highly of the latter. To Kiyosaki, business ownership "provides people with the necessary skills, mindset, and capital for a successful venture into the I quadrant, where they can finally live off their investments" (Fridman 2016, 50). To Bum Young, in contrast, business owners always put profit before humans. In order to make money, they cannot but profit off of the "tears and blood" of other people. Their greed, he continued to argue, aggravated capitalist harms. Throughout his lectures, it was made clear that Ten in Ten Academy aimed to "promote the model of the investor, but not the business owner."

As exemplified by the discourse of *saeopga*, Bum Young diverged from his own guru by offering a critique of inauthenticity. Importantly, the critique of *saeopga* was boundary work for setting authentic wealth apart from inauthentic wealth and linking the former type of wealth to the investor. Branding investors as authentic seemed to be imperative given the South Korean context where rich people were often decried and the legitimacy of their wealth was commonly questioned.[9] Echoing such sentiments, Bum Young associated those who acquired wealth through business with excessive commodification, reckless pursuit of monetary gains, and conspicuous consumption. He cast investors as the opposite of such decay, and instead as an emblem of authentic wealth. According to him, in contrast to *saeopga*, investors do not have to turn things into commodities; they do not have to turn their back on workers (which is one of the most inaccurate and troubling views); more broadly, they are able to offer genuine care for human life. Here, Bum Young did not consider all "investors" as fitting the model of the I. Those who should be categorized as I or S according to Kiyosaki's original theory were called *saeopga* if they were deemed inauthentic. Real estate investors were a case in point. Bum Young thought that real estate investors were more like inauthentic speculators, thus similar to *saeopga*, and not like the investor. From his point of view, real estate investors took advantage of the underclass while stock investors took up the fight against rogues in the market. One day, Bum Young declared as he put up a slide showing Kiyosaki's image of the ESBI quadrants:

> Frankly speaking, I think there are very few Investors out there. We need to have more Investors to make the world better. [...] But I have seen very few people who strike a balance between stock investing and real estate investing. It seems like most rich people are just *saeopga*. I regard those who invest only in real estate as *saeopga*, not as investors. Imagine a person who buys thirty homes by bidding on foreclosure auctions. I consider such a person *saeopga*. They might think they are doing asset tech, but real estate investing is like running a business.[10]

His argument was that wealth acquired at the expense of others, like the wealth made by *saeopga,* is "easy bucks." Real estate speculators are therefore to be seen as *saeopga*, and not as representing the investor. In providing an indictment of inauthentic business owners and identifying real estate investors as belonging to that category, Bum Young saved stock investors from the taint of inauthenticity and hailed them as true investors ("the Investor"). While business owners were described as selfish, insatiable, and manipulative, the Investor (i.e., stock investors) was painted as autonomous and socially conscious. In this way, stock investing was put on a pedestal and was considered to be the pinnacle of asset tech.

## The Critique of Development

Fridman comments that Kiyosaki does not take issue with capitalism itself and sees it as "not necessarily unfair" (2016, 47).[11] Ten in Ten Academy's core recommendation was similar to Kiyosaki's in the sense that both encouraged participants to create their own system of assets instead of holding the state accountable for providing citizens with systematic financial security. Nevertheless, it is important to acknowledge that Bum Young was rather unequivocal about inequality being inherent in capitalism. Bum Young's critique of inequality was most pronounced in his critique of the developmental state. That his critique of capitalism was mapped onto the state reflects the South Korean context where capitalist development was driven primarily by the state during the second half of the twentieth century.

Kiyosaki posits that individuals are solely responsible for their (im)mobility within the four quadrants. In his theory, only individual effort determines one's movement from the positions of E or S to those of B or I. Bum Young deviated from his own guru by bringing into relief the structural conditions that determine one's position. Specifically, he developed a compelling account of how the state placed weighty hurdles that made it nearly impossible for ordinary Koreans to grow financially. To him, hellish inequality was entrenched in the national economy from the moment it took off in the 1960s. This view was in stark contrast to the way South Korea's rapid economic development has been narrated. Commonly dubbed "The Miracle on the Han River," South Korea's economic growth is often told through "the triumphalist lens of market capitalism and liberal democracy as a *fait accompli*" (Han J 2011, 147). To Bum Young, however, the process of development testified to the fundamental inequality embedded in capitalism. In recounting the victorious story of South Korea's development as a tale of capitalist inequality, Bum Young provided quasi-sociological critiques of national development.

In his critical reading of state-led development, the state manipulated citizens in order to benefit large corporations in the name of national development, which impeded the financial thriving of ordinary people:

> [During the era of rapid growth, circa the 1960s–1970s,] the savings rate was like 50 percent. All those savings were given to whom? People sacrificed for whom? Large corporations.[12] [...] They were able to take out tens and hundreds of millions of dollars in bank loans. We couldn't. From the beginning, we were prevented from starting businesses, because we couldn't borrow capital from banks. Only business owners were able to take advantage of bank loans. What's the result now? We've come to work the longest hours among the OECD countries.[13] That's how we developed the economy. Who reaped all the benefits? Large corporations. See? This is the structure of capitalism. Our parents have mostly gone broke by now.

In this passage, Bum Young summarized how the state reassured people to tighten their belts and save aggressively while they could not access bank loans. This created a contemporary wealth gap, he argued. Several decades later, many industrious citizens who had cooperated with the state campaign for hard work and thrift found themselves on the brink of poverty. Bum Young continued to develop his account: "Rich people today are mainly those who bought real estate in the past" instead of sticking to what the state told them to do.

Such a critique could very well have come from scholars critiquing the Korean developmental state and "the state-banks-*chaebol* nexus" (Shin and Chang 2003). Indeed, many scholars have criticized how South Korean authoritarian regimes took a firm grip on commercial banks and mobilized the nickels and dimes of ordinary people in order to channel domestic capital to *chaebol*. Carried out in the name of export-oriented growth, the state-controlled banks rendered loans completely unavailable to average citizens while mobilizing their savings to the fullest extent (Chang 2019; Kim D 2018a, 2018b; Song 2014). Economists Jang-Sup Shin and Ha-Joon Chang (2003) call this model "the state-banks-*chaebol* nexus" or "Korea Inc.," which, they argue, operated as the backbone and central feature of the Korean economic system prior to neoliberal financialization. According to them, South Korea's development model "operated on [*sic*] a close cooperation and consultation among the government, commercial banks, and big businesses" (119). Bum Young's comment that most wealthy people today were those who had invested in real estate reflects the *chaebol*'s path for expansion as well. They have long benefited from favorable loan terms and "many of the *chaebol* invested their borrowed funds not in the intended productive activities, but in speculating in the curb market itself and in real estate" (Nelson 2000, 17).[14]

Bum Young extended his critique of national development to the more recent past, by grieving the sacrifice citizens had to make when the IMF crisis broke out. He contended that, in the same way that the government during the 1960s and 1970s achieved economic development at the expense of ordinary people, Korean citizens were once again called on to sacrifice during the IMF crisis. This diagnosis is similar to the academic discourses on the experience of the crisis for South Korean citizens and workers. For example, sociologist Chang Kyung-Sup (2019, 5–6) writes that, in the wake of the IMF crisis, Korean citizens were "told to sacrifice themselves once again"—in the same way they had been during the state-led development—"in order to rescue their national economy from a supposedly impending collapse."

A nationwide movement called the "gold collection campaign" (금모으기 운동) was a case in point for both Bum Young and the scholars. Faced with the national debt crisis, in January 1998 a public television network (KBS) aired a live campaign asking viewers to contribute to repaying the national debt by donating gold items. The government, civil society, corporations, and financial institutions soon joined forces to propel the campaign into a national movement (Cheon 2017; Cho H 2007; Kim and Finch 2002; Song 2009). In response, more than three million people turned up at gold-collection centers across the country. Not just celebrities and high-income earners but middle-class and lower-income citizens brought their personal gold treasures, including necklaces, coins, medals, wedding jewelry, and infant rings (a common gift item for a Korean baby's first birthday) to be melted down into ingots for sale on the international markets.[15] The campaign was successful as 225 tons of gold were collected, equivalent to US$1.8 billion (*Yonhap News* 1998). This campaign was heralded at the time, as well as during the following decades, as a sign of patriotism. For example, in 2016, *Forbes* described the event as "one of the most moving shows of patriotism and self-sacrifice the world has ever known" (Holmes 2016). Mainstream discourses in and beyond South Korea have invoked the gold-collection campaign as a historical marker of national prowess, the unity of people, and civic virtues (Cheon 2017, 85).

This story of a victorious nation was recast in Ten in Ten Academy as a tale of capitalist exploitation sanctioned by the state. "Look, how awful capitalism is," Bum Young said. To him, the gold-collection campaign was a coordinated act of deception by the state and large corporations: "We overcame the IMF crisis by collecting gold when the economy was struggling. But look, in the time of a crisis, who should be damaged the most? The large corporations that [...] took out the biggest loans, right? But it was not the case. Strangely, the government protected them."[16]

Indeed, as a scholar of Korean consumer culture has shown, the gold collection campaign effectively eschewed holding the domestic culprits accountable for the economic crisis; it instead had recourse to the patriotic sentiments of the people (Cheon 2017). Scholars also point to deceptiveness in the ways in which the government mobilized consent for the post-IMF labor reforms, which involved massive layoffs. It was through the discourse of "burden-sharing" (고통 분담, also translated as "pains-sharing") that the government persuaded workers to accept the harsh terms of the restructuring. The slogan suggested that the state and businesses "would equally share whatever sacrifices were required for the emergency relief of the national economy" but the post-IMF restructuring "was not conductive to pains-sharing at all" (Chang 2019, 6). Millions of workers were let go but big businesses were bailed out in the name of "too big to fail." Bum Young raised his voice:

> They fucked with us. They said they should fire 30,000 employees. They forced us to use scrap paper and spend less on lunch. They undercut the price for subcontractors. This is the capitalist system. Then, the society

must suffer. Nonregular workers increased, as did dispatched workers and part-timers. It's the logic of the game, the capitalist game.

Bum Young continued to make the criticism that the economic recovery did not bring jobs back to the workers who had been asked to sacrifice. As Chang (2019, 105) points out, workers continued to suffer, during the following two decades after the crisis, due to "the stagnation and even decline of wage income across society in a stark contrast to the phenomenally swelling corporate dividends and financial transaction profits accruing to foreign investors." Bum Young continued:

> When things got better, after corporations began to reap higher profits, did they hire back the previous employees they had sent away? Definitely not. It was usually called the rationalization of management, improvement of industrial structure (기업 체질 개선), or the enhancement of competitiveness. That's how the rules of the game work.

Prior to the crisis, many *chaebol* companies used to call themselves "family" (가족), like "Samsung *Gajok*" and "Daewoo *Gajok*" (Chang 2019, 66). "One's true colors are revealed when we have a hard time," Bum Young scoffed. "When things were great, they said we were all family. But when things got hard, the 'family' killed all of us, didn't they?"

## The Critique of Finance

In the same way that the Ten in Ten Academy offered a quasi-sociological critique of national development, it critiqued the financial sector as well. Bum Young's understanding of financial capitalism eerily paralleled postcolonial and poststructuralist critiques of finance, which demonstrates that reading the economy critically has become a mode of financial consumption in contemporary South Korea. His critique of finance had two strands. On the one hand, Bum Young criticized, albeit in a very rudimentary form, US-centered global financial governance, thereby sounding much like the academic discourses amplified by postcolonial critics after the 2007–2008 global financial crisis (Bahng 2018; Chakravartty and Silva 2012; Kang LHY 2012; Kim J 2022). On the other hand, he also liked to talk about how the contemporary financial market itself was operating on a shared belief or fantasy, which was similar to the observation made by some poststructuralist critics (Bjerg 2014; Haiven 2014).

Bum Young provided a brief account of the financialization of the global economy, strongly condemning the US-dominated governance of global finance. I juxtapose here his accounts with the postcolonial critiques on the post-Bretton Woods system of global finance. Bum Young was able to talk about the hegemony of US dollars without the help of such terms as "the gold standard," "the Bretton Woods system,"[17] or "the Nixon Shock." He contended that, ever since the US had unilaterally put an end to the convertibility of the dollar to gold and instead made the dollar a global reserve currency, everyone had been in a *game*, "the capitalist game of growth that the United States created." Previously, when the US dollar had been convertible to gold, Bum Young continued to explain, there was no big difference between the growth of the real economy and the growth of the financial sectors. Suddenly, however, "the motherfucker United States began to print dollars and started the game. *All the standards are now set by them.*" If we look at postcolonial critiques, Jodi Kim writes in strikingly similar language that "the United States rigged the game of world finance in 1971" (2022, 50). Due to its growing trade deficits largely caused by the Vietnam War, the US did not have enough gold holdings and thus Nixon ended the Bretton Woods system in 1971. According to Jodi Kim:

> Nixon's de-pegging of the dollar from gold made it into a nonconvertible or fiat currency. This in turn made it possible for the United States to exercise full monetary sovereignty: the power to issue not only its own currency but also specifically a fiat currency not tethered or pegged to gold or another currency.
>
> (2022, 51)

Similar to Jodi Kim's account, Bum Young explained that while the US can print dollars in a self-serving way, the dollar's value does not plummet because it is the global key currency, which indicates how arbitrary its value can be. In this way, he introduced the participants of the Ten in Ten Academy, who were eager to learn about asset tech, to the vernacular critique of global financial governance. Some readers might find this jarring, thinking that I am trying to establish an affinity between his underarticulated form of criticism and the sharp observations made by postcolonial critics about post-Bretton Woods global finance. I do *not* intend to argue that Bum Young's insights were as elaborate as those of postcolonial thinkers. Nor do I believe his comments to be original. Instead, I am interested in the ways in which this vernacular, quasi-postcolonial critique, however rudimentary, was mobilized as a rationale for popular investing and for what was called financial freedom. This critique of global finance built up to the claim that foreign investors had dispossessed

Koreans of their own stock market, and that stock investing was an act of resistance against global capital.

The post-Bretton Woods system had consequential effects on the economic life of South Koreans, just as it probably did all over the globe. Above all, the floating of US dollars and the proliferation of derivatives—the latter was seen as one of the crucial culprits of the 1997 IMF crisis as well as the subprime crisis ten years after—were closely linked to one another. As Lawrence Grossberg notes, the explosion of risky derivatives was "at least in part a response to, first, the move from gold to money as the universal equivalent on a global scale and second, the denial of the universal equivalent" (2012, 33). Indeed, the floating of US dollars and the rise of the financial derivatives markets all happened "when capitalism in the United States and European contexts had to restructure itself vis-à-vis the emerging markets of the 'Asian tigers'" (Bahng 2018, 16; see also LiPuma and Lee 2004). Multilateral organizations such as the IMF served the interest of the US, which has been increasingly beholden to Wall Street interests (Ji 2013; Kang LHY 2012; Jodi Kim 2022). The IMF pushed for "privatizing public enterprises, lifting trade restrictions, opening up capital markets, and cutting public expenditures" (Kang LHY 2012, 423) in many countries across Asia and Latin America in the post-Bretton Woods era. In South Korea, such measures exacerbated "the vicious cycle of the very processes that caused the [IMF] crisis in the first instance" (Jodi Kim 2022, 11). In this regard, Bahng (2018, 5) asserts that "the fundamental governance of the global financial system has been dominated entirely by US and European economic interests" and "the financial colonization of the future builds on preexisting disparities of wealth held over from earlier histories of empire and neocolonial enterprises." Likewise, Laura Hyun Yi Kang concludes that "economic and financial globalization is crucially organized by 'discriminatory inclusion and segmentation' rather than horizontal inclusion and multilateral cooperation" (2012, 424).

Meanwhile, Bum Young's oft-said word "game" also bears some resemblance to a poststructuralist critique of the financial market. He did not believe that finance creates value. He instead stressed that "the economic game is a game of inflation. It is a game of virtuality, a game of allocating money, collecting money." This capitalist economic game, according to his theory, runs on a mutually shared belief in financial institutions—the belief of consumers that their claim to value can be fulfilled whenever they want. This narrative of a shared belief (or fantasy) underlying financial capitalism corresponds to poststructuralist accounts of the financial economy as running on a "social fiction" (Haiven 2014). Scholars such as Max Haiven and Ole Bjerg have developed such critiques by using the example of the fractional-reserve banking system. To them, this system exemplifies how financial capitalism is entirely built upon a fiction. The fractional-reserve banking system allows banks to hold dollar reserves in much lower amounts than their deposit liabilities. Thanks to this system, banks loan out far more than they actually hold in their depositories. According to Bjerg (2014), banks these days commonly operate with a reserve ratio as low as 1–2 percent. Arguing that "it is an open secret of modern banking that banks *create* credit money," he writes:

> [T]he issuance of a bank loan is essentially the creation of money out of nothing. The bank lends out money that it does not have. [...] [A]s long as the money created through the loan does not come back to the bank for redemption in cash, the bank makes a profit equivalent to the difference in interest between the lending rate and the deposit rate. [...] [T]his profit is made on the basis of money that the bank did not have in the first place. In brief, the bank makes money out of nothing and then profits on the interest margin for as long as the credit money is kept in circulation.
>
> (Bjerg 2014, 136)

With fractional-reserve banking, the operation of banks is dependent on their customers entertaining the fantasy that they can exchange their deposits for the entire amount in cash at any time. As long as the fantasy is maintained, banks can get away with profiting from the money that they make out of nothing. Haiven describes this fantasy as a social fiction and contends that the reproduction of financial capital both depends on that social fiction and perpetuates it at the same time. While the price of financial assets is "a hallucination, a conjecture created when multiple claims to the same underlying surplus value were sold to multiple parties," it can double and triple as "promises built upon promises" (Haiven 2014, 28).

These critiques are analogous to the ideas reverberating in the lecture hall of the Ten in Ten Academy. Bum Young devoted large portions of the second day of his program to explaining, if not hammering on about, the ways in which financial services firms (e.g., banks, insurance companies, brokers, credit card companies) worked. Like Haiven and Bjerg, he stressed that the operation of the financial services industry was founded upon people's belief. "We're made to believe it's real," he asserted. "Banks can't fail because otherwise people begin to doubt." As I mentioned in the previous section, Bum Young's notion of *saeopga* included not just business-owning individuals but stockbrokers, market professionals, and asset tech coaches as well—even if many of them were technically employees or self-employed—in the sense that they were inauthentic. His contention was that most of them were mere con artists who profited off ordinary people. Now, he extended this critique to the entire financial services industry, not just the people working in it; the industry is inauthentic or, more bluntly, fake because it cannot be sustained without the fantasy it creates for consumers. The industry is phony not just because of its excessive commodification but because it is built upon a fiction to begin with.

Another point Bum Young made was related to the ways in which ordinary people have been increasingly and unavoidably entangled in the financial market although they are systematically disadvantaged in it (cf, Bryan and Rafferty 2018). Bum Young held that banks rip off ordinary workers by requiring them to have their salaries directly deposited into their accounts. While the banks give just 0.1 percent or lower in interest back to the savers, "they lend our savings out to others without our permission." Bum Young took as a marker of the inauthenticity of banks the fact that most workers these days are required to receive their wages through direct deposit without being given a fair return on these wages. A more advanced but similar critique has been made by scholars who contend that channeling the wages of workers into financial institutions in the form of various retirement savings is a pivotal mechanism that tethers wage workers to financial markets (Langley 2008; Lapavitsas 2011; Mulcahy 2017). With portions of their wages automatically invested in financial markets, wage workers increasingly have a stake in the markets even if they do not buy stocks on their own. Such indirect ownership of equities has a powerful effect on the conduct of earners since, as Lazzarato (2009) puts it, "it splits each person internally into a 'schizophrenic' double, torn by the different, possibly opposite, rationalities" (125). In the past, wage workers had to worry about collective bargaining, but now they have to act like shareholders at the same time.

Lastly, Bum Young denounced financial services firms for their affective marketing.[18] Academic critics of financial capitalism note that such marketing draws on and incites the fear, anxiety, and insecurity of consumers. By using various "affective devices" (Thrift 2008), financial services firms heighten anxieties around uncertainties to prod consumers into participating in markets (Anderson 2007; French and Kneale 2009). In South Korea, the clichés of affective marketing include terms such as "aging society" (고령화), "slow growth" (저성장), and "involuntary early retirement" (조기 퇴직). Pundits and popular coaches often present, in dazzling charts, tables, and numbers, the rapid aging of the Korean population and the stagnation of the economy in tandem, unsettling the audience by asking whether they are prepared for the doomed future. Bum Young took a different path by debunking such affective strategies used by the wider financial services sector. "Suddenly there's a new era. The aging society and slow growth." He moved on to ask his students: "Who do you think incites insecurity and anxiety about these things?" Answering himself, he argued that financial services firms are the ones who publish the data indicating that many people are unprepared for retirement. He said that the financial services industry capitalizes on the fear of dying too soon in order to sell life insurance and amplifies the fear of living too long in order to sell annuities.

It is important to acknowledge where Bum Young's critiques diverged from the scholarly critiques with which I have juxtaposed them. The poststructuralist scholars analyzed the social fiction and affective marketing of financial capitalism in order to show how detrimental it is to workers, consumers, and citizens. In contrast, Bum Young's critiques boiled down to an emphasis on self-directed investing: do not believe in financial institutions; do not rely on brokers; educate yourself and become an autonomous, authentic stock investor! The postcolonial thinkers brought attention to how the financial economy has reinforced the imperial dominance of the global North and vice versa, i.e., how the ongoing legacy of imperialism and colonialism plays a role in the organization of global finance. In contrast, Bum Young's popular critique mobilized participants into the stock market by defining stock investing as an act of resistance against foreign capital. He argued that, under the capitalist game that the US created, foreign capital has dispossessed Koreans of their own stock market. The fruit of South Korea's growing economy has not been evenly shared among Koreans but is instead monopolized by foreign capital. The amalgam of quasi-postcolonial and quasi-poststructuralist critiques of finance ended up nonetheless as a bizarre form of advocacy for returning to finance: becoming a stock investor yourself is the only way to claim your share of the national growth and to prevent its drain into foreign pockets. Bum Young asserted:

> Our country will do well. So, take your share of the growing pie. Will the rich give back? Will the state give back? They say they will, but they won't. You should learn and take care of yourself. [...] Economic growth gives us the opportunity. It is a matter of seizing the opportunity or not.

## Conclusion

Ten in Ten Academy was in no way short of critiques. In contrast to the global guru Robert Kiyosaki, Bum Young criticized capitalism for its oppression and inauthenticity. Similar to the critiques posed within the academy, Bum Young offered quasi-sociological critiques of national development and quasi-postcolonial and quasi-poststructuralist critiques of finance. Although critiques were rampant in the classroom of critical capitalism, they were *not* harnessed to transformative ends. Instead, the critical reading of capitalism, with a focus on power, structure, and history, was mobilized to define self-directed stock investing as an act of resistance against entrenched wealth and foreign capital.

Acknowledging the limitations of such vernacular and populist critiques is as important as understanding the critiques in themselves. The reduction of critique to a defense of individual financial freedom might have been a necessary result of the apolitical nature of the investors' critiques, which significantly differed from other salient non-academic critiques, namely by workers and labor unions. The factory workers of the 1970s and 1980s, for instance, shared with the lay investors of the 2010s the grievances and resentment against "extremely abusive and despotic work relations" (Koo 2001, 16). In contrast to the asset seekers who tried to game the system, however, working-class laborers resisted the dominant structure of social control. Politics were central to their struggles in demanding not just higher wages but justice and greater representation (Koo 2001; Lee Y 2011). Even in the 2010s, a group of workers who had been laid off by Ssangyong Motor developed a radical critique in their resistance against layoffs as they refused a simple return to the status quo, i.e., returning to the factory. In building solidarity with others and imagining a different way of life to transcend the capitalist order, their radical critique called for rebuilding society and changing how we relate to one another (Choo 2022). Ten in Ten's critique differed significantly from workers' radical critique in that it lacked a political and ethical vision of "what kind of society one wants to establish" (Laclau and Mouffe 2001, xix). To borrow from Eleana Kim, who comments on freedom in a different context, such apolitical critique ignores "the radical unfreedom of people around the world, many of whom are unfree precisely because of" the new capitalist order that lay investors reinscribe (2022, 118).

It is also noteworthy that reducing critique to a defense of individual financial freedom shows the abiding force of the late cold war (Jung 2015; Kim E 2022). South Korea's notion of freedom has been developed within the complex history of imperialism and colonialism, and its Cold War roots have had a sweeping impact. In many postcolonial countries, the Cold War broke the link between freedom and equality, setting the stage for free market ideology (Chakravartty 2018; Grandin 2011). Likewise, anti-communism in South Korea hindered freedom from being tied to social solidarity, and instead gave the US-led Cold War ideal of freedom—which was associated with liberal democracy and the "American Way of Life"—a transcendent valence. As a result, the pro-democracy movement of the 1980s led by a broad coalition of intellectuals, students, workers, and ordinary people became largely content with political liberalization in 1987, rather than further demanding economic democracy and justice. After toppling the military dictatorship, the urban middle class was quickly demobilized and their previously favorable and supportive attitude toward labor was overturned (Choi JJ 1993; Koo 2007 [2002]). This facilitated the subjection of labor to the demands of capital and the state in the 1990s (Lee N 2022). As such, South Korea's two crucial roots of freedom—anti-communism (반공) and anti-dictatorship (반독재)—shared in common the veneration of personal liberty and the free market,[19] which led to the simultaneous development of democratization and neoliberalization in the late 1980s and onward.[20] Ten in Ten's critiques should be contextualized within this complex history.

FOUR

# Emotional Wounds

On one of the last days of Ten in Ten Academy in 2015, I was walking with Heewon, a mother of two in her mid-30s, to the location of the afterparty. We chatted about the lecture we had just listened to for more than three hours. When I asked how she thought the lecture went, Heewon said in an appeasing tone, as if she were soothing a baby, that "I wanted to say to Bum Young, 'Aww, I know *how much you have suffered.*' I wanted to comfort him." Heewon's sense of sympathy, expressed in an emotional and maternal way, had to do with Bum Young devoting the entire session of his program's last day to telling his personal stories. In what was similar to the narrative form of the "hero's journey" mentioned in chapter 2, Bum Young's story was about the lonely striving of a rebellious boy born into a lower-class family. His father was abusive and his mother, who had little schooling, had to support the family by peddling vegetables in a village market. His story included the external hardships that had caused him to suffer on an emotional level as he came of age, at college, during his military service, and in the workplace, as well as in his married life as a husband and father of two children. He spoke about how he endured and overcame various obstacles including the social ostracization he experienced due to his non-conformist dream of financial freedom. This story of self-realization concluded with a reaffirmation of his confidence as a freeman. Heewon felt that Bum Young's personal stories resonated with her more deeply than any other aspects of the program content, which demonstrates the effectiveness of the alliance between the ideal of self-realization and the narrative of suffering.

Such an emotionally charged response as Heewon's was not new to me. One Saturday afternoon in the summer of 2012—three years prior to meeting

Heewon—I was sitting in the Ten in Ten Academy for the second time. Trying to find a research site for my doctoral dissertation, I was eager for firsthand observations of how Koreans were dominated by monetary reason and how they were obsessed with investing. I enrolled in the program after three sessions had already occurred, and my second day was therefore the last day of the program for other participants. As in the first meeting I had attended the prior week, I walked away from the lecture feeling puzzled and having a lot to process about the instructor's unexpectedly critical stance towards capitalism. I headed to the afterparty without knowing that I would run into a more eye-opening moment there. In one of Seoul's typical taverns known for fried chicken and beer, I sat next to two married women in their 40s, Hana and Jahee. Like the other participants, they appeared to be quite spirited. They seemed to be emotionally boosted and experiencing a moment of camaraderie. Both were expressively grateful for Bum Young's passion, honesty, and "unique" character.

Hana did not have particularly high expectations when she enrolled for Ten in Ten Academy. She had taken a number of other asset tech classes before, and they had all felt the same. The 41-year-old realtor had once aspired to become a lawyer, but her dream had been frustrated after she failed the national bar exam several times. She gave up and took a part-time job when she reached 30. She met her husband there, a man she had never been in love with. Her husband was not financially independent. He did not have a regular job but occasionally helped with his parents' small business. Describing him as jobless, unfaithful, and abusive, Hana told us that the lives of women of her generation were no different than the traditional lives of her mother's generation. She choked up again when she mentioned that she had almost cried during Bum Young's concluding lecture. Hana found Bum Young's class especially touching because he put his passion into practice, which she believed she had failed to do. Hana felt her inner self was consoled. Tearing up, she remarked, "I saw some hope."

I did not get to meet Hana again afterwards and it remains unknown to me what actions she took for her self-realization after that highly emotional moment of awareness, or how she connected it to her financial project. However, the ethnographic encounter with her brought my attention to the ways in which asset aspirants responded to emotional discourses, even more than to calculative techniques for managing assets. We often think of emotional and economic discourses as contrasting with each other. However, the language of psychology, psychoanalysis, and therapy was as pivotal in discourses of asset tech as the language of economics. In Ten in Ten Academy, taking care of one's emotions had more than a tangential relationship to financial freedom. Paradoxically because of this, emotional *wounds* were expressed out loud repeatedly. What Ten in Ten Academy shows us is that the instructional site of asset tech became a space for the performance of emotional wounds. In order to trace the centrality of emotional wounds in the discourses of asset tech, this chapter examines various narratives of emotional suffering created by asset seekers.

I begin by reviewing Eva Illouz's discussion of the centrality of emotional wounds in therapeutic practices and, more broadly, in contemporary capitalism. As she notes, "emotional capitalism realigned emotional cultures, making the economic self emotional and emotions more closely harnessed to instrumental action" (2007, 23). My own analysis pivots on the incorporation of therapeutic practices by Ten in Ten Academy. I show that its afterparty became a ritualized space for performing the wounded self. The next section provides additional examples that illustrate how the narrative of emotional wounds structures the ways in which asset seekers articulate their aspirations. I close the chapter by circling back to the lectures of Ten in Ten Academy, arguing that claims to emotional wounds neutralize critiques of structural inequality.

## The Therapeutic Emotional Style and Afterparty

In her discussion of "emotional capitalism," Eva Illouz (2007) provides a lucid account of why emotional wounds occupy a significant position in contemporary capitalism. During the twentieth century in the US, she observes, the self-help ethos came to be intertwined so closely with psychology that the two became virtually indistinguishable. Self-help discourses promise that one can accomplish liberation and self-realization through a deep commitment to personal needs. Individuals are seen as having an inner reservoir of power that can be accessed through just the right use of the right technique. Therapy, which posits self-realization as the goal of the self, is conceived as one of these techniques (Rimke 2017). Precisely because of the alliance between the self-help ethos and therapy, "psychic misery—in the form of a narrative in which the self has been injured—has now become a feature of the identity shared by both laborers and well-to-do people" (Illouz 2007, 42). A narrative of suffering seems contradictory to the ideal of self-realization, but it paradoxically sets the process of achieving self-realization in motion by making an individual responsible for alleviating her or his own misery.

Illouz points out that therapeutic narratives in effect produce "un-self-realized" and sick people. Therapeutic narratives problematize particular inner states as obstacles to self-fulfillment. For example, those who are afraid of fully realizing their capacities are considered sick. They are urged to face those inner fears, anxieties, and traumas that prevent them from optimizing their capacities. Echoing the liberal view that self-development is a right, the thera-peutic narratives of selfhood have been pervasive in popular culture, talk shows, literature, workshops, and self-help kits. Therapeutic discourses, therefore, play a central role in making the self amenable to monitoring, diagnosis, and evalua-tion; these discourses thereby operate as a neoliberal technology of government that relies upon the self-realizing capacities of free, autonomous individuals (Seo D 2011).

If emotional and therapeutic discourses were swamping the discourse of asset tech in South Korea, they were not just limited to Ten in Ten Academy. Psychological discourses have permeated the discursive field of asset tech since its early days. Sunam Joung (2011) points out that the spread of asset tech dis-course after the early 2000s owed a lot to psychological discourses. At first, asset tech discourses relied heavily upon the vocabulary of economics, finance, and business management; but after incorporating the lexicon of psychology, asset tech became widely taken up. By placing greater emphasis on habits, minds, and attitudes, and by using accessible language, psychological discourses in advice literature stressed that transforming one's inner states was as crucial as the acquisition of knowledge when it came to becoming affluent. In this regard, Joung continues, it was psychology that "democratized" asset tech by present-ing it as feasible to everyone, not just to those with capital.[1] Bum Young was also heavily influenced by the western ideal of self-help and "the therapeutic emotional style" (Illouz 2007, 6) was prolific in Ten in Ten Academy. He hailed asset tech as a cure for the underdog (*yakja*) who had been ground down by the cruelty of capitalism. Ten in Ten Academy purported to "heal hurt souls" and "raise up those who have fallen" so that participants could empower themselves to prepare for the capitalist war. Participants were encouraged to engage with the self emotionally as part of the pathway to successful asset tech.

Illouz points to support groups, talk shows, counseling, rehabilitation pro-grams, and for-profit workshops as the social sites where therapeutic narratives, or the "talking cure," are prevalent; these are the sites in which one narrates one's life stories and performs the confessional (see also Peck 1995; Skeggs 2009). In South Korea, asset tech seminars such as Ten in Ten Academy became one of those crucial social sites where the wounded self was staged and the thera-peutic narrative of self-realization triumphed. In particular, the form of the social event called the "afterparty" (뒤풀이, *dwipuri*) lent itself to the thera-peutic emotional style. It is very common in South Korea to hold an afterparty following any kind of event, be it social or professional. If a main event like Ten in Ten Academy's lecture denotes formality, the afterparty evokes infor-mality, socializing, and play. Involving food and drinks, afterparties can follow virtually any occasion, for instance, wedding ceremonies, sports games, reunion

events, lectures, and work-related activities. While I was in college and graduate school in South Korea, I went to afterparties for a variety of occasions such
as after working on a team project, spending a day in street demonstrations,
completing finals, or even after just a regular class meeting. While the English
word "afterparty" tends to suggest a smaller, invite-only group of participants
following a main party, South Korea's afterparty is not necessarily about exclusivity. Anyone who attended the lecture at Ten in Ten Academy, for instance,
was welcome to go to the afterparty each day. As I will discuss later, the Korean
term that is equivalent to afterparty (뒤풀이, *dwipuri*) denotes that something
is unexhausted; that there is something further to be done. If there is no afterparty following the main event, some Koreans may feel that they aren't yet
ready to go home.

Because the afterparty usually entails food, drinks, and socialization, it is
similar to the idea of *hoesik* (회식; which means "dining together") that often
refers to after-hours socializing in a work context. Seen as "a central genre of
South Korean office social life" (Prentice 2022, 138), *hoesik* typically involves eating, drinking, and singing in a karaoke room with coworkers. As anthropologist
Prentice points out, workplace *hoesik* events involve a dual sense as both escape
and obligation. It is a form of corporate sociality that includes play and leisure,
but it has its "own forms of normative coercion" and has become "a locus for
complaint about South Korean office culture" (25). For those who are resistant
to it, *hoesik* is about unwanted excessive drinking, having to cheerlead for drunk
superiors and their inappropriate jokes, and being pressed to perform loyalty.
As seen in the previous chapter, Bum Young utterly despised *hoesik*, taking it
as corporate Korea's ugliest example of collectivism and as a form of unnoticed
oppression that dragged wage workers into "slavery."

Like the corporate *hoesik*, however, Ten in Ten Academy's afterparty began
with alcohol being served and Bum Young giving a toast, "Here's to Ten in
Ten!" The difference was that the Academy's afterparty was a social escape
without obligations. For an event that felt like it took the form of *hoesik*, but
with only comrades and no annoying boss around, participants found the
Academy's afterparty surprisingly hospitable. For the cost of about US$5—as
the program fee covered most of the afterparty costs—one could share meals,
drinks, and conversations with like-minded strangers. Certainly, participants
did not come to the afterparty without a sense of purpose. Many attended it
hoping to exchange information about their stock holdings, financial products and services, or the real estate markets. They shared money-making tips
they overheard elsewhere from brokers, fund managers, acquaintances, or other
asset tech programs. Many also discussed how they were trying to keep up
with the markets, which online forums were helpful, etc. However, despite such

instrumental ends, the afterparty was also a mundane occasion for drinking that many Koreans found themselves frequently attending. They could drink as much as they wanted without a boss forcing them to drink, sing, or dance against their will. Participants were ready to open up, get loose, and share deep conversations. However, this form of the afterparty did entail a sense of obligation to perform emotional wounds, as the next section will unfold.

## The Therapeutic Pedagogy of Asset Tech and the Performance of Emotional Wounds

I met Kyunghee (36, F) and her friend (34, F) at one of Ten in Ten Academy's afterparty occasions. It was the second round of the night at a casual restaurant serving soju and kimchi stew (meaning that the first session of the afterparty had been somewhere else and we had moved to this place for another session). The group was relatively small—only seven including Bum Young and me—and we managed to sit around two adjacent tables. During the previous round at a Japanese-style barbeque restaurant, Bum Young invited everyone to introduce themselves and I learned that Kyunghee and her friend were colleagues working as civil servants in the same office. Kyunghee's friend aspired to buy a condo apartment someday and prodded Kyunghee to take the class with her. Also among the party were Sihoon (40, M) and Jisu (37, M), the latter being one of the asset enthusiasts I mentioned in chapter 2 who wrote a fan letter to his real estate star.

It was a small enough number of people that we could chat as a whole group without private side chats. Conversations developed organically and spontaneously on many seemingly random topics. At afterparties, Bum Young liked to talk about his personal stories, usually about his family. He would share relatable, ordinary happenings in his family, but he often talked about their ongoing lines of conflict as well. That night, he boasted about himself being the kind of cool daddy who bought his teen daughter an expensive concert ticket for her favorite band. It was his gesture of emotional care for his daughter who was in serious, constant conflict with her mother. Bum Young dominated the conversation for a while, trying to apply his knowledge of psychology to the family conflict. He interpreted his daughter's challenges to his wife as a sign of the daughter's developing self-esteem.

Such storytelling by Bum Young often became an icebreaker and a catalyst for the performance of emotional wounds by others. Bum Young was strategically personal himself and encouraged others to be vulnerable. He would jokingly invite others to share their personal stories or, to be more precise, their personal "issues." It was after listening to Bum Young's recounting of the family conflict that the quiet Kyunghee began to speak in a way that implied that her marriage was difficult. Five years into her marriage, it seemed that she did not have a say in the couple's decision-making. Kyunghee's friend, single and two years younger, prodded her to "say everything here." When I asked the friend what she meant, she whispered to me, "Whenever her husband disapproves of her doing things, she just obeys." When all of us noticed that Kyunghee's marital relationship was on shaky footing, others began to encourage her to share more of her stories, just as her friend did. "You must have a communication issue with your husband," Bum Young said. To signal that he was ready to listen and be supportive, Sihoon also nudged the hesitant Kyunghee by saying, "If you don't speak to your husband openly, he can't know how you feel." Kyunghee's friend intervened, "But it's impossible to talk with him. I've witnessed that."

Kyunghee finally confessed to us that her husband did not trust her, which sometimes led to ugly troubles. Kyunghee's friend added her testimonials while Kyunghee continued, which helped listeners read between the lines: "When I see this couple, Kyunghee is great and she doesn't nag at all but her husband does a lot of nitpicking." "There might be something wrong with me," Kyunghee trembled. Sihoon, who had appeared to be reticent, became surprisingly opinionated: "You really need this program. Find yourself, improve your self-esteem, and make sure to attend the afterparty more than the lecture." Sihoon was not alone in believing that the afterparty had its own function in addition to the exchange of investing information. Many participants were as blown away at the afterparties as they were in the lectures. Afterparties provided participants with an ideal space in which they could share memories of suffering and emotional wounds. To help loosen up his participants, Bum Young, as a skillful conversation facilitator, shared his personal and private stories on various matters, including his family issues, childhood traumas, and investment failures. In this way, the afterparty often turned into a group therapy session for asset seekers. "People need to heal [by] resolving pent-up feelings," Bum Young said. He added to Kyunghee, "You have low self-esteem. It's not your fault. You deserve love, just by being yourself."

When Bum Young comforted Kyunghee and gave her emotional support, he was following the therapeutic script of self-help: asking someone to identify a pathology, building connections between the pathology and the past, and making oneself responsible for changing it (Illouz 2007). In therapeutic discourses of self-help, one needs to exercise "one's memory of suffering in order to free oneself of it" (Illouz 2007, 54).[2] Therefore, the narrative of self-help and self-realization is intrinsically a narrative of memory and, in particular, the memory of suffering. It casts individuals as damaged and injured, but also as "redeemable from within" (Rimke 2017, 6). Bum Young was positive when he spoke for Kyunghee—instead of asking her to identify a pathology and connect it to the past: "She needed to be recognized and loved by her parents when she was a child but wasn't." He continued, "Marriage works better when the husband loves the wife more than the other way around. But as it is not the case for her, her husband doesn't respect her enough. It's not her fault."

Kyunghee teared up and everyone else began to talk about their own inner wounds. Some tears were shed and laughter rose around the table, followed by supportive and cheering words. While the conversation was going on, Kyunghee noticed on her cell that she had missed several calls from her husband. With worried eyes, she disappeared to the restroom to return the calls. Kyunghee came out soon to get her friend since the husband wanted to talk to the friend in order to verify that his wife was indeed out with a female colleague. Everyone else, including me, was a bit surprised. Kyunghee and her friend stayed in the restroom for quite a while. When Kyunghee returned to our table with even more worried eyes, both picked up their purses and left quickly. After the two were gone, I was the only woman remaining in the group, so I too departed. It was around 10 p.m.

***

Examples of the performance of emotional wounds abounded at the afterparty. If "emotions have become objects to be thought of, expressed, talked about, [and] argued over" under emotional capitalism (Illouz 2007, 36–7), a drinking event that spurs emotional intensity made a perfect stage for this.[3] One night, the afterparty went on until 3 a.m. The group of people who were there would later constitute a tightly knit alumni group, which I will discuss in the next chapter. Three women and seven men, from their early 30s to early 50s, sat around in a tavern that served traditional Korean rice wine. On this night, the participants consumed lots of alcohol and got carried away with the performance of emotional wounds. Sharing their personal issues related to marriage, childhood, and finances, they talked about how damaged they were, on the one hand, because of violent parents, an abusive husband, a crazy, nagging wife, or troubled children; and, on the other, because of the bad economy, financial troubles, or distressing work.

Tactically vulnerable, Bum Young confessed that he found it difficult to show affection to his family because—invoking his psychological and therapeutic knowledge—his own father was a tyrant (*pokgun*) when he was a child and rarely had conversations with him. A traumatic incident during childhood and the improper development of early relations with parents are some of the most common tropes in the talking cure and are seen as a major cause of the flawed, pathological self that continues into adulthood (Rose 1999). Youngjoo, an unmarried woman of the same age (44) as Bum Young, agreed with him enthusiastically, recalling that her father smashed a rice cooker when she was a child: "My mom still talks about it. 'I took the plunge to buy an Elephant [a brand name] rice cooker. And your dad smashed it on the day I got it.'" Chulsung (41, M) concurred: "Our fathers were all violent at that time." Half-sentimental and half-joking, Youngjoo added, "The Elephant rice cooker was a Japanese import. My mom had finally bought it after a long resistance and dad destroyed it right away, and my mom would repeatedly say throughout her life, 'Oh, such a pity (아이고, 아이고)!'"

Youngjoo's performance of the suffering self continued as she changed the subject from her violent father to the difficulty of being a single woman at her age. She implored, "I'm doing well. I live normally. But why do people keep [asking me]?" Bum Young made a joke about it, saying to me, "Don't analyze her. She's doing well on her own." Youngjoo continued, "Do you know what questions people ask me? 'What do you do at home after work?' 'What do you do during the weekend?' They always ask me such questions." The empathetic Chulsung responded, "Damn it! It has nothing to do with them!"

The narrative of suffering dominated the afterparty as an important genre of speech. For Changhee (45, M), his biggest injury had to do with constant conflicts with his spoiled wife. According to him, his wife was a stay-at-home mother who rarely stayed at home. She often became verbally, physically, and emotionally abusive to Changhee and complained that his salary was too low. Furthermore, whereas he treated his in-laws with due respect, his wife was not willing to relate to his parents. Changhee said, "I should embrace my wife as she is, but I can't. So we fight a lot and we are becoming more and more distant from each other." An older male, Hongkoo (51), advised him to communicate his feelings more openly: "You should express yourself. You should tell her that you feel hurt when she bad-mouths you." Youngjoo later added her thoughts, saying that women should have jobs and earn money. Changhee clapped his hands in agreement.

I was not alone in thinking that the emotional wounds as performed were amplified. Two days later, I interviewed Hyeri (34, F) who had also been at the afterparty. She was a more reserved observer and would not come back to afterparties in the following weeks. She told me that that night felt like watching a shaman's *hanpuri* (한풀이; releasing or unbinding unrequited grievances) (see Kendall 2009, 22). It was an interesting parallel to make, given that both the terms "afterparty" (*dwipuri*) and "*hanpuri*" share the suffix "*puri*," which denotes resolving, releasing, or untangling. In typical afterparties outside of

Ten in Ten, what is to be released is not always emotional wounds. To the contrary, an afterparty can be characterized by unexhausted merriment and fun, for instance, as in the afterparty following someone's wedding ceremony. In Ten in Ten's afterparties, participants certainly wanted to untangle their social curiosity about each other and their pragmatic curiosity about asset markets; but the emotional injuries deep in their minds were taken to be the most pivotal ones to be untangled—similar to the feelings *hanpuri* evokes ("unrequited grievances"). Hyeri added more of her thoughts: there seemed to be three types of people who came to the afterparty—the knowledgeable ones, the networkers, and the emotionally wounded ones. For the wounded ones, Hyeri speculated that Ten in Ten Academy provided them with a unique opportunity to open up: "They must *not* be talking about money, asset tech, or their wife on other drinking occasions or when they hang out with friends, because they don't want to lose face."

Although it is not uncommon to use the word *hanpuri* in quotidian contexts, the word denotes—as it does in Hyeri's usage—a shamanic performance or ritual. Looking back at the 19 afterparty occasions I observed, holding an afterparty after each lecture was a conscious choice, not a mere cultural habit. The performed quality of emotional wounds shows that the afterparty was a central component to Bum Young's pedagogy of asset tech, as important as his lectures. At many afterparties, he visited each table, inviting every single person to talk about their injury. By confessing their inner wounds, participants were encouraged to identify their pathologies that were preventing them from self-fulfillment. Injury had to be generated so that a cure could be achieved. In this regard, the afterparty was not an appendix to the lectures; it completed Ten in Ten Academy, integrating "investing 101" with therapeutic self-help.

Not everyone liked the excess of this therapeutic emotional style. Sihoon later complained to me about the ways conversations were channeled into quasi-therapy: "We weren't allowed to talk about asset tech. Bum Young captivated the audience with his stories. [...] Even if we wanted to talk about asset tech, he led conversations in another direction. [...] Seems like we *have to* talk about something human or personal, according to him, at the afterparty." Frustrated with the sense of obligation to be vulnerable, however, Sihoon also generally believed in the therapeutic efficacy of afterparties, illustrated by the suggestion he made to Kyunghee that she take afterparties seriously. The emotional therapeutic style—in combination with critiques—enthralled Sihoon and led him into the discourse of asset tech. This 40-year-old man lived below the poverty line most of his life. His father had been a construction worker his entire working life and had only recently retired in his mid-70s due to an injury. Sihoon had to take on "whatever jobs were available" after high school to make a living and to contribute to the family income. After floating around as a casual laborer, telemarketing was the first full-time position that gave him a sense of stability. When I met him, he was running a franchise convenience store. In our interview, he gave me a long account of how the contract between the franchise corporation and franchisees was fundamentally unfair. Sihoon contextualized in detail the recent tragedy of a retiree (probably laid off in his 50s) who opened a franchised convenience store but soon took his life because of the predatory terms of the franchise corporate that led the store runner to incur debts instead of profits. Sihoon also wished he could walk away, as he had to work more than 12 hours a day just to get by. He said, "the kind of unfairness I have felt viscerally? I definitely felt it throughout life," and added that Bum Young articulated his inarticulate feelings in using the words "slave" (노예) and "exploitation" (착취). He also felt "empathy" with other participants, most of whom belonged in the middle of the economic class ladder, as opposed to Sihoon, who saw himself at the bottom. He interpreted the central message of the Academy as "the current way of living is not the only way. Another way of living is possible."

On one afterparty occasion—the night when Heewon became sympathetic about the young Bum Young—Bum Young said, "I am choked up whenever I talk about my mother. Something visceral comes up from deep in my heart." Many participants thought Bum Young revealed a new persona at the after-parties. While he appeared cold and rational in the classroom, he felt warm and softhearted at taverns. Sharing a comment he had heard from a past attendee, Bum Young himself said to me, "When I talk about something macro and rational, I should be cold, hard-nosed, because I should make people become conscious [of capitalism]. [...] But if you go to the afterparty, you should listen to the microscopic stories of people, for example their family issues."

## Making Inroads to Asset Tech through Suffering

If the afterparty offered a stage where participants performed emotional wounds, the narrative of suffering continued to structure the ways in which participants articulated their financial aspirations. In many participants' narratives, their motives for asset tech were centralized on the suffering self. The narrative of suffering as a genre of speech for South Korea's asset seekers had an important role to play: offsetting the culture of development. Koreans in the 2020s may no longer live with a felt stigma about the pursuit of unearned income after the Donghak Ants Movement, but the abounding narratives of suffering that existed during my time in Seoul testify that many still found themselves in the 2010s in need of defending their desire to generate income from assets. Narratives of suffering helped asset enthusiasts and hesitant novices justify their orientation to the asset market and define their practice of asset building as a cure for their wounded souls.

To Teo (37, M), his wounded self had to do with his lost passion and lost authenticity. When I first met him in 2013, he looked inspired, like many other participants, at the afterparty on the last day. Late night in a place offering only alcohol and snacks, Teo brought a burger meal from outside because he did not have time to eat dinner between work and the class. We happened to sit next to each other and he quickly unfolded his suffering self. Teo had never imagined that he would ever take an asset tech class. He used to be a free-spirited soul, playing guitar in a college band and performing salsa dance. A 37-year-old father of two, he was now working for a marketing team at a *chaebol* company, known as one of the highest-paying firms in South Korea. Teo nonetheless found himself miserable and emotionally debilitated. "I don't need a brain at work. I work like a cog in the machine." Finding himself to be a soulless corporate machine and breadwinner, he said, "I hate to talk about things like how much an apartment costs, what about rent, blah blah, but I've found myself looking at that stuff." At this point, Teo's roadmap for asset tech and self-realization was not clearly drawn. He said, "I want to create a system for cash flow and, after that, I wanna do what I really wanna do."

I met him again for a formal interview a year after. Teo responded favorably to my request, yet we had to reschedule the interview several times because of his unexpected overtime hours. When I finally got to see him in person, he looked burned out, making me wonder for a moment if I should send him home without asking any questions. Teo had changed quite a bit during the span of a year. He had been taking action in order to explore asset markets sooner rather than later. Teo had come to the conclusion that real estate suited him better than stocks. With so much time spent on work, he was left with insufficient time to read advice books. Wanting to break into the market as soon as possible, Teo came up with an idea that would allow him to read more advice books while he was at work: listening to audio books rather than surreptitiously reading paperbacks. With earbuds on and the audiobook app hidden on his desktop screen, Teo could behave like he was just working rather than distracting himself with audiobooks on real estate. During my time in Seoul for fieldwork, Teo transitioned into an even more aggressive learner and investor. He began to attend other workshops, organize discussion groups on social media himself, and hold offline gatherings to find fellow investors. Although I never did so, Teo prodded me to participate with him in a meeting he discovered online where people would gather to play Kiyosaki's Cashflow board game.

For Yoo (38, F), her suffering self was centered on the filial burden of repaying her family's debts. We have already met Yoo in chapter 2 as one of the asset enthusiasts and followers of Expert Seo. One of the motives behind her dedication to assets was to compensate for the pain that she had suffered due to her father's unsuccessful business. He defaulted when she was young, after which she and her older sister became breadwinners for the entire family, including a younger brother in high school. Since her early 20s, Yoo had spent the springtime of her life working overtime in the fashion industry every year for half the year. Yoo described the industry as women-friendly; most of her coworkers were women and benefits for mothers were secure. Still, the job was emotionally and physically exhausting. Overwork was a must and competitions were intense. She and her sister were able to repay their family's debts in their entirety before Yoo quit her designer job. They also financially supported their parents in purchasing a home.

"In fact, there wasn't a lot of new information or anything shocking to me," Yoo said about Ten in Ten Academy's lectures. This was mainly because she had joined Café Ten in Ten back in 2003 and was familiar with Bum Young's overall approach. More than the lectures, it was the afterparties that she found interesting. Yoo described herself as shy and reserved in meeting new people, but she found the afterparties rather comfortable. She described the afterparty as "an occasion where I got to talk about my story openly." Like many other participants, she also thought that the afterparty went as it did because Bum Young "opened up with his private stories first." Because "he felt candid and unassuming," she was able to converse with him "authentically."

It was not just the lecture material that Yoo had been familiar with. She also came with rich prior experience in the therapeutic emotional style. Overall, therapeutic discourses gained traction in South Korea after neoliberal financialization and the word "healing (힐링)" became one of the most prolific buzzwords in the 2010s (Kim EJ 2015; Park JK 2016; Park and Hwang 2018; Ryu 2012; Shim B 2013). As Eunjung Kim (2017, 19) notes, "the proliferation of books, lectures, and services that focus on healing seems to indicate that psychological and physical sufferings have become universal." As someone who enjoyed learning new things, such as foreign languages, baking, and dancing, Yoo had previously participated in a three-day workshop called the Landmark Forum. An "international personal and professional growth, training and development company," Landmark is headquartered in San Francisco and has more than 50 offices around the world. The Landmark Forum is its signature workshop that purports to "bring about positive, permanent shifts in the quality of your life—in just three days."[4] Strongly recommending it to me, Yoo described it as "a program that [helps participants to] wrap up the past and create the future."

It was her unending, emotionally unhealthy relationship with her father that she came to put an end to by participating in the Landmark Forum.

I did not know much about the Landmark Forum when interviewing her, but the name reappeared in a pile of books when I reviewed Illouz's analysis of emotional capitalism. Illouz herself had participated in the three-day workshop where she observed how the program used the therapeutic narrative of self-realization. According to her, the program asked participants to "focus on a dysfunctional aspect of their life" (49), build "causal connections with the past" (50) and make oneself responsible for changing the pathology—similar to the ways Bum Young guided many of the afterparty participants, including Kyunghee. A childhood incident in which "the self was presumably diminished" was a common theme that participants identified during the process. The Landmark Forum programs are also used by Silicon Valley tech companies, which have been increasingly investing in the emotional and spiritual health of employees. One start-up employee who attended an all-expense-paid retreat with the Landmark Forum said that it helped him "confront the childhood trauma of feeling like a failure" against his parents' impossibly high expectations (Chen 2022, 64). Like this Silicon Valley tech worker, Yoo felt that she had become much more of a whole person emotionally due to the Landmark Forum. She used to blame her father for the sacrifice she had to make, but she realized through the Landmark Forum experience that "every moment in my life I've created who I am right now. So, the sacrifice I made was my choice." The Landmark Forum remained a compass in Yoo's life.

Investing her time in asset tech rather than in her designer job was a manageable action she came up with in order to part ways with her past suffering self and carve out paths toward the future. To Bum Young's claim that wage workers are capitalism's "slaves," she "couldn't agree more." Yoo said:

> When I worked that hard, sales increased. But that's not mine. I worked like a slave. I am certain that it is right to get out of this situation. I worked for really long hours. If it had been my own business, I would own more now. I was a slave.

As mentioned in chapter 2, it was in the seminar called "Investing secrets of a 35-year-old investor who has bought 200 apartments" that I ran in to her the next year.

Mina (41, F) was a storyteller. Friendly, personable, and witty, she opened up quickly and always liked to talk about asset tech and her family. Her storytelling also often took the form of a narrative of suffering, with a more direct link made between suffering and asset tech. She turned her passion away from her children's education and redirected it to asset tech in order to distract herself from her ongoing conflicts with her son. To the nurse and mother of three, asset tech had not been her priority at first; education was what she had focused on. Mina deprecated herself, saying that she used to be a sort of helicopter mom (*hyeonmo*, 현모),[5] particularly to her first son whom she believed to be a gifted child. However, he found her expectations too high, while Mina thought he never tried his best. When she could no longer control her son and their relationship became "toxic," Mina decided, "Alas, I have to make money instead."

Mina also suffered emotionally and financially because of economic disparity. The first day we met, on our way to a subway station after a day of Ten in Ten, Mina began her story by mentioning that her children were surrounded by rich kids because of where they lived. Mina's family won a lottery for a long-term public rental apartment (largely due to the bonus points they earned for having three children) in Banpo, one of Seoul's most affluent neighborhoods. Her first son, a ninth grader, found that whenever a brand-new phone was released his classmates brought the new device to school the next day. Mina said:

> We are outliers. I don't necessarily want to make big money, like 10 or 20 *eok* won. I just thought "Aww, I can't even buy my kids a cell phone." […] When my kids say they have a craving for beef ribs, I have to tell them, "Let's just eat pork belly at home instead." So, it's not that I want to become rich. I just want to get them a cell phone and beef.

Mina was the main breadwinner since her husband had lost his job during the IMF crisis. After failing to keep a full-time job, he now delivered food part-time and was mostly a stay-at-home dad. Mina often contrasted her humble lifestyle with the glamorous ones of other women whose educational and income levels were comparable to hers. Importantly, however, Mina measured her financial suffering against those she aspired to be like. As will be shown in the next chapter, Mina was actually a homeowner but was using the property for rental income while her family was occupying the public rental apartment. Many Koreans regarded the public rental program as like winning the Powerball lottery. The rent was significantly lower than market values, the lease was for 20 years, and Mins's high-rise apartment was in a brand-name complex located at the heart of Gangnam. It was something that poorly paid, financially suffering Koreans aspired to have but could not access. Her rental arrangement, which was called Shift (시프트), was a new program for non-homeowners developed by Seoul City and a public housing company. Although this program was launched "to provide an alternative to homeownership—a decent place to live" for 20 years, anthropologist Jesook Song indicates that it was "not destined for working-poor people because it [was] becoming promising real estate for the middle class" (Song 2014, 45). Her research participants, mostly under-waged precariats, testified that "Shift targets middle-class professionals who can afford to pay high utility bills and interest on the bank loan they need to come up with the lease deposit" (Song 2014, 45).

Mina was a doer and a high achiever. She often put into action what she had learned before it slipped out of her memory. If someone recommended an advice book, for instance, Mina began to read it the next day. This woman of action did not end her story with an account of suffering. Like Bum Young, who concluded his narrative of suffering by affirming the ideal of financial freedom and self-realization, Mina's story also ended with the self to be realized in the future:

> I've got confidence now. I think I will be able to make more money. [...] Before taking this course, I used to complain at work with my colleagues about the intensity of labor. I used to criticize managers behind their backs. But now, I have stopped complaining because I will quit this job soon, because I will become rich.

Mina's conclusion that there was no need to complain came after she narrated a long story about unfair, intense work at her hospital. As the interview went on in an informal and unstructured way, she later added that she "objects to universal welfare (보편적 복지)" because "economic growth should come before welfare." In the next chapter, I will present more of Mina's stories to show how she aspired to become a foreclosure investor willing to evict other tenants.

### Flight from Critique to Repair[6]

A contradiction emerged in Ten in Ten Academy between its structural critique of capitalism and its exhortation to tinker with the system. On the one hand, the advice to build one's own system of assets and cash flow signaled that the current system was broken and not to be relied upon. However, Bum Young was clear that there was no alternative to capitalism; those below the poverty line should be supported by welfare, but wage workers could find leeway within the system. Therefore, it was highly contradictory when capitalism was said to be fundamentally and systematically unequal, and capitalist development was seen to scapegoat ordinary people, and yet participants were advised to make changes to their lives within the system.

In the end, the therapeutic emotional style resolved this contradiction by neutralizing structural criticisms. Narratives of suffering united various forms of psychic pain and economic suffering within the universality of emotional wounds. As I showed in the previous chapter, Ten in Ten Academy provided an array of critiques of capitalism, including a quasi-sociological critique of development and a quasi-poststructuralist and quasi-postcolonial critique of finance. While Ten in Ten Academy acknowledged the power relations that caused structural inequity, its therapeutic emotional style provided participants with the tools for translating structural problems into inner wounds manageable on the individual level. In critical capitalism, the harms that corporations, the state, and global finance had caused were transposed into psychic misery as a shared and democratized identity across class.[7]

Take the example of national development. While the state-banks-*chaebol* nexus was seen to have disadvantaged commoners systematically (see chapter 3), all participants were interpellated as victims and wounded souls who had been heartbroken by the capitalist state. The sacrifices that ordinary people had to make for the sake of economic development and the structural inequities that systematically disenfranchised them were now identified as inner traumas that obstructed individual self-realization. Along with other forms of emotional suffering and injury, the inner traumas were seen as commonly and equally shared by average Koreans, and qualitatively similar to other types of psychic pains that supposedly prevented one's self-realization. The same goes for the example of global finance. While the critique that global finance was governed primarily by US interests—which were themselves driven by Wall Street—was forceful, this was once again transposed into the national psychic misery of the Korean people as a whole, as a shared and democratized identity across class. Drawing on the scripted therapeutic narrative that combined suffering and self-help, asset tech discourses described financial self-realization as a route to repair. As such, emotional wounds made a perfect hinge linking critiques of capitalism with dedication to the financial and asset markets. Once the structural and social issues had been identified as an inner obstacle, they were to be addressed within the self. The therapeutic emotional style and the narrative of suffering therefore made each individual responsible for alleviating their own misery even when the underlying issues were acknowledged to be systematic.

Some more tangible examples of the flight from critique to repair can be found in seemingly insignificant moments in the lecture. For instance, Bum Young was talking about the importance of frugality when he attributed over-consumption to individual psychic issues. He showed a slide of Maslow's hierarchy of needs and raised the question: "Why would people buy Chanel or Mercedes?" A woman jokingly responded, "For self-realization." Bum Young dismissed it immediately, connecting luxury consumption to low self-esteem. People with a low level of self-esteem, he insisted, want to be recognized through what they possess. With his charismatic persona turned on, he suggested that participants find therapists if they were to be successful in asset tech:

> When your friend went to an expensive show and posted it on social media, it wouldn't bother you if you believe it's your choice not to go to the show. But, you think, "Why did I marry this loser guy from a struggling family? [I'm screwed] because of this stupid man ..." [...] How foolish is that! Think about how you always curse capitalism and hate riches. Isn't it because you guys are jealous of rich people? Observe yourself in terms of what it really means when you criticize others [...]. Sorry to say this, but you decry, "The rich are disgusting. They are villains," just because your self has been wounded. [...] Take a psychology class, please. See a therapist and try to understand what your trauma is.

This comment, made in passing, shows how therapeutic discourses took on a straightforward significance in his pedagogy. Capitalism is bad but a repair cannot be made if one does not resolve one's own inner problems first. Ten in Ten's afterparty was intended to provide a therapeutic space, but participants had to find a real therapist to be successful in asset tech. This was also a moment where the structural critiques imploded and the fundamentally sexist assumptions beneath critical capitalism surfaced. Not only was luxury consumption, which was connected to self-esteem issues, presumed to be women's behavior, but also discontent with capitalism was reduced to the jealousy and psychological issues of those with critical views.

However contradictory it was, the therapeutic emotional style was effective in championing the idea of individual repair. The memories of suffering and the emotional wounds that successful persons revealed—such as Bum Young, lay experts, and others at the afterparty—gave the idea of individual repair an even more respectable aura. Bum Young's success story came across as powerful due to his suffering, which he openly acknowledged, including a difficult childhood, social ostracization, and painstaking endurance of market volatility. At one afterparty, a male participant, who was similar in age to Bum Young, confessed that he had lost almost 1 eok won (about US$94,966) on the stock market. He said, "If we were told of only success stories, I would've suspected this program is predatory, but Bum Young has failed a lot. He is a human being." Another man added his own comment, "What's important is moving forward even after you have failed." Attributing the current wealth gap between himself and Bum Young to their individual capacities, this man exhorted the youngest male at the table—who had just graduated from college—to "try buying stocks with as little as 1 million won (US$949) and try bidding on real estate."

## Conclusion

This chapter has traced the prominence of emotional wounds in the field of asset tech. The profuse recounting of emotional wounds pertained to the ideal of self-help that is central to the discourse of asset tech. Drawing from the custom of afterparties, Ten in Ten Academy opened up a space in which the instructor and participants shared emotional suffering, turning the afterparty into a quasi-therapy session. The narrative of suffering also played a role in counteracting the residual culture of development, i.e., the ongoing sense of stigma toward unearned income. If the afterparty for Ten in Ten Academy offered a stage where participants performed emotional wounds, the narrative of suffering became a genre of speech for lay investors and continued to structure the ways in which they articulated their financial aspirations. I have argued that the emphasis put on emotional wounds reveals underlying contradictions in the Ten in Ten discourses. While these discourses presented forceful critiques of capitalism and the structural inequality it entails, the therapeutic emotional style quickly translated systematic issues into inner wounds and psychic misery. Emotional wounds were invoked to bridge critiques of capitalism and the project of asset building. Critiques were neutralized and left to implode. Emotional wounds were ordinary—as much as critiques were—and found to be universal.

# PART II

Social Reproduction,
or the Dilution of Critique

# Flipping Homes, Flipping Victimhood

One day, I was having coffee with Juyun (45, F), a stay-at-home mother who was residing temporarily in Seoul. Her daughter was in college and I asked casually about her daughter's major, without knowing what a vexing question this could be. I quickly realized something was going on when Juyun was hesitant to answer this question that I was not even terribly curious about. She smiled shyly as if she had been asked about something difficult or embarrassing, and insisted that she had already talked about this in our prior interview. I could not recall what her answer had been. After beating around the bush for a while, she finally gave me a confession that her daughter was in the Department of Real Estate Studies. Juyun was quick to add that a real estate studies major could lead to many different career paths. It was Juyun who had encouraged her daughter to choose this major so that her daughter could learn about real estate investing early on. Later I reviewed Juyun's interview transcripts, but we had never talked about her daughter's college major.

During the early 1980s, some universities and colleges began to establish real estate studies as a new area of study. It appeared to be a popular major among students and employers in the 1990s and gained stronger traction after the IMF crisis, as broader asset tech discourses encroached on the ivy tower.[1] Not just real estate studies but other courses with shaky academic merit, such as "Theory of Asset Tech" (재테크론) and "Affluent Studies" (*bujahak*, 부자학; translation from its founder), found a place in colleges of different tiers.[2] With the new dominant culture of neoliberal financialization, asset income seemed to be very much legitimized in higher education as well as in media culture. Juyun's reservation, though, tells us a different story. We were on a

93

spontaneous coffee date, after I thought we had already established a good rapport. Juyun was aware that I was eager to hear anything about her interests and that I would not judge her daughter's major. She still looked ashamed about putting her daughter in the real estate major—even while having been openly passionate about learning real estate investing.

Through the lenses of Juyun and the Alumnigroup she was part of, this chapter describes how Ten in Ten Academy's participants negotiated the tensions surrounding real estate investing. In the Academy they attended, Bum Young harshly and openly disregarded real estate speculators and flippers.[3] He would posit stock investing as a solitary game between an individual and the market with no visible group of victims involved, while seeing real estate investing as impinging directly on the dreams of other people. Alumnigroup picked up where Bum Young left off by selecting the foreclosure auction as the very first topic of their group study. By looking at how foreclosure investing was discussed in Alumnigroup, I track an afterlife of Ten in Ten to see how critical capitalism is enlivened and where it takes its participants.

This is a story of the social reproduction of investing subjects and of asset capitalism. For asset capitalism to be sustained, it is necessary to produce shared values, frameworks, and habitus. De Goede (2005, 9), for instance, states that the idea of finance as "a rational, normal, scientific, and respectable practice" was made possible through contested historical articulation and rearticulation. Similarly, Preda (2009, 2) contends that the emergence of the investing public required a shared interpretive and dispositional framework that shaped "a willingness to accept investment activities (and markets with them) as legitimate and highly desirable." I find that study groups such as Alumnigroup played a key role in South Korea in generating and maintaining such shared meanings that are essential to the reproduction of the contemporary economy. Investing was a relatively new field of knowledge, and many asset tech adherents I observed found study groups to be an effective way to navigate this new realm. The stakes were particularly high for foreclosure investing since it had been a moral hot potato. It involved more complex economic and moral stakes than those entailed by investing in the regular market, and thus foreclosure investing was one of the most contested strategies of asset tech and was often questioned by asset seekers themselves. Foreclosure investors felt that society disapproved of them and that they were tarnished even within the community of asset tech. Foreclosure seemed to be asset tech's most disliked aspirational practice. This chapter brings to light how Alumnigroup navigated this predicament, illuminating how the subjectivity of foreclosure investors was reproduced under the culture of critical capitalism.

In essence, members of Alumnigroup worked together to generate new meanings about foreclosure deals, translating speculative purchases of foreclosures into a common good for the national economy. The discussion of morality and the performance of victimhood occupied a central position in this process. Even though foreclosure investing had already become part of the dominant culture of neoliberal financialization in the post-IMF era, Alumnigroup saw it differently; instead, a moral stigma toward real estate investors was actively invoked and described as part of the *dominant* culture. To be clear, the moral repugnance was actively felt as part of the *residual* culture of development. As Raymond Williams (1978) has stressed, a residual culture should not be confused with a dominant culture—even though the residual culture is still active as an effective element of cultural processes in the present. It was through this deflection that foreclosure investors claimed victimhood and acquired moral capital. I argue that Alumnigroup went beyond offering a simple justificatory narrative for foreclosure investing; they developed a new art of "seeing like an investor." This emerging art of seeing like an investor involved more than developing the analytical ability to assess investment risk. It was about crafting new narratives to valorize their interest, shape an ingroup identity, and reassure fellow investors as well as other members of the public. By developing the art of seeing like an investor, the pursuit of rent was normalized and so was asset capitalism. It was through this process that the investing subject who treated homes as things to speculate on and flip for rent and profit margins was socially reproduced. In contrast, the idea of home as a place to live was marginalized and the displacement of propertyless people was rendered invisible. The social reproduction of investing subjects, therefore, unavoidably entailed the dispossession of others.

I chose to tell the stories of Alumnigroup partly because they were one of the most convivial, diverse groups of participants. They were composed of both men and women, single and married, ranging in age from 30-something to 50-something, ranging in income and occupation from those who earned less than 20 million won (US$18,993) a year[4] to an affluent businessman, from a casual laborer to a stay-at-home mother to a retired fund manager. The amount of investing capital each participant had ranged from zero to several hundred thousand dollars. Alumnigroup epitomized what critical capitalism was. They became champions of capitalism through generative community practices and collective reflections on existing capitalism.

In what follows, I first foreground the historical context surrounding the popular obsession with real estate investing and explain how the foreclosure auction emerged as one of the dominant strategies for asset seekers after the IMF crisis. The next section contextualizes the residual culture—the moral dilemma foreclosure investors had to redress—with a focus on the vulnerability of tenants within South Korea's unique rental system. A close reading in the following section of one of Alumnigroup's study meetings demonstrates how its participants developed the art of seeing like an investor, including the intentional obfuscation of what was dominant and what was residual. By positioning their interest as oppressed by the dominant, and by juxtaposing their practice with a common good, they claimed victimhood and acquired moral capital. This reversal of victimhood is further discussed through the lens of a legal case study carried out by Alumnigroup.

## The Dominant: The Rise of the Foreclosure Auction

In July 2020, South Korea's finance minister apologized for having failed to stabilize the real estate market and promised to tax short-term flippers and owners of more than one home more heavily. This apology came after the government had already implemented a series of measures, all of which proved unsuccessful, to curb inflated home prices.[5] Confronted with a public outcry and a dropping approval rate, the Moon Jae-in administration (2017–2022) urged top government officials to sell their second homes. This was not the first time the real estate market had gone out of control despite regulation. The Roh Moo-hyun administration (2003–2008), for instance, released regulatory measures for the property market more than 30 times, only to meet its own failure in stabilizing the market (Jung H-M 2017). It seemed that Seoul's real estate was permanently haunted by the ghost of speculation.

Popular interest in home resale values and house flipping has been widespread ever since the 1970s. The popular obsession with real estate profits is deeply entrenched in the country's history of rapid industrialization and speculative urbanization. It only took around 22 years for South Korea to reach a five-fold increase in its initial real GDP per capita—a process that took 160 years in the UK, 100 years in the US, and 75 years in Japan (Dunford and Yeung 2011). Such highly compressed growth came with all manner of socioeconomic issues, including massive rural-to-urban migrations and consequent housing shortages in Seoul. Responses by the developmental state were inadequate at best. The state used housing construction as a stimulus for economic growth, focusing on supply through large-scale development projects rather than on the provision of affordable public housing or improving lending conditions for low-income citizens. Furthermore, the state intervention was made under its strong alliance with *chaebol*, which often resulted in *chaebol*-friendly policies (Ronald and Kyung 2013; Shin HB 2008; Shin and Kim 2016; Yang 2018).

State policies were spatially uneven as well. Beginning in the 1970s, the authoritarian state picked a then undeveloped area in Seoul (Gangnam, now Seoul's richest district) to build infrastructure through mega-construction projects. As a result, Gangnam witnessed a thousandfold increase in land prices between 1963 and 1979 (Yang 2018, 74–5).[6] Sociologist Myungji Yang, who has studied the relation between spatially uneven urban development and the expansion of the middle-class, notes that many families who bought homes in booming areas by pure chance ended up significantly more affluent than others with similar household incomes and occupations who bought homes somewhere else. According to Yang, it became a common practice beginning in the 1970s for middle-class families to move frequently in order to turn real estate profits. Crucially, apartment flipping was the most prominent means for climbing up the class ladder; it was of higher importance than educational credentials and technical job skills (Yang 2018).[7] It is against this backdrop that speculating on homes has been highly envied and stigmatized simultaneously (Abelmann 2003; Nelson 2000; Yang 2019). The following two figures show that real estate investing was taken to be the most important practice for asset accumulation in ordinary life, well before the neologism "asset tech" ever emerged.

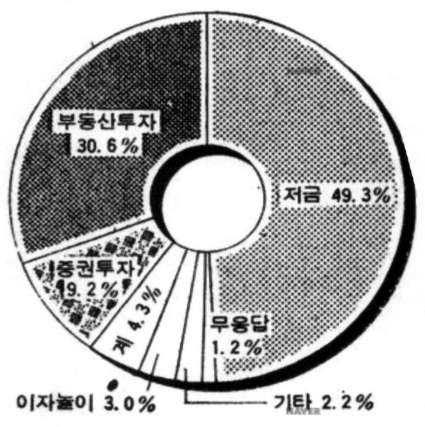

# 가장 좋은 재산증식방법

부동산투자
30. 6 %

저금 49. 3 %

증권투자
9. 2 %

계 4. 3 %

무응답
1. 2 %

이자놀이 3. 0 %

기타 2. 2 %

Figure 3. A Poll: The Best Methods of Wealth Accumulation (Source: *Donga Ilbo*, January 4, 1980.)

This figure shows a 1980 poll published in one of Korea's major newspapers. Among respondents, 49.3 percent picked savings as the best way to accumulate wealth, followed by real estate investing (30.6 percent), stock investing (9.2 percent), rotating credit association (*kye*) (4.3 percent), and private lending (*ijanori*, 이자놀이) (3.0 percent).[8] The high preference given to real estate investing is in line with Jesook Song's contention that the urban real estate market has operated as "a major source of both asset accumulation and class polarization in South Korean history" well before neoliberal financialization (2014, 47).

Figure 4. Advertisement for an Asset Tech Conference (Source: *Maeil Business Newspaper*, September 19, 1996, p. 5.)

The Maeil Business Newspaper company, the financial media corporation that spearheaded an asset tech boom in the 1990s, held a four-day conference in 1996 to bring together financial services firms and consumers. It was the very first event among numerous others to come. Asset tech conferences burgeoned in the 2010s, organized by a network of financial services firms and media conglomerates. Shown in the middle of this advertisement are thick coins stacked up, with an egg-shaped object next to them that is probably a golden egg representing wealth, albeit the black-and-white print would leave the interpretation ambiguous. In the bottom right corner (in a darker box) are captions promoting a competition to be held during the conference to stack coins. The tagline at the bottom in bold reads: "Do you want to build assets? Everything about making money will be revealed for first time ever." That this advertisement translated asset tech as "Property-Technology" (*sic*) might denote more than just a mistranslation. Above the call for the coin competition, a couple additional lines of text explain what types of information would be offered at the conference. Although this includes "banks, stocks, insurance, financing, lottery, financial asset tech products," the information leans heavily toward real estate investing.

It was after the IMF crisis that Koreans began to stake out foreclosure sales for greater profit margins. Shrewd investors could buy foreclosures for far below market price at court auctions and resell them to make a fortune. Foreclosure auctions (*budongsan gyeongmae*, 부동산 경매)—which are also called "court auctions" as they are managed exclusively by the courts—began in 1960, but it was not until the early 2000s that they were widely taken up as an investing strategy. While foreclosures in many other countries involve a mortgage lender (i.e., a formal financial institution) as a creditor, in South Korea foreclosures had been closely connected to the informal financial sector.[9] This is because ordinary people could not access credit through official financial institutions under the state-banks-*chaebol* nexus and therefore private loans prevailed. In place of mortgage loans provided by banks, it was common for Koreans to rely on familial support and private lending to purchase a home. When a homeowner borrowed money on their property, either for home purchasing capital or for something else later, and then failed to repay the loans, creditors (including private individuals) would bring a case to court. With the court's approval, the property would be foreclosed and put up for auction.

Due to credit restrictions and the absence of mortgage loans, almost all private transactions before the IMF crisis, including real estate, were conducted using cash. This is why, for decades, foreclosure auctions were not much of a viable option for lay investors.[10] As a comparison, real estate in the US was seen, for a long time, as "an opportunity for poorly capitalized individuals to generate investment portfolios far beyond what would be possible with stocks or bonds" (Garboden 2021, 2). Long-existent mortgage loans established such a belief, because purchases were leveraged and barriers to entry felt fairly low. In contrast, Korean asset seekers—for whom leverage was not thinkable until the early 2000s—believed that the threshold was high for real estate investing because it required high capital and could incur big losses.[11] In this regard, neoliberal financialization was a game changer for many, with the sudden extension of credit to ordinary consumers. More crucially, US-style mortgage loans were introduced in 2004. As housing finance became widely available to the public, the leveraged purchase of real estate was made possible in Korea.[12]

It was against this backdrop that lay investors turned their attention to the foreclosure market. With the newly available mortgage loans, shrewd investors realized that they could purchase a foreclosed property with borrowed money for greater margins. In the mid-2000s, prospective buyers began to pack the courthouses where foreclosure auctions took place. The number of bidders increased by 59.89 percent between 2000 and 2005 (Choi J 2006). I recall that one of my aunts was frantically on the hunt for foreclosures during these years. She had always been a money-savvy person, but she was noticeably busy during that time, making trips to check out foreclosed properties, making bids at the courthouse, and going to real estate offices to resell apartments. The auction boom peaked in 2007, setting record-high sales before it was hit hard by the global market crash in the following years (Seo 2016). Having lost my father's retirement savings to the stock market earlier, my own family moved around during these years to occupy some of the apartments my aunt could not flip immediately.

The emerging hype of asset tech was certainly another motor driving the foreclosure boom. Pundits on the subject appeared in the media and overpriced private classes mushroomed.[13] The pundits urged citizens to ride the wave of new capitalism and promoted the foreclosure auction as an especially profitable path. Once a property has been won by a successful bidder, the argument went, the auction winner can generate profits either by flipping it or renting it out. The former is a way of making profits within a price range. In the latter case (renting out the property), returns are generated as cash flow. Pundits said that mixing the two (i.e., selling the property after renting it out for a certain period) could generate the highest returns.

When I was conducting fieldwork in the first half of the 2010s, the auction market was on the rise once again. After years of slumps following the 2007–2008 global financial crisis, the market was boiling again and many people I met were turning their eyes back towards foreclosures. If each property had three to four bidders on average during the prior boom in the mid-2000s, the number jumped to 5.21 in 2012 and to 6.21 in 2013 (Moon and Lee 2013). During the first half of 2015, each property listed in a court auction had 7.9 bidders on average and the average successful bid was at 89.4 percent of the appraised value, with both of these numbers at their highest in ten years (Kim S-M 2015).

## The Residual: Moral Dilemmas of the Foreclosure Auction

The back story behind the investing booms in foreclosures is that these booms often took place in tandem with rising debts and defaults. The initial boom (i.e., 2004–2007) was driven not only by the introduction of housing finance but by other sorts of consumer debts that were soaring. After the IMF crisis, the government unleashed consumer credit in order to revitalize the economy through domestic consumption. Consumers were recruited, in the words of Nelson (2006), "to the economic frontlines to take up the slack of global demand" (201). In line with the government policies that promoted consumption through credit, in the post-IMF era credit card companies set up street booths and peddlers, and any adult-age individual, including students and the unemployed, was able to obtain a credit card on a street corner. As a result, the number of credit cards issued doubled between 1998 and 2002 (Kim S-Y 2011, 22). The rapid uptake of consumer credit changed ordinary economic lives, and South Korea witnessed a drastic increase in debts and delinquency. Between 2002 and 2003, for instance, household debt grew by 30 percent (Nelson 2006, 204)[14] and the number of credit-delinquent individuals soared from about two million in 2000 to 3,824,000 in 2004 (Kim S-Y 2011, 16). These rising debts and defaults set the backdrop of the foreclosure investing boom. Those failing to settle their credit card debts had to see their homes foreclosed and, thus, listings for the court auctions grew significantly. There was some truthfulness, therefore, to Bum Young's statement that foreclosure investors took advantage of the misfortune of others, and Juyun's uneasiness had to do with this reality.

It becomes even more controversial if we consider not just defaulting home-owners but the tenants who reside in foreclosed properties. Indeed, foreclosed properties are often occupied by tenants. Although this might also be the case in other parts of the world (see Grynberg and Anderson 2018), the level of dis-possession created by foreclosures tends to be more significant in the Korean rental market. Simply put, many tenants put down massive deposits in place of monthly rent and their lump sum money becomes imperiled if a foreclosure auction occurs. I will describe in the next few pages South Korea's unique rental system in order to highlight the heightened vulnerability of Korean tenants. In distinguishing between vulnerability and victimhood, Chouliaraki (2021, 10) defines vulnerability as "an embodied and social condition of openness to violence." I likewise consider vulnerability as an embodied and socioeconomic *condition* that makes one susceptible to dispossession. The particular vulner-ability of tenants has added a dilemma for amateur investors when it comes to foreclosure auctions.

South Korea's most prevalent rental system (*jeonse*, 전세; also transliterated as *chŏnse* or *chonsei*) is different from the monthly rental system typical in many other countries, although the latter type (*wolse*, 월세) also exists. Predominant for more than a half century, a *jeonse* lease, which usually runs for two years, requires its tenant to put down a massive deposit in lieu of monthly rental pay-ments. The deposit that a tenant should pay upfront depends on market condi-tions. It had typically been 50–80 percent of the rental home's sale price (Song 2014),[15] but it shot up as high as an unprecedented 90 percent in the mid-2010s (The Economist 2014). The landlord returns the deposit when the lease is up, without interest, and the tenant moves out. Importantly, a landlord can use the deposit for any purpose during the lease, as long as he or she returns it to the tenant at the end of the contract. Therefore, the landlord "in effect collects rent in the form of bank interest on the deposit paid and often uses this income as principal capital for business and so on" (Kim S-H 2011, 184). Under the *jeonse* system, the transaction between the tenant and the landlord is essentially a loan where the tenant is the lender, the landlord is the borrower, and the house is the collateral (Phillips 2014).

*Jeonse* emerged as a self-help funding mechanism under the state-banks-*chaebol* nexus in which 90 percent of bank loans were directed to *chaebol* and households had almost no access to credit. In the absence of mortgage loans or any other forms of consumer credit, the *jeonse* lease functioned as an informal, private credit system. As Song points out, for the landlord, "it is a promising business, because he or she is able to access funds, in the form of the lump-sum deposit, on which to earn interest" (2014, 53). The landlord did not even need to have the deposit money in hand to return to the tenant at the end of the lease. Conventionally, the landlord, the outgoing tenant, and the incoming tenant met at a realtor's office where the incoming tenant's deposit money was passed on to the outgoing tenant. Tenants also tended to prefer *jeonse* to other arrangements, including the monthly rental system, which many tenants think of as "throwing away money every month" (Nelson 2000, 54). In this sense, the *jeonse* system was "a saving mechanism" for tenants and "a credit-loan opportunity" for landlords (Song 2014, 11).

Nevertheless, the *jeonse* system worked to homeowners' and rentiers' advantage (Han D 2019). The system was a convenient means for them to quickly expand capital. When the interest rate was high, simply putting the lump sum of money in a savings account generated a good amount of cash flow. Moreover, informal financial markets thrived under the state-banks-*chaebol* nexus, which made private loans highly lucrative. Landlords were able to lend the tenant's deposit to someone else in the curb markets at a high interest rate. They could also use the deposit to buy another property. Indeed, acquiring lump-sum deposits from tenants was a crucial strategy for people to buy homes. A home-buyer could match their cost to the price of the home minus the deposit they would receive when they lease the home. The *jeonse* system therefore has often been used as a means of speculating in homes with small amounts of cash and this has contributed to the polarization of the financial classes (Kim S-H 2011; Song 2014).[16]

Because of the large sum of money at stake, *jeonse* tenants became severely vulnerable to dispossession in the event of a rental home's foreclosure. If the defaulting landlord does not give the tenant their money back, the tenant is entitled to a refund when the property is sold at court auction. However, it has often been the case that a foreclosed property has multiple creditors—due to the lack of affordable lending from official financial institutions and thriving curb markets for private loans—and there is insufficient money to repay all the creditors after the property has been sold. The court distributes money to each creditor according to the order of priority designated in the property's title document. Secured creditors have higher priority than unsecured creditors, meaning that they are paid first. Many tenants often have the lowest priority among secured creditors or, in the worst-case scenario, they are unsecured creditors.[17] It is nearly impossible for tenants to recover their deposit fully if the foreclosed home is underwater with preexisting creditors. In many cases when landlords default and properties are sold at auction, tenants fail to fully recover their lump sum. In 2013, of those tenants whose leased properties were sold at court auction, 79.31 percent did not fully recover their lump sum payments; this percentage has increased every year since 2010 (Song H 2013). To *jeonse* tenants, not just the fear of eviction but the likelihood of losing a significant sum of money is inherent to their lease contract, which conditions their vulnerability. An auction winner frequently has to evict the tenant of the previous owner, which often ends in a teary drama. Staking out foreclosures for the purpose of one's wealth acquisition, therefore, is a particularly charged topic, much more so than buying shares of stocks or investing in the regular real estate market.

## The Emergent: Seeing Like an Investor

A few weeks after the Ten in Ten Academy had concluded in October 2014, nine participants met in a Gangnam barbeque restaurant to discuss how to run a cohort group. Rough plans and some initial rules were established at this meeting: group study would take place once a month and members would take turns giving a presentation on any topic related to asset tech that they were relatively familiar with. The topics and presenters for the first three meetings were chosen as well. It took only a moment for them to reach the unanimous decision that Changhee (45, M) should lead the first meeting on the subject of foreclosure auctions. Having spent five weekly gatherings of the Ten in Ten Academy together, participants were aware that they had a shared appetite for this topic. As a firm believer in real estate, Changhee habitually said that wage workers could not get ahead and stressed the joy of finding hidden gems in the foreclosure market. Having learned that Changhee was into foreclosures, other participants wanted to hear about his experience, and he happily agreed to be the first presenter.

For monthly regular meetings, they met in one of the places called a "study café" near Gangnam Station. A study café is an establishment that combines a tea house and a seminar space. As a trendy space for students, freelancers, and working professionals, most study cafés are clean, spacious, comfortable, and equipped with brand-new audiovisual equipment. However, sticking to the frugality motto emphasized in the Ten in Ten Academy, participants chose the most affordable option among many such places. Located in a rundown building on a residential street, the study café where Alumnigroup met cost US$1 per hour per person. The place seemed to have been repurposed cursorily, several participants conjectured, from an old *noraebang* (a song bar, or karaoke bar) that had gone out of business.

A manager of an advertising firm, Changhee brought slick presentation slides. They were simple but attention-catching. The first slide was just an image of a red die, shown from an angle exposing its three dimensions. This slide visually epitomized the whole point of his talk: a thing has multiple dimensions and so does the foreclosure auction; thus, do not judge it from a narrow angle. Insisting that morality was a complex, multidimensional issue when it came to the foreclosure auction, Changhee contextualized the die with the following opening statements:

> There seem to be a lot of misconceptions about the foreclosure auction. I want to debunk those misconceptions before giving you some practical tips. Let's say this die is a foreclosed property to be auctioned. [...] A die has the numbers one, two, three, four, five, and six, but people see just one dimension. You always see just one dimension of the foreclosure auction and say it's awful because the tenant of the property is kicked out. But as with everything else in our life, we should see the foreclosure auction from many different angles. Seeing just one dimension is not good.

According to Changhee's account, the dominant view of the foreclosure auction was apparently highly negative and disapproving. For the next hour and a half, he elaborated on how such a disparaging view should be challenged. "The foreclosure auction benefits *everyone*," he repeated several times. The conventional wisdom Changhee sought to revoke was that the buyer benefitted from foreclosure deals whereas the defaulting homeowner and the tenant fell prey to them. He instead argued that the foreclosure auction benefitted *all* stakeholders, not only the bid winner (i.e., the investor) but also the defaulting homeowner, the tenant who was living in the distressed property, the creditors, and the state. A defaulting homeowner can pay off debts to creditors, Changhee specified, tenant(s) can have their deposits returned, creditors can collect their money, the state can earn taxes, and a bid winner can purchase a home at margin. He pleaded:

> So please don't focus solely on the negative aspects of the foreclosure auction. What about the state? All of us are better off when money circulates. When a house is valued at 200 million won (US$189,933) but 700 million won ($664,767) is lent on it, the economy is stuck. The foreclosure auction unblocks the clogged blood vessel and puts the economy back into a virtuous cycle.

The significance of the foreclosure auction, according to his view, lay in its ability to repair a broken national economy. This idea presumed that "the economy," as a fixed category detached from sociocultural realms, must exist in a certain state in which capital continues to flow. As Timothy Mitchell (1998) points out, however, understanding "the economy" as an autonomous, coherent structure and a self-evident totality was a discursive construct of the twentieth century. By means of this discursive construct, the nation-state found a new way to claim legitimacy and a novel conception of politics as growth was invented. In South Korea, the notion of the national economy served primarily to justify capitalist development driven by military dictatorship. Changhee's claim essentially brought us back to the familiar repertoire of national development while leaving ambiguous what sacrifices were to be made. In other words, his claim doubled down on the idea that a healthy "national" economy reigns supreme over equity. By linking a personal, speculative enterprise to the health of the national economy, Changhee framed the foreclosure auction not as an entitlement but as a *duty*,[18] which invoked the same sense of responsibility as the gold collection campaign of 1998 that was carried out in the name of saving the indebted nation (see chapter 3).

Investing clubs are commonly seen as creating a *cognitive* map of the market in order to pick items to buy and sell collectively (Harrington 2008). Alumnigroup differed from such investing clubs since, of greatest importance, participants did not pool capital to invest as a group. Moreover, in urging us to change our point of view on foreclosure investing to envisage it not as a means for personal profit but as a project for bettering the wider community, the novelty of Changhee's approach had to do with his focus on the virtuous and moral dimensions of real estate investing. Having attended several seminars focused on the foreclosure auction, I was expecting Changhee's talk to focus on what was commonly known as the "analysis of entitlements" (*gwolli bunseok*, 권리 분석). Just as many stock investors rely on the analysis of the fundamentals, foreclosure investors perform an analysis of entitlements. To understand the entitlements of each creditor of a foreclosed property, the analysis of entitlements requires extensive research on the part of a prospective buyer. It is considered essential for foreclosure investors to comprehend the credit status of the property, details of the financial stakes of each creditor, and the tenancy of the property (including the possibility of it being occupied by tenants who do not exist on paper). For an analysis of entitlements, a prospective buyer has to closely read the title document of the property and other related documents, which requires a high level of legal and financial literacy. Most of the paid seminars and "cram schools" instructed participants on such analytical skills with concrete examples, highlighting that a thorough analysis of entitlements helps buyers avoid potential complications and hidden risks. The provision of investing statements (see chapter 2) was also a common instructional method so that the audience could learn the breakdown of costs, payment schemes, and estimation of returns. Changhee departed from this typical pathway, illustrating that the emerging art of seeing like an investor was more than developing financial acumen or analytical proficiency. Going beyond drawing a cognitive map of the market, Alumnigroup charted out a moral framework for the market itself to reassure both those inside and those outside of the market. To see like an investor was to draw and embrace this moral framework.

Changhee's claim was clearly a reassurance for someone like Juyun who wanted to turn real estate profits but had reservations about it. While Juyun and Changhee did share a felt sense of moral repugnance toward their own interest—a visceral response to the active residue from the pre-IMF era—I maintain that there was an intentional obfuscation of the dominant and the residual. Investing in foreclosures has been part of the dominant culture of neoliberal financialization since the early 2000s, but Alumnigroup forged a world that was still punitive to foreclosure investors. The effect of positing their interest as oppressed by the dominant was that they could claim a victim status. In other words, the intentional obfuscation of the dominant culture with the residual one worked to flip the vulnerability of tenants over into the victimhood of foreclosure investors.

Memories of eviction complemented Changhee's presentation in amplifying middle-class victimhood. A few participants in Alumnigroup had the experience of their tenancy being foreclosed. This experience had been particularly harsh for Youngjoo (44, F) since she was thrown out from the first place she rented on her own after leaving the parental nest. She graduated from high school in 1990 and took a clerical job. She was able to save enough to rent a bedroom in Seoul in 1997 for a *jeonse* deposit of 23 million won (US$24,129) by living frugally, saving most of her paychecks, and accruing interest in the informal lending markets. Her independent living was short-lived though, as her landlord defaulted when the IMF crisis hit. The house was sold at a foreclosure auction and Youngjoo had to leave without recovering any of her deposit. All she had was 500,000 won (US$357) of relocation money that the new owner provided as a courtesy.[19] She moved back in with her parents, quit her job, and lived like a hermit for a while.

About 20 years had passed when I met her in Alumnigroup. Stylish, never married, and highly conscious of her looks, Youngjoo habitually spoke of Gangnam as a fashionable and cultured place while diminishing the rest of Seoul. Operating as a free-floating lender in a curb market, she now owned two rental homes and was eager to purchase more properties at the auction. Despite her current wealth and comfortable life, the memory of eviction always prevailed in any discussion of foreclosure investing. Her narrative of suffering seemed to provide an alibi for her speculative projects. Her memory of eviction did not just evince the past vulnerability she had suffered through while she was a member of the financially marginalized. It was a vehicle for victimhood in the present, a means of transposing the moral value accruing to the vulnerable group of tenants to the individual who had transiently experienced it. Based on the reversal of victimhood, foreclosure hunters defined themselves as those who were unfairly judged by society despite their suffering and despite the contribution of their economic practice to the common good.

Alumnigroup provided a unique social context in which such memories of eviction came to validate their current practices. Participants discussed trading strategies and technical details on a number of occasions, but they carried on the ethos of Ten in Ten: pondering the mandates of asset tech, keeping a critical eye on the economy, and valuing the community experience they generated. In this sense, Alumnigroup was less similar to the investing clubs that operate like small businesses (Harrington 2008) than to the Bible study groups that are seen as a site of "knowledge production and disposition formation" (Bielo 2009, 11).[20] But Alumnigroup's distinctive focus on individual presentations was an organizational feature that separated it from either of these types of groups. At regular meetings in North American investing clubs, members pitch or articulate their reasons for wanting to buy or sell stocks, although some members might have more to say than others (Souleles and Hansen 2019). In the context of group Bible study, collective reading is the most crucial practice, with discussion led by a facilitator (Bielo 2009). In comparison, the study meetings of Alumnigroup were run in a traditional lecture setting where one person taught the rest of the participants—in the form of a presentation—just as in the for-pay programs such as the Ten in Ten Academy.[21] Much as the online community of Café Ten in Ten lent itself to the emergence of lay experts and their followers, Alumnigroup became a platform for lower-level lay experts to arise. This setting metaphorically resembled what participants tried to do: it authorized the expertise of the speaker and, in so doing, authorized the topic of presentation as worthy of serious discussion. By having a lay expert share his knowledge generously in a community setting, Alumnigroup generated "experiential qualities of detachment and independence" (Stout 2016) from the supposedly judgmental outer world. Instead of linking the memory of eviction to collective struggle for social justice, it reinforced the victim status of the participants.

Juyun also shared a similar experience, although she managed to avoid eviction. A few years earlier, her *jeonse* apartment had been foreclosed when her landlord defaulted. Her family would likely have been kicked out of their residence without getting their full deposit money back. They were fortunate, though, to have enough capital to bid on their leased apartment when it was listed for auction. They lived in a southern province where condominium apartments were much more affordable than those in the Greater Seoul area, and Juyun's husband was in a lucrative industry and had brought home a stable income for almost 20 years. They won the auction, became homeowners, and minimized their losses. It was this past experience that opened Juyun's eyes to foreclosure investing. In Alumnigroup, Juyun would often confess to her inner conflict. At the afterparty that followed Changhee's presentation, she said, "I'd like to make money by buying foreclosures. But I feel undecided because I know someone like me can fall prey to it." Yunna (34, F) responded supportively: "Even if you don't do it, someone else will." Changhee quickly reiterated his point, telling them that the [defaulting] homeowner is the biggest winner when their home is foreclosed and sold in an auction. The authorized speaker encouraged Juyun to walk away from having a tenant disposition and to see like an investor instead.

## The Reversal of Victimhood and the Social Reproduction of Foreclosure Investors

The reversal of victimhood became more pronounced during Changhee's presentation as he moved on to a legal case study, a mode of learning commonly adopted by foreclosure investors. The tenor of his account was an emphasis on individual responsibility and the distinction between tenants deserving and undeserving of legal protection. Contending that most tenants lose money just because of their naivete, Changhee held tenants accountable for their vulnerability. In stressing that legal protections for tenants were already in place and in effect, Changhee asserted that, "legally speaking, everything has been done to protect tenants. They suffer because they don't know about the laws. […] What else can the state do for them?" The legal protection he was referring to is the Housing Lease Protection Act (HLPA), which ensures that tenants with smaller deposits can recover their money first (all or partial recovery) in the case of their rental homes' foreclosures, even though there are preexisting creditors who have established prior liens.[22]

Changhee projected onscreen a newspaper article (Yoon HJ 2014) reporting on a case where an eligible tenant was denied his HLPA rights in court. The tenant, who was in a wheelchair and was the father of two, burned himself to death after his *jeonse* apartment was foreclosed and his family was removed from their home without their deposit returned. The sum of the deposit he put down for the three-bedroom apartment (approximately 1170 sq. ft) amounted to 25 million won (US$23,741), which was seen as notably lower than the market average. To begin with, the father was the victim of a lease fraud instigated by the landlord and a phony broker. The landlord intended to rake in cash by renting out the underwater property before he was to default. In complicity, the real estate broker reassured the tenant that the HLPA would protect his deposit. Right after the tenant family signed the lease and moved in, the landlord stopped paying the monthly mortgage. The apartment was foreclosed in two months, and the family was evicted by a new owner the next month. It took only three months from move-in to eviction.

According to the HLPA, the deceased tenant was entitled to receive 88 percent of his deposit (about US$20,892) when the apartment was sold at auction. The court declined to recover the funds, however, on the grounds that the tenant himself contributed to the landlord's fraudulent activity. The court saw that the property was already underwater (i.e., the total sum of loans on the property was already much higher than its market value), and thus its foreclosure was foreseen at the time the tenant signed the lease. It is important to understand how this verdict failed to take into account the tenant's point of view. Not only was it difficult for the tenant to predict the course of action the landlord would take (i.e., whether the landlord would walk away from his debts or not), it was also hard to gain a full picture of the landlord' financial condition beyond one given property (i.e., whether the landlord had capital beyond the underwater property). In fact, it remained unclear if the victim was aware of the extent of the indebtedness of the apartment. If he was aware, he might have taken the risk anyway because there was no better option. The tenant took his life on the day that his family was forced out.

Changhee placed the blame on the tenant by referring to the court ruling. He maintained that the tenant was an emblem of a moral hazard intensified by tenant protection programs. According to Changhee, the verdict confirmed that the tenant violated the rights of the preexisting creditors. The fact that the tenant signed the remarkably affordable *jeonse* lease, Changhee argued, testified to the unscrupulous character of the tenant:

> What I mean by seeing [the foreclosure auction] from multiple angles is, thinking that "Aww, the tenant had a disability and he immolated himself" is just focusing on the tenant's perspective. It means that you don't think about his unscrupulous wrongdoing. He was too greedy. [...] The deposit was nonsensically cheap. ... How on earth can a three-bedroom apartment be 25 million won (US$23,741) in Incheon? He must have known [that it was fraud]. Greed brings about a disaster. The law protects only deserving people. [...] Do you still think the most sympathy-worthy party is tenants? No. It's creditors.

In fact, however, the newspaper article he was referencing defined this case as a white-collar crime targeting poor tenants. Such crimes, committed not by neighborhood hustlers but by corrupt financial and legal professionals, were observed to be on the rise. By contrast, Changhee's recounting of the case focused on dividing between deserving tenants and undeserving ones, which reflected South Korea's broader post-IMF logic of neoliberal welfare citizenship that "discriminat[ed] between 'deserving' welfare citizens and the 'undeserving'" (Song 2009, xi). By putting emphasis on individual responsibility,

Changhee generated a reactionary narrative to contest the fact that poor tenants were dispossessed in foreclosure markets. In a reversal of the moral hierarchy between the supposedly irresponsible, naïve, and even unscrupulous tenants and others involved in the foreclosure auction, foreclosure investing was transformed from the act of dispossessing the vulnerable of their money and space of life to the virtuous act of resuscitating the economy.

On the reversal of victim status, Chouliaraki and Banet-Weiser write that we need to ask not only who the victim is but "from which position this claim to victimhood is made; who gains from such a claim and who is set to lose" (2021, 5). In Alumnigroup, the reversal worked to portray the vulnerability of tenants not as a socioeconomic condition but as related to one's moral character. Tenants looking for affordable housing were portrayed not as a group susceptible to dispossession but as individuals who were likely to violate the rights of others and who were therefore undeserving of legal protection. As seen in the court ruling, once tenants were deemed undeserving, this had real consequences including the loss of money and life. It was often working-class and poor tenants who were seen as undeserving because the *jeonse* deposit was often discounted if the property had preexisting liens. An affordable *jeonse* home often had higher loans on the property than its market value and involved a number of creditors, and these homes were the most likely to be occupied by tenants having lower economic, educational, and social capital.

Meanwhile, foreclosure investors and wannabe investors gained moral capital by claiming victimhood. Individuals come to possess moral capital when their moral virtues are acknowledged, and moral capital provides its bearers with a specific kind of power by defining them as legitimate economic actors (Wilkis 2018). Likewise, what the participants of Alumnigroup gained was moral legitimacy for house flipping. They were set on pursuing speculation and avoiding moral repugnance or inner conflicts that would potentially hold them back.

"I'm completely sold!" Mina gave a shoutout to Changhee when his presentation concluded. As mentioned in chapter 4, Mina's family had won a lottery for affordable, public, long-term rental housing; even better, their unit was part of a high-end apartment complex at the heart of Gangnam. The lottery system had a set of priorities including one for parents. Having three children, her family earned big bonus points and was prioritized. The extroverted and chatty woman had opened up quickly from day one; however, for a long time she did not disclose that she bought a house after winning the lottery. She had been self-conscious about taking advantage of the affordable public rental—which was very rare in South Korea—while being a homeowner herself but renting out her own place for monetary gains. As mentioned in chapter 1, she had been also secretive within her social circles about taking asset tech classes and would lie that she was taking humanities classes instead. She was emboldened, however, by the community practices of Alumnigroup, the newly created narrative about foreclosure deals, and the moral capital acquired through this new narrative. It seemed that she was set free from a moral indebtedness that had been incurred by being involved in the displacement of propertyless others. The helicopter mom-turned-asset enthusiast (see chapter 4) was taking a fee-based class on foreclosure investing and reading advice books zealously. In a self-deprecating way, Mina said that just reading a book alone was not very helpful: "I've never bid. [...] It was like scratching the surface. Learning just a theory is very limiting. So I think it's essential for us to learn by actually bidding, purchasing, and kicking out tenants."

## Conclusion

We see that the participants have arrived at the point where it is risible to view them, in any way, as critics of capitalism. The practices of community and emotion are strongly held, but the critique has run out of steam. Although Alumnigroup discussed a variety of items in asset tech including stocks and funds, it is significant that they took up the foreclosure auction as the first topic of group study, a path particularly conducive to speculation. Crucially, the practice was harshly detested in the classroom of Ten in Ten. In discussing the foreclosure auction, members of Alumnigroup developed the art of seeing like an investor, which required much more than financial acumen. The attainment of moral capital was key to their emerging art, which was made possible by amplifying victimhood and translating foreclosure deals into a common good for the national economy. The moral capital they accrued empowered the participants to take a stand, without any moral reservation, in the foreclosure market where poor people were severely dispossessed. The way in which participants were socially reproduced as foreclosure-investing subjects, therefore, involved justifying the dispossession of the propertyless. While many in Alumnigroup and in the broader community of foreclosure hunters described that their devotion to the foreclosure auction was an act arising out of necessity (e.g., to supplement wage income, to prepare for retirement), their involvement often turned out to be outright speculative. Changhee, for example, was anxious about a looming layoff that he felt was just around the corner. It felt as though he had been "standing on the edge of a precipice." The foreclosure auction seemed to be his last resort, until he told me later that his family "impulsively" purchased one floor of a building in its entirety. The account that I have given in this chapter is not just about one of Ten in Ten's afterlives; it exemplifies a living afterlife of critical capitalism as well. Critical capitalism socially reproduces the investing subject, which has consequences for the economic underclass.

# SIX

# Single and Wanna Be Rich

I met Sangbo (37, M) in 2015 at a monthly meeting of Singlesgroup. The two-hour meeting was centered on his talk on what it means to approach asset tech as a principle of life. Sangbo's presentation was like an extended motivational speech, but the tone was gentle and far from an aggressive pep talk. Sangbo seemed to have put a great deal of work into preparing his content and presentation. His PowerPoint slides were full of cartoon images and humorous references. Making his content accessible to the lay audience, Sangbo also managed to avoid jargon and engage effectively. After the talk came to an end, a dozen participants headed over to a pub for beer and chicken wings. As people arrived at the afterparty site in twos and threes, Sangbo came over to greet to me. His cheeks were bright red after the long presentation. He seemed to be excited, relieved, and proud at the same time at having successfully completed the nerve-racking, on-stage performance. Because it was my first time meeting him in person, another participant, Jinwook, introduced us to each other.

I had heard of Sangbo before from several other participants, and it seemed that he was also aware of why I was there. As though he wanted to help my research, Sangbo spoke to me for a while without any prompting. He talked about what motivated him to participate in Singlesgroup by asking a rhetorical question: "Why would I spend so much time volunteering to give a presentation for this group? To learn asset tech? I can learn much more elsewhere. It is because of the comfort I feel with these people. I can be myself here without worrying about social norms." The norms he mentioned were about the normativity of marriage. Singlesgroup was mostly composed of those who were born in the 1970s. Although late marriage was becoming increasingly common in South Korea,[1] many participants in Singlesgroup felt insecure about their extended singlehood. Sangbo explicitly hailed social, relational, and emotional satisfaction as his primary motivation for participating in Singlesgroup, while understating its pragmatic ends. This tendency to place greater emphasis on personal relationships and the sense of community was one of the most prominent traits shared by members of Singlesgroup.

This chapter looks closely at the tangled pursuit of assets, community, and personal relationships through the lens of Singlesgroup. Made up of dozens of 30-plus, unmarried men and women interested in asset tech, Singlesgroup provides a privileged window through which to discuss the social reproduction of investors within the context of urban singles. Singlesgroup performed community through socialization, group study, and information sharing. Its participants were socially made into and reproduced as investors through community practices while also enacting a particular form of singlehood.

Singlesgroup was made up of 74 unmarried people (almost all were never married rather than divorced or widowed), including 33 "lurkers" who did not participate in offline activities or in online interactions. Of the 41 "non-lurkers," nearly half (n=20) were women and the other half (n=21) men. While everyone was unmarried at the time that the group was formed, five members got married over a few years. Three members found their spouses outside of Singlesgroup and the other two met within Singlesgroup and surprised the other members by announcing their wedding. Participants came from many different professions, ranging from freelancers to white-collar office workers, public servants, teachers, and so on. It is safe to say that many of them had secure employment that came with middle or higher incomes. Still, the group had members who were at a much more precarious end of the workforce, including those who worked in retail, bakeries, or fashion. There was greater variation among them when it came to investing knowledge and experience. Participants ranged from those who might be seen as lay experts with a long history of self-directed, informed investing to novices with minimal or no financial literacy to those who were not doing any form of investing and were only using savings accounts. New members were admitted via referrals, mostly from existing users of Café Ten in Ten.

In tracing how Singlesgroup was brought into being, I discuss its significance as a community for asset-minded singles in relation to South Korea's long-held marriage normativity. Through spontaneous meetups (called "lightning"), participants took socialization seriously and Singlesgroup became a key site for enacting a heterosexual singlehood linked with mobile, flexible, and connected lifestyles. At the same time, financial virility was another emphasis put on the heterosexual singlehood they performed through group study and online information sharing. The next sections delineate the multiple ways in which social activities spurred participants toward asset tech, including financial socialization, risk management, and self-entrepreneurship.

## Making a Social Club for Asset-Minded Singles

Singlesgroup was formed by two men who met through Café Ten in Ten. Mr Seven and Smoothie were both white-collar workers of the same age (44), with secure employment and income.[2] Smoothie was struck one day by Mr Seven's posting entitled "Ten *eok* won is my goal. Will I really accomplish it?" Describing himself as "an old bachelor" (*nochonggak*, 노총각), Mr Seven listed his asset portfolio, which was valued at approximately 650 million won (about US$593,607). He had a diversified portfolio including annuities, a variety of savings and cash management accounts, and all manner of funds. Concluding the post, Mr Seven expressed an interest in meeting like-minded people:

> I am a wage worker. My salary is not that high, a little more than 50 million won (US$45,662). It's been 17 years since I started working for this company, and I have continued to save 80 percent of my paychecks. I was able to save like this because I had a goal. Making ten *eok* won is my goal and my dream is traveling around the world. Of course, I don't have a girlfriend. Some people say marriage is also a path to asset tech and remaining unmarried is my biggest flaw. People also say you should have rich people around you if you want to become rich. I will work hard in order to make an additional 350 million won (US$319,634). Where do you put your money? I want to organize an asset tech meeting. Leave a comment if you are interested. For those born in the 1970s and 1980s, let's meet and share information.

This posting seemed to be a sneak peek into what Singlesgroup would be about: the single life presented as aspirational but lonesome; the assertion of financial prowess juxtaposed with the anxieties around financial disadvantages for single households; and the desire to pursue social networks, a potential spouse, and material assets simultaneously. Smoothie responded to Mr Seven's call and their meeting quickly came about. The two met in Seoul's bustling business district, packed with towering office buildings. It was a rendezvous between an enthusiast and a socializer, which would later define the nature of Singlesgroup. At this meeting, Smoothie learned some more specifics of Mr Seven's portfolio. "We met, you know, inside of the G building at Euljiro. The

H company has been leasing the building. Mr Seven said he's the building's investor. I was, 'What? In what ways can he invest in the building?'" Smoothie continued to explain. "It turned out that he was holding shares of a dividend-paying fund and the fund was investing in that building. There is a thing called 'dividend funds.' They invest in real estate, receive dividends, and distribute the dividends to shareholders. [...] I found it fascinating."

Apparently, Smoothie had not been very familiar with asset markets before he met Mr Seven, even though he had been a regular at Café Ten in Ten for several years. It was after he became a homeowner that Smoothie developed an interest in asset tech. He was everything that a typical Korean man of his generation was not: shy, polite, sweet, and allergic to alcohol. He would cover his mouth with his hands when laughing, a behavior typically associated with a traditional feminine demeanor. He lived at his parents' house, put most of his paychecks into installment savings plans, and was able to buy a new condominium apartment in 2011 with a minimal bank loan. It was around this time that he became a regular user of Café Ten in Ten.

As a fixture of its Beautiful Singles board, Smoothie represented the playful investor or socializer; he was nowhere close to being an enthusiast or a lay expert. He "got to know many people and came to be more reflective about [him]self" by using Café Ten in Ten. One of Smoothie's posts (2010) read:

> [Café Ten in Ten] offers the knowledge and information we can't get from the mass media. [...] We can [...] learn about aspects of human life through various stories on dating. By interacting with different people, we get to know each other's worldviews. This is the best strength of the Internet, and I've learned a lot from this Café. I'm very thankful.

As seen in this post, Smoothie found Café Ten in Ten meaningful to his life and particularly appreciated the lively culture of the Beautiful Singles board that he contrasted with "a tedious life centered on work."

As discussed in chapter 1, Café Ten in Ten created an environment conducive to the transformation from a socializer to an enthusiastic investor. For Smoothie, getting to know Mr Seven catalyzed his transition. It was through their meeting that Smoothie was socialized into the world of various financial products and full-fledged asset tech:

> We moved to the Starbucks across from the building to talk more. We introduced ourselves to each other. He works at such-and-such company, and I work at blah-blah company. Both of us are single. [...] He told me how he made money so far, and I was really surprised. [I realized]

"Wow…there are these really innovative, really amazing methods that others don't know." He is already all set for retirement. He talked about how to build assets, how to choose annuities, and how he was preparing for retirement, etc. I said it's great and it'd be helpful for beginners.

The two men came up with the idea of finding more people to create a tight-knit group. The idea was to organize "a small group of five or six people who are good at asset tech to share information together." Smoothie posted on the Beautiful Singles board to invite interested users to an offline meeting. About a dozen people showed up and almost everyone expressed interest in meeting on a regular basis. An online group was created to arrange group activities to follow, and the shy Smoothie took up a leadership role.

One of the keywords participants frequently brought up when describing their practices was "*chinmok*" (친목; being close, friendly, and harmonious) which denotes socializing. Smoothie recalled that he intended to make Singlesgroup not just a place for discussing asset tech but also a space of *chinmok*. His attention to socializing was indeed amply found in the online space of Singlesgroup. "We created this group," Smoothie posted, "not just for the purpose of asset tech, but also to make a social group by sharing empathy and friendship with each other." In our interview conducted more than a year after this post, Smoothie stated that the social aspect of Singlesgroup had grown significantly, to the extent that it was overwhelming the mandate of asset tech: "Asset tech is only ancillary. What's going on now is mostly *chinmok* activities."

Many of the participants felt that creating a meaningful social space for singles in their 30s or older was much needed, given South Korea's long-held marriage normativity and the stigmatization attached to late singlehood. Nelson (2022, 74) writes that "the *inevitability* of marriage was built into Korean social structures and cultural practices" and "marriage universality was reinforced through repetitive representation in fiction and nonfictional media, […] in the commercialized matchmaking industry, and in the constant hectoring of unmarried young people by parents, friends, teachers, and coworkers." While she traces marriage normativity back to premodern Confucianism, she also notes that heteronormative marriage was definitional to biopolitical administration and the labor structure during the second half of the twentieth century. Under the presumed universality of marriage, Nelson concludes, the existence of unmarried women was historically erased from view, and "South Koreans reacted as though not being married was inconceivable and unprecedented" even at the turn of the millennium (83). Similarly, Song (2014) documents extensively how contemporary single women experience marriage pressure from the family and elsewhere. Her ethnography presents a painfully vivid picture of how single women were labelled as "deficient" by coworkers (63) and were subject to "the constant matchmaking discussions and the invasive comments about their appearance intended to make them more suitable for the marriage market" (22).

Even though both Nelson and Song focus their discussions of singlehood on the experience of women, many single men I interviewed felt they were hit hard by the privileged status of marriage as well. They were far more advantaged financially than unmarried women since men had higher incomes and promotional opportunities, which afforded them higher chances for loan approvals and higher credit line. They were also subjected to parental and societal regulations significantly less than single women were (Song 2014). They nonetheless experienced social isolation and infantilization because of marriage normativity, which regarded marriage and parenthood as one's entry into normal adulthood.[3] As seen in Mr Seven's posting, they also shared anxieties about the financial advantages provided to married couples that they were missing out on.

It was Dongsoo (44, M) who invited me to Singlesgroup. An IT administrator in the financial services industry, he was well versed in funds investing and had been using Café Ten in Ten actively for almost a decade. A softly spoken man with a receding hairline, he was often asked to repeat himself since he spoke too quietly to hear. When I first met him at the Ten in Ten Academy, he would sometimes be placed in an awkward situation. One night, for instance, Bum Young threw out an ice-breaking question to Dongsoo, who had remained silent most of the time at the afterparty. Bum Young asked Dongsoo if he lived alone, independently from his parents. Dongsoo said "no," and other conversations halted immediately with an awkward moment of silence. It seemed as if everyone had been left speechless by the idea of a man in his mid-40s who was still in the parental nest. Not only did the silence make Dongsoo uncomfortable but it also implied his social infantilization and emasculation.

Seven years younger than Dongsoo, Sangbo would rage over the damning social situations where he was often grilled about his unmarried status. "If you work in Korea," he said, "you get questions everyday about why you don't get married. If you go to a wedding or a baby's first birthday party (doljanchi), it's a lot of pressure on people of my age." Sangbo went on to elaborate, "I went to the wedding of a junior colleague last weekend. I thought in the morning, 'Oh, I will get a ton of questions today.' […] If you sit at the wrong table, you think 'Shit! I just wanna leave no matter how good the food is.'"

In this broader context of marriage normativity, Singlesgroup offered a neutral ground for singles in their 30s and 40s where they took such pressure off while enjoying themselves and sharing interests. This is why Sangbo firmly believed that "the members are *not* here for asset tech. Asset tech-related conversation is like a mere dessert, which takes up only 20 or 30 percent of conversations."

## Meet Like "Lightning" (Spontaneous Meetups)

If asset tech was a mere dessert, the main dish for Singlesgroup was socializing. Lightning illustrates the preponderance of socializing in Singlesgroup and the type of singlehood it produced. "Lightning" (*beongae*, 번개) is a slang word for an online-instigated meetup. Although its meanings have been significantly broadened compared to its use in the 1990s when it first appeared, it still denotes an Internet-enabled meeting that has a degree of spontaneity. The size and purpose can vary, ranging from a one-on-one meeting to a gathering of dozens, from hanging out to chatting to eating out to carousing to filmgoing, etc. The level of spontaneity varies as well. Some meetups are planned ahead of time and others are held on the spur of the moment. Café Ten in Ten's Beautiful Singles board had a rich tradition of lightning, without which Singlesgroup would not have been created to begin with.

After Singlesgroup took shape, lightning evolved into "ritualized entertaining" (Osburg 2013) that enacted a particular type of singlehood. In his ethnography of China's elite networks of nouveau-riche entrepreneurs, state managers, and government officials, Osburg (2013, 26) observes that "the bulk of the relationships that make up these networks are forged through ritualized leisure" such as banqueting, drinking, singing karaoke, and cavorting with female hostesses. According to him, it is through these shared experiences that homosocial intimacy is created, which is a key component of business in contemporary China. Likewise, my contention here is that ritualized entertaining such as lightning made Singlesgroup a key site for enacting a heterosexual singlehood linked to financial productivity as well as to mobile, flexible, and connected lifestyles.

In Singlesgroup, a lightning meetup usually took place when one participant suggested online a spontaneous lunch meeting, coffee break, or after-work drinks. Such a gathering happened if anyone responded to the suggestion. After a lightning meetup had taken place, participants posted photos and brief reflections to keep the rest of the members updated. Most lightning occasions were spent engaging in chitchat, eating, drinking, and hanging out in places such as restaurants, coffee shops, and taverns. I also saw numerous meetups that entailed less spontaneity and more planning (e.g., picnics, hiking, outings to hidden gem restaurants, housewarming parties).

At one of the lightning events I attended, participants welcomed back two seasoned members who had been gone for a little while. GreySky (35, M) had been an active participant in Singlesgroup, but had disappeared for months while he was dating a new girlfriend. Even though he had been hopeful that the relationship might lead to a marriage, they eventually broke up and he made a return to Singlesgroup on the day of the lightning event. GreySky became the butt of teasing at this gathering. No one talked about asset tech. Instead, most conversations were in the form of jokes focused on dating or marriage. Self-mockery about being single was a constant theme throughout my fieldwork, not solely that night. Participants had moved to a different pub for a second round of drinks when another longtime member joined us. He had returned that same day from a six-month trip overseas. After welcoming greetings, the adventures he went on in Southeast Asia became the new subject matter for conversation.

Smoothie wanted to wrap up a few hours after, but the rest of the participants wanted to stay longer and consume more beer. Smoothie whispered to me, "What do you think about the character of our group? Aren't they quirky?" I laughed. Sangbo, one of the most ambitious, asset-minded enthusiasts, recalled the night as fun because he was able to "hang out without thinking." On my way back home, I took a subway with GreySky. Having observed so much interest in dating, I asked him why there were no flirtations or romantic relationships within Singlesgroup. GreySky was very sure that "people are all checking each other out implicitly."

Lightning was, in part, a way for participants to keep each other company and enjoy leisure activities when many of their old buddies had been taken away by marriage and parenting. At the same time, lightning paved the way for unmarried people to find like-minded dates. Many in Singlesgroup wanted to date and/or get married, but they found it increasingly difficult to develop such connections as they grew older. Most members were in their late 30s or above, a cohort stuck between changing and abiding norms. In the middle of the 2010s, this range of ages was viewed as too old to remain unmarried, whereas younger cohorts were more actively exploring other options such as online dating, hookups, and/or opting out of marriage. At a time when many members were seen as faltering due to their unmarried status, Singlesgroup offered a space where they were able to pursue sociality, bonding, and intimacy through lightning. Such practices marked an alternative to the stereotypical image of late singlehood. Instead of being socially isolated and seen as incapacitated adults unable to start families, they created experiences of singlehood linked with mobility, flexibility, and connectedness. Such lifestyles were reaffirmed by means of frequent online chats and spontaneous gatherings.

Although not everyone had the luxury of having a high income and flexible work hours, many were afforded at least one of these. Those who worked mostly outside of offices and those doing shift work exemplified flexible hours. Yongmi (39, F) worked for an insurance company, where she was in charge of consumer instruction. Her daily duty was to visit different firms to speak to the employees, which required her to travel to multiple sites every day instead of sitting in an office chair. Moving from one site to another via the subway, she often listened to podcasts related to asset tech, browsed Café Ten in Ten, or checked out the online space of Singlesgroup. As a seasoned socializer on the Beautiful Singles board, she had attended numerous meetups before joining Singlesgroup. She first participated more than ten years ago in a two-day getaway. Dozens of unmarried users of Café Ten in Ten gathered at a large vacation rental to enjoy cookouts, share drinks, and play games, which Yongmi recalled as "having fun like college kids." Afterwards, she would go to a lightning when she "wanted to get to know new people" or "felt down and happened to see a lightning notice for drinks." Singlesgroup became her social home after it came into being. She no longer had to hover around in search of social events but was able to turn to Singlesgroup for meeting and talking to regulars. She was excited whenever a lightning post popped up on her phone and she would stop by as she traveled from one work site to another.

Picasso (37, M) was another socializer who oriented his mobile and flexible lifestyle toward socializing and dating. He joined Café Ten in Ten in order to ride an investing boom back in 2007, but he was more blown away by its vibrant culture of lightning. Since he was doing shift work at a public firm, he was able to attend plenty of meetups at various times during the day. Like Yongmi, he would go to a meetup to kill boredom; but he was more straightforward in our interview, adding that "[I participated in lightning] for the purpose of meeting the opposite sex." With the shaping of Singlesgroup, the backbone of his social circle changed from Café Ten in Ten to Singlesgroup. Picasso pinpointed *chinmok* as his favorite aspect of Singlesgroup. Although he did not think of anyone in the group as his "bestie" *per se*, he always felt welcomed in the group even though he would sometimes ghost on it.

### Invest Like Virile Men

Many participants acknowledged the heightened significance of socializing in Singlesgroup, but this did not mean that the pursuit of asset tech was halted. At the end of the day, Singlesgroup was a collection of asset seekers—those who wanted to socialize not just with random singles but with financially responsible and asset-minded singles. Participants seemed to gather primarily to enjoy each other's company, but the practices of *chinmok* entailed interest, not just intimacy. Participants worked to improve their own investing skills by sharing information and learning from one another. Group study and online information sharing were the two pivotal activities that allowed them to expand their horizons in asset tech. More importantly, it was also through these two practices that participants enacted a heterosexual singlehood linked with financial productivity in a highly gendered form. Male participants were more vigorously engaged than women in instructing others and sharing information, and they saw the gender divide as a sign of women's ineptness. In this sense, Singlesgroup offered a space in which male financial virility was exhibited in the course of creating an alternative singlehood.

It was a pressing issue for unmarried people to get a strong handle on finances. Marriage normativity not only associated old bachelors and maids with economic unproductivity, but it also institutionalized financial advantages for married couples in a variety of ways. In regard to the former, Nelson's comments on marriage normativity in the premodern era merit further consideration: "Although the household shared both production and consumption, there was no recognized role for unmarried adult women in their natal home, and in the premodern era the options for self-sufficiency outside the family were limited for men and even more tightly constrained for women" (Nelson 2022, 75–6). Although modernization and industrialization allowed many unmarried men to live a self-sufficient life outside their parental homes—which also became slowly available to some unmarried women—a never-married Korean was still considered a less mature, complete person and more unproductive and wasteful. For instance, Bum Young initially targeted married couples when creating Café Ten in Ten as he perceived them as the most productive demographic with promising odds to thrive financially. He regarded never-married people as an economically unproductive population, depicting them as self-indulgent, reckless, and unprepared for asset tech. He did not shy away from speaking out on his belief that married people were more responsible and serious. The following statement, which he made during a lecture, is just one instance among many similar iterations:

I am saying people become mature only after getting married. That's why I don't want to give advice to single people. Unmarried people just spend money, they go on a trip as they wish. They see a musical ten times. They are that immature. They have nothing important in life— only themselves. [...] You grow up when you start a family.

Underlying this statement was a deep prejudice that saw unmarried adults as unformed and infantile; Bum Young regarded them as irresponsible, not even worthy to receive financial consultation.

Probably more consequential were the real policy frameworks designed to offer marriage premiums. Unmarried people were disadvantaged in different ways when they applied for the purchase of new apartments or bank loans for rental housing,[4] since housing policies were based on the normative family. For instance, Jesook Song (2014) points out that unmarried people younger than 35 could not apply for bank loans for *jeonse*. One of her informants said that marriage was the only option if a woman under 35 sought a loan approval for rental housing. Given that home ownership has been the most predominant way for Koreans to build assets, such disadvantages for single households posed formidable roadblocks for unmarried people. This contextualizes Mr Seven's statement that "some people say marriage is also a path to asset tech and remaining unmarried is my biggest flaw."

Against this backdrop, group study and online information sharing provided a crucial space in which participants could pursue financial stability and create an alternative singlehood. Study meetings were set to take place on the first Saturday of every month.[5] Each meeting consisted of a presentation or two, followed by a short discussion and an afterparty. The group relied heavily on a pool of seasoned investors, and presenters were selected either when someone volunteered or by Smoothie's invitation. Several members, including a tax accountant, a realtor, and a National Pension Service employee, were tied professionally to fields closely linked with asset tech. They also occasionally gave talks on subject matter related to their fields. Examples of presentation topics included: "Foreclosure Auction for Wage Workers," "Introduction to Brazil Government Bonds and ELS [Equity-Linked Securities] Funds," "Stock Investing for Beginners," "A Slightly New Perspective on Value Investing," "Introduction to the National Pension," and "Airbnb and the Sharing Economy." Most presentations were based on the presenter's own investing and/or professional experience, but a research overview or a summary of a guidebook was sometimes presented as well.

A common complaint among active presenters was that they were predominantly men. Many of them saw this gender divide between information givers and receivers as a sign that women were less serious about asset tech, less learned, and/or less generous in knowledge sharing. Intended or not, many male participants were projecting the predominant societal view of unmarried folks as self-indulgent and immature onto the group of single *women*. For a long time, Korean women were often assumed to be financially ignorant, even though it was common for them to be in charge of household financial management. The work of housewives in many homes, for example, involved saving and investing; this included "the complicated work of real estate speculation, such as gathering information about different neighborhoods, predicting future housing values, mobilizing resources from kinship networks for credit and deciding when to resell" (Choo 2021, 149). However, such intellectual labor was often dismissed as illogical and inapt. For instance, the stigma of economic irrationality often clung to women's participation in *kye* (rotating credit associations); although, as Janelli and Yim (1988) observed, when a Korean woman decides to join a *kye* "she knows exactly what her receipts and payments will be from its very first meeting until its last" and "she usually calculates in advance exactly what her net income or expense will be" (167). This longstanding gender stereotype was reproduced within Singlesgroup as well.

The lesser willingness of female participants to give a presentation, however, had to do with the fact that women investors were more reserved and modest, and they did not feel the urge to show off their financial prowess as much as their male counterparts. Duffy and Pruchniewska (2017) observe that female digital entrepreneurs who work in a field where assertive self-promotion and pep talks are the norm still conform to traditional prescriptions for femininity. Likewise, although Singlesgroup had a good number of self-directed female investors who continued to have positive returns, they tended to think that they were not smart enough to teach others. Plumtree (38, F), one of the small number of women whom male members believed to be financially intelligent, would resist the idea that she could be resourceful to others. She thought that she did not know much and found it daunting to give a talk. It is also worth mentioning that financially literate women tended to be more participatory in information giving online—albeit less recognized—through comment threads and by reposting news articles and events related to asset tech.

It is also noteworthy that gift giving is not always purely altruistic, and informational gift giving is often driven by status seeking (Belk 2013; Campbell, Fletcher, and Greenhill 2009; Lampel and Bhalla 2007; Velkova 2016). To male participants, sharing information, advice, and knowledge was a means of putting their financial virility on display. Certainly, it was an altruistic and generous act that many participants found helpful. At the same time, it redeemed their masculinity, which had been damaged due to their unmarried status in a world dominated by marriage normativity. Dongsoo, for example, regularly posted various forms of information about fund investing. In addition to reposting news articles or market reports published by financial institutions, he put together information based on his own research and analyses, such as a list of top-performing mutual funds, the returns on particular funds,

and a list of recommended funds that he had handpicked. Such posts garnered much attention among other participants especially because Dongsoo
had revealed his asset portfolios early on, almost immediately after he had
joined Singlesgroup. Like Mr Seven, Dongsoo broke down the list of his
assets—composed of savings, funds, stocks, bonds, and real estate—saying
that the value of his assets reached 800 million won (about US$707,338). He
also attached his "Life Master Plan", using a template Bum Young provided in
the Ten in Ten Academy (see chapter 2). In his plan, Dongsoo articulated his
mission statement as becoming "a smart investor who contributes to society
and helps the social minority people."

Knowing that Dongsoo was relatively new to the group and did not excel
at reading social cues, I was concerned that other participants might gossip
about his arrogance. However, this proved to be a mere prejudice of my own.
Dongsoo's post drew lots of admiring and celebratory replies. Members con-
gratulated him on his hard work, discipline, and merit. This post set Dongsoo
up for recognition by other male investors as someone who was capable and
worth listening to. As I became more familiar with the culture of Singlesgroup,
I came to understand that sharing asset portfolios was a common practice in
the group, widely accepted, and mostly done by men. It was a symbolic act of
creating a singlehood that was financially productive and competent. Creating
such an alternative image that challenged the long-held stereotype of old singles was most urgent for the aging unmarried men who were seen as effeminate
and infantile.

## The Social Reproduction of the Investing Subject

The tangles of asset tech and sociality were observed in the variety of ways
in which participation in Singlesgroup had an impact on financial practices,
for both beginning and advanced asset seekers. Singlesgroup socially reproduced investor subjectivity by providing spaces of financial socialization for
novices and spaces of risk management and entrepreneurship for experienced investors.

### The Financial Socialization of Novices

The socializer Picasso had been far removed from direct ownership of equity
but was eager to save. He kept his consumption simple and maintained a frugal
lifestyle. Constantly on the lookout for high-interest savings products, he had
always chosen mutual funds or low-risk financial products if he invested at all.

After joining Singlesgroup, however, Picasso began to buy shares of stocks in keeping with what many others did in the group. He also began to spend his off days attending asset tech events based on the information shared by other members. While Picasso identified *chinmok* as his favorite perk of being part of Singlesgroup, he also believed that the social network created by Singlesgroup provided him with practical aid in achieving his financial ends:

> If I have a question, for example, if I am curious about real estate, then I can text Smoothie or Pyungchan. Those are my important assets. If I have a question regarding stocks, then I can ask Top Trader or Sangbo. It's like, *now I have the infrastructure* where my questions are answered.

Yongmi's experience likewise demonstrates how Singlesgroup socially reproduced investing subjectivity for novices. The bubbly and humorous woman was a self-proclaimed "fool" in asset tech. She had "tried to invest in funds, stocks, and real estate but without any research." She had never turned any profits and would often laugh at the outcomes saying that she was living "a minus life." One of her most devastating incidents had been taking out massive loans to purchase an apartment for an investing purpose. She made this decision six years ago by following a colleague who seemed to be a shrewd investor. Yongmi "invested there because he bought there" without knowing that the housing bubble was at its peak. She intended to flip it, but the town was hit hard by the market burst and the apartment was still giving her a big headache when I met her.

During my fieldwork, Yongmi was far from being an avid learner; nonetheless she had a strong presence in group activities, describing her primary motivation as keeping herself stimulated:

> Also, there are many successful investors here, whether in real estate, funds, or stocks. [...] I see they do their homework really hard. They are savvy when it comes to judging if this neighborhood is worth investing in, something like that. I have one property. It hasn't been sold yet. I ask questions, seek advice, and listen to what they say. And I get stimulated by looking at how these people invest and make money.

The word choice of "stimulation" denoted both her current incapability to invest and ongoing interest in investing in the future. As she was stuck with the underwater property, she did not have capital in hand. In addition, she was a procrastinator and did not want to study:

I actually don't invest much these days because I still don't do research on my own after attending other members' presentations. [...] I participate in Singlesgroup in order to be stimulated. Rather than actually investing, but to keep myself stimulated. [...] By "stimulation," I mean, I wish I could invest, but now I don't have the capital.

Even if Yongmi did not define herself as an investor *per se* but rather as financially illiterate, her participation in Singlesgroup did socialize her into asset markets, particularly into the stock market. By forcing herself to be exposed to asset tech talks, she began to learn some of the terms that are important in the vocabulary of asset tech, albeit superficially, and became motivated to dig into it more:

Previously, I didn't even know terms like "value investing." I didn't know at all. What I knew was just if investing generates a profit I earn money, and I lose money if a return is negative. But [by participating in the group], I got to learn that it's a good strategy to invest your spare money in a strong company for a long time.

Saturated with the information shared by other participants, she got up the nerve to dip a toe into the stock market again: "So, recently, I bought some stocks again, because many people [in Singlesgroup] are successful." Her return was negative by the time of our interview, and she laughed at herself again, "I shouldn't invest." To novices like Picasso and Yongmi, hanging out with experienced investors and listening to their strategies were some of the most significant ways to approach the asset market.

### Expanding the Horizon for Experienced Investors

Engaging with Singlesgroup had a meaningful impact on the investing practices of self-made investors like Plumtree. Growing up in a struggling family, she had to go to a high school focused on vocational training—instead of college preparation—despite her strong academic performance. Her family poverty had forced her to establish a frugal lifestyle since her formative years; she developed early on the habit of saving money and using account books. Only a year and a half after getting her first job at a non-banking financial company, the IMF crisis broke out and she decided she might as well quit her job and prepare for the college entrance exam. She was admitted to both a four-year college that granted a bachelor's degree and a two-year college focused on vocational training. She chose the latter, again because of its brighter job prospects. Plumtree believed that it was a solid choice and she now earned about 34 million won (about US$30,061) yearly.

Unlike the socializers Yongmi and Picasso, Plumtree had studied asset tech over an extended period of time. She began to read asset tech books and economic newspapers in her early 20s. She grew to be a firm believer in value investing and boasted more than ten years of experience in it when I met her. The most important lesson that she gained from her self-directed research was the importance of seeing "the forest" rather than "the trees." If the former was a metaphor for big economic trends, the latter entailed technical details such as the daily fluctuations represented in graphs and charts. Participating in Singlesgroup, however, brought her attention to technical details more often and opened her eyes to a wider range of investing items than she was previously familiar with. As she was trading about eight foreign funds and four domestic funds, I asked when she would sell them. Plumtree said, "We'll see. There's an uptrend these days so I am still looking, not selling." I caught the nuance that she was leaning more toward the opposite of value investing, since terms such as "uptrend" or "looking" were more frequently used by chartists than by value investors. I asked, "When you say 'looking,' how do you check them out?" Plumtree responded:

> I told you I didn't care much in the past. I used to follow only the big news, like, the Chinese economy is doing well, or China is suffering, something like that. Things like KOSPI hit 2,000 or 1,800, big news like that. [...] Upon participating in Singlesgroup, I came to look more closely.

Plumtree specified that, whereas previously she used to pull out her investing accounts once a month or even once in a quarter, she now tracked the performance of her holdings every day. "In Singlesgroup, people talk a lot about asset tech." She laughed and went on, "Well, I think I'm checking them out at least several times a week."

As a highly experienced, self-directed investor, Plumtree said that the information shared in Singlesgroup was "mostly shallow, frankly speaking." She would nonetheless find something helpful that she thought was worth more research. "Then I try to find related books or newspaper articles. [...] Also, [because] other people keep investing and talk about how they invested in such and such ways and how they gained profits, I get to know that 'Oh, there are such things out there that I didn't know about.'" Dividend stocks were one such territory she had yet to explore.[6] When someone in Singlesgroup presented on dividend stocks, the enthusiastic Plumtree felt that she should look into it more. She researched dividend stocks and bought shares in such stocks. "So far," she said, "returns are good."

*Risk Management for Enthusiasts*

To some participants, social networking through Singlesgroup was directly tied to risk management. Risk acceptance has been key to the process of financialization and to the construction of its subjects. As Randy Martin (2002) writes, financialization "insinuates an orientation toward accounting and risk management into all domains of life" (43). To many enthusiasts, meeting other asset-savvy folks was a crucial means of enhancing the diversity of information, which was taken to be a starting point to managing risk. Although many participants described *chinmok* and asset tech as two separate realms brought together simply by accident, the two were closely and inherently interwoven in practice. Smoothie, who quickly transitioned from a socializer to an enthusiast, once wrote to articulate the intent of Singlesgroup:

> These days I'm thinking one shouldn't be an egotist when it comes to investing. When we are mutually helpful, being together rather than being alone, investing becomes safer, and we can enjoy a diversity of information. This is the goal our group was created for: becoming mentors for each other.
>
> (April 28, 2014)

His emphasis on mutuality for the sake of "safer" investing is reminiscent of Randy Martin's point that financial risk management engenders an "awareness very different from what is presupposed in narrow self-interest" (2002, 101).

Joong-Ki's account was more telling about such awareness. As a 38-year-old man working to become an airline pilot, he had been investing in real estate for nearly a decade. He was financially erudite and seriously "geeked out" about the property market. Other participants would jokingly refer to him as "Doctor" as it was clear that he was a walking dictionary in the field of asset tech. He posted articles online every single day, and the information he shared was overwhelming both in quality and quantity. He often posted, for example, news articles on government policies, legal issues, analyst reports, and the like, which rarely drew any comments from the audience. Joong-ki appeared to be aware that he was an oversharer, and that most participants rarely clicked on those articles he reposted. Nevertheless, he still valued the readership of Singlesgroup: "If I were to talk about something I share with Singlesgroup to my ordinary friends in society, I would be treated as crazy. I'm too invested."

Indeed, his engagement with Singlesgroup was not aimless but highly intentional. To him, managing risk was about sifting through the information that saturated the Internet and finding reliable human informants. It all began in the early 2000s when Joong-Ki realized that gathering information from the mass media was limiting and biased. He believed that the mass media tended to report government policies favorably, which he thought was not always helpful to his investment. Having second thoughts about the mass media, he signed up for a number of online communities. Online communities were inundated with information that Joong-Ki found enormously helpful. According to him, those online communities (including Café Ten in Ten) used to have a much more intimate feel in the early 2000s and the information circulated was of high quality and lucrative. However, an irony appeared when they hit a critical mass of users. As investing became a popular activity for ordinary people, online asset tech communities drew a huge number of users, and the quality of information circulating within these large online forums deteriorated. In other words, Joong-Ki found that the more open, expansive, and popular an online financial forum became, the less helpful it became. He noted that many big names within Café Ten in Ten in its embryonic phase began to stop sharing their lucrative tips when the Café became widely known and new members increased.[7] Implied quite explicitly here was the moral ambiguity of such tips, which likely entailed morally questionable practices and maneuvering through legal loopholes. The days of hunting information online were over and risk management had now evolved into the burden of building new personal relationships. "Low-end information is shared online, and quality information is shared in person," Joong-Ki asserted in our interview. This was the primary reason why he participated in a small-sized group like Singlesgroup that centered on offline practices. Whereas Joong-Ki's informational gifts did not seem to be reciprocated at all, he stated that there were a good number of adept investors in the group who were not actively present online. As a result, he was trying to develop one-on-one relationships with them.

Sangbo also commented on the importance of offline networking and interpersonal relationships. More than the need to find valuable information, Sangbo demonstrated the awareness that managing financial risk is largely contingent on the actions of others. Similar to Joong-Ki, Sangbo was putting intentional effort into expanding his opportunities to individually meet other participants in person. In explaining how he studied asset tech, he began by describing the limitations of relying on books or the Internet:

Reading is the easiest and fastest way for indirect experience. [...] After you've got a solid understanding of the books, then you can also look up the Internet and see some data, which means you begin to develop your own thoughts. Then you put yourself out there and meet people.

To my request to elaborate on why one has to meet people, Sangbo stressed the need to be connected with others to manage a risk. He believed that he should take a "contrarian" approach to the stock market (see Souleles and Hansen 2019), but being a complete outlier was too risky. In order to strike a balance, one had to have conversations with other investors. To Sangbo, therefore, meeting people was a response to the "growing interdependence on unknown others" (Martin 2002, 137) and an ongoing effort for "a daily practice of decision and affirmation, research and reflection" (Martin 2002, 107). Sangbo explained:

> If you want to be successful [...] you should do things in a little bit different way from the ways others do them. What I mean by "different" is, you can't be the only one although you should be different from most people. There should be some folks who are similar to you to a degree. I learned this when I did investing. [...] My approach can work only when there are some people who practice investing in the ways that I do. But it shouldn't be the same. In order for me to compare such things, I need to meet people out there. There are no asset tech prodigies in Singlesgroup, so my approach is very unique here. But if I meet those who are really good at asset tech, we share a lot in common in terms of how to approach asset tech.

During the span of my research, Sangbo gradually became cynical about the socializing activities of Singlesgroup. He found them emotionally fulfilling at first but would scoff at the heavy emphasis on *chinmok*, finding it disorienting and discouraging. Still, he valued the opportunity to leverage sociality for risk managing:

> Still, I can observe trends [in Singlesgroup]. "Oh, many people these days use such and such methods." [...] If my approach is used by no one, then the chances are one or the other: it's either a jackpot (*daebak*, 대박) or a bankruptcy (*jjokbak*, 쪽박). The fear of bankruptcy is bigger. Its risk is higher. I'm not the kind of person who can bet all in and lose everything. [...] The uniqueness shouldn't be too high, so I test it and adjust it.

The consequence of risk acceptance, Martin (2002) writes, is that "the actions of others take hold of your fate" (121) because "the information gathered, the risks taken, the gains realized will be affected by what others have done" (101). Sangbo likened stock investing to walking on a tightrope held by the hands of others and he wanted to reduce risk by having a better understanding of how other investors were acting.

## Community as a Testbed for Self-Entrepreneurship

More than improving his investing skills or strategizing about risk management, Sangbo's trajectory shows that he took up Singlesgroup as a testbed for his entrepreneurship, exemplifying the tangled pursuit of community and assets. Similar to Bum Young's path to entrepreneurial communitarianism in which he assetized himself by building communitarian networks, Sangbo tried to develop his career by contributing to Singlesgroup. He was emblematic of how asset tech participants pursued enterprise not just as a chance for capital gains but as a mode of self-making and a whole way of life. Community practices such as socializing and information giving were central to this process. He was a generous giver of informational gifts both on- and offline. Unwilling to provide stock recommendations as he believed such spoon feeding would be unhelpful to novices, Sangbo still periodically posted about particular stocks, trading strategies, and market prospects. Offline, he gave several presentations in study meetings, as exemplified in this chapter's opening vignettes. His lectures always had good turnouts and were very highly spoken of. For instance, when I first consulted Smoothie about my plan for participatory observation, Smoothie asserted that Sangbo's presentations would be helpful for my own future well-being, not just for dissertation research. Sometimes, Sangbo seemed to be the glue for Singlesgroup. His participatory and generous activities reproduced Singlesgroup, which simultaneously reproduced his broader self-entrepreneurship.

In general, Sangbo approached the stock market carefully and conservatively; he loathed chartism, had been performing value investing (fundamental analysis[8]) for years, and was leaning more toward dividends instead of profit margins by the time I met him. If value investing was a more conservative investing style than chartism, focusing on dividends instead of profit margins would be perceived as even more conservative and less risky. As he mentioned during one of his presentations, it would be hard to realize profit margins with stocks that generated good dividends. A long-term devotee of value investing, Sangbo was trying to switch his target holdings from value stocks to dividend stocks. More unique to his tenet was the belief that work was the best policy for asset tech. In his presentations, he would stress that making money through investing is never easier than earning money through work. He asserted, "the most important investing is 'no-risk investing' which is your job."

The emphasis on dividends rather than profit margins, and on work rather than investing, was in line with his belief that asset tech had more to do with one's attitude to life than with mere techniques. He believed that, just as one should do in life, one should approach asset tech with continued research and reflection. Risky investing was likely to fail, and leaving the labor market was just as reckless. He was critical of fellow lay investors who chased capital gains without self-directed research. He also believed that the notion of financial freedom became a kind of empty signifier and scoffed at those who blindly pursued it. "You want to travel around once you have achieved financial freedom? It's most disgusting to me." Traveling around the world was indeed one of the most common tropes mentioned by asset tech enthusiasts. Mr Seven wanted to travel around the world, and another person I met outside of Singlesgroup dreamed of surfing in Hawaii after accomplishing financial freedom. Sangbo continued in our interview, "they say they want financial freedom, but no one can answer what they want to do after achieving it. They should establish a goal before talking about financial freedom."

The importance of having a job in order to do asset tech put Sangbo in a deeply contradictory position, since he was highly discontent with his job. Finance presented itself as a means of self-realization in place of a job that used to be a lifetime calling; this resonated with Sangbo. Growing up in the middle class, he majored in business management in college because it was "chosen precisely by my parents." After college, he got his current position in the IT team of a commercial bank. He felt that he had lived for good grades and good schools only to end up spouseless and disillusioned with a supposedly good job. While he found his job labor-intensive, hierarchal, and thankless, Sangbo took pleasure in exploring asset markets. He immersed himself in studying the stock market during his spare time even though his day job demanded frequent overtime late into his nights and weekends. He would cut back on sleep to read the financial statements of corporations and analyze fundamentals. Whereas his job was holding him back, the practice of asset tech was a freedom machine, an enabler of individual autonomy. His daily endeavors and discipline were, in his own words, "about asset tech in a narrow sense but it's about passion in a broader sense." Asset tech allowed him to develop a better self and it thus became integral to his self-entrepreneurship.

Sangbo's dismay at his career continued to surface in his self-reflective online postings, many of which revolved around why he was interested in asset tech. According to him, he saved, researched, and invested "in order to design the life [he] wants to live." The same posting continued, "I don't want to be confined to the situation in which I always have to choose a job merely based on its salary, without being able to do *what I really want to do*" (my emphasis). Another posting reiterated a similar concern: "When I was younger, I thought asset tech was a means of getting rich and quitting a job, literally unearned income. Now, I would say asset tech is a means of allowing me not to give up on *what I really want to do* due to money" (my emphasis).

Despite his continued emphasis on passion and autonomy, he immediately turned defensive in our interview when I asked him what he really wanted to do. It took long, tense harangues until he confessed that he was still undecided. The predicament he found himself in was that asset tech was a means to individual autonomy, and he believed that his demeaning job was essential to his ability to pursue asset tech. He loathed the blind pursuit of financial freedom by asset-seeking herds, but his personal dream remained unarticulated under the likewise hollow parlance of self-autonomy. In other words, he was subjecting himself endlessly to work that he found menial in order to accomplish autonomy.

Sangbo tried to resolve this paradox by making asset tech his job; he decided to explore the possibility of developing a career in asset tech coaching. He began to see his experiences of information giving in Singlesgroup as a vital springboard, and he began to receive invitations to give talks to various asset tech communities and study groups outside of Singlesgroup. He also began to give lectures at his own workplace. While still professionally bound within an IT team, he began to develop a personal reputation as a coach and a speaker on the subject of asset tech.

Sangbo's employer was one of South Korea's major commercial banks, and it was not impossible for him to be transferred within the same firm to a financial services team. However, such a transfer from IT support to customer wealth management rarely happened. Therefore, seizing the opportunity to give lectures to his colleagues was a significant milestone for his new career dream. When I spoke to him on the phone for a follow-up interview a year after our initial interview, Sangbo was engaging significantly less with Singlesgroup on- and offline. Recalling that he had given 19 talks at different venues during the previous year, he said that addressing members of Singlesgroup—most of whom he perceived as indifferent to asset tech and financially illiterate—had been helpful in developing an understanding of his wider audience:

> It can be said that I did a sort of testing with Singlesgroup. [...] I can say that Singlesgroup became a bridge for me. At first, I didn't know how to address a general audience. If I make materials too easy, then my lecture would be the same as average advice books. To the contrary,

if I just throw out my own investing skills, then [the general audience] would find it too difficult and lose interest, like when you can't follow anything. I learned how to find a middle ground from Singlesgroup.

## Conclusion

If Alumnigroup tried to redress the moral stigma toward the foreclosure auction, participants in Singlesgroup wanted to forge a social space insulated from marriage normativity and the stigmatization attached to late singlehood. Their recurring practices of socializing, group study, and online information sharing demonstrate the dynamic ways in which 30-plus singles pursued opportunities to bond with other asset-minded singles, socially and financially. This chapter has described Singlesgroup as a key site for reproducing a heterosexual singlehood alternative to the dominant stereotypes associating an extended singlehood with asociality, selfishness, and immaturity. This alternative singlehood was a markedly gendered one, I have shown, linked with the performance of male financial virility. The process of enacting this particular singlehood also heralded the social reproduction of the investing subject. The mix of rookies, devotees, geeks, and maestros in the asset markets socialized novices financially, expanded the horizons of experienced investors, and helped enthusiastic investors manage risks. For some participants, the community of Singlesgroup was also leveraged for advancing self-entrepreneurship.

When I revisited Seoul in 2016, I hung out with Smoothie and Jinwook. Smoothie had recently undergone surgery and had been hospitalized for a week. He and Jinwook had not seen each other for months, partly because Jinwook got married at the end of 2015 and moved to a province two hours away from Seoul. Since Smoothie missed greasy food, we went to a small restaurant for American homemade-style burgers. Catching up over our food, Smoothie brought up an idea of asset tech for Jinwook, who had recently cashed in his dividend-paying fund due to his risk-intolerant wife. Smoothie's suggestion was to start a "room salon (룸살롱)" business. Designated as adult entertainment establishments, room salons are a particular type of bar for male customers that sell not only alcohol but also hostess services. Smoothie had recently made a field trip to such an establishment, run by his acquaintance, in order to investigate its financial potential. He emphasized that the biggest strength of opening room salons was that most transactions were made in cash, not on credit cards. This has to do with the fact that room salons are positioned in a legal gray area. Room salons are legal so long as sex is not for sale on the premises. However, most male patrons go to room salons in anticipation of not just groping the hostesses but also engaging in intercourse, whether on the premises or in nearby motels. A room salon has been seen as a "never-fail" business item in South Korea even when the economy struggled (Kang J 2011). As Joohee Kim (2020) notes, financial services firms began to offer special loans designed specifically for such adult entertainment establishments, demonstrating how the financial services industry restructured South Korea's sex industry. This means that the bodies of female sex workers are securitized as investing items and they are now subjected to the sex industry in more complex and subtle ways than before. Such special financing was provided only for big-ticket establishments in Gangnam with a great number of hostesses; small-scale establishments outside of Seoul, like the one that Smoothie had conceived, were not eligible. But Smoothie explained to us that, while Seoul was oversaturated with room salons, it could be still lucrative in the provinces where there were large incoming populations of male factory workers. It would be ethnographically inaccurate to read Smoothie's idea as suggestive of selling sex or other illegal practices. He was just throwing out an idea within the bounds of legality for Jinwook, whose paths for asset incomes had been thwarted. Nevertheless, I conclude this chapter with this vignette as a telling instance of how socially reproduced investors, empowered by the experience of convivial community, can be surprisingly insensitive to the vulnerability of the socioeconomic underclass (e.g., tenants or sex workers) and to their own involvement in perpetuating such vulnerability.

# Epilogue

This book has argued that critique, emotion, and community comprise South Korea's new spirit of capitalism. Critical capitalism, as a simultaneous critique and legitimation of capitalism, has become the cultural and affective backbone of South Korea's financialized asset economy. Cultural studies scholar Randy Martin wrote more than 20 years ago that "financialization promises a way to develop the self, when even the noblest of professions cannot emit a call that one can answer with a lifetime. It offers a highly elastic mode of self-mastery that channels doubt over uncertain identity into fruitful activity" (2002, 9). I have asked in this book if investing has become not just a path for self-realization—not to mention a means of climbing up the economic ladder—but a vehicle for "dissent," mobilization, and even therapy. My interlocutors were insightful theorists of their own experience, critics of capitalism, and wounded rebels rallying collectively against the broken economy. It seems that contemporary capitalism was thriving on critiques of it.

A culturally significant moment that was widely cited as a harbinger of South Korea's neoliberal financialization was a TV commercial by a financial services firm in which a top actress looks into the camera and gives a shout-out to the audience: "May you become rich (여러분, 부자 되세요)!" Broadcast during the 2001–2002 new year holidays—not too long after Café Ten in Ten was created—this campaign generated a wild buzz. Forever more, the phrase wishing for someone's wealth replaced conventional greetings such as "Happy New Year" and "May you live long and prosper." It became a historic saying that Koreans would routinely use in the decades to come.

This TV campaign has been commonly cited by the critics of neoliberal financialization, who indicate that it presaged the state of affairs South Korea would soon find itself in: the blind pursuit of monetary gains. But it is precisely this kind of stale critique that this book wants to challenge. Ever since the 1997 IMF crisis normalized popular investing, progressive narratives have often seen asset seekers as pathological, comparing them to brainwashed cult followers or drug addicts. A 2013 news article, for instance, reported that "for the last ten years, many fell into the temptation of *the new cult of asset tech* only to find themselves ending up penniless or even massively indebted" (Choi and Seo 2013; emphasis added). A 2009 piece in another national newspaper described amateur investors as "addicted" and as "the market's *slaves* losing their low wages to the stock market" (Lee and Kang 2009; emphasis added). As unpacked in chapter 3, however, such criticism of the "slavery" or "addiction" to contemporary capitalism that people experience was even more forcefully articulated in the classroom of asset tech. I have chronicled the surprisingly dynamic and compelling practices that asset tech unfurled—including critical, communal, and therapeutic ones—in the hopes of highlighting the scant attention that progressive scholars have paid to such emerging practices.

A primary motivation behind my research was my curiosity about how capitalism is reproduced when its rosy promises keep failing. My family lost my father's retirement savings on the stock market around the same time that the abovementioned TV commercial came out. On another personal note, my activist friends, who had taken to the streets vehemently calling for workers' rights and economic justice under the liberal government of Roh Moo-hyun (2003–2008), immediately began to discuss stocks and real estate the moment they left college. Overall, it is frustrating that, in a country known for its rich history of popular protests, South Korean citizens have been surprisingly reticent about the economic injustice exacerbated by financialization. *Critically Capitalist* has illuminated how Koreans have become active conformists and contributors to capitalism, not only by chasing after speculative profits but by expressing compelling critiques of capitalism as well.

South Korea is a quicksilver place, and its ethnography becomes recent history rather quickly. After I wrapped up my fieldwork in 2016, South Korea witnessed several remarkable investing booms, such as a bitcoin frenzy in 2017 (Jeong 2018; Lee SC 2022a)[1] and the Donghak Ants Movement in 2020 and onwards. Especially in the post-COVID 19 climate, it seems that asset tech has become unquestionably mainstream. More people now have stakes in the stock market and believe that investments are necessary, not optional.[2] Numerous media reports sketch out how young people from diverse backgrounds—from wage workers to college students to professionals—are organizing study groups for asset tech, watching YouTube videos for investment advice, and chatting with other investors on social media. Beyond such entrepreneurial communitarian practices, more self-assetizing people have become content creators in asset tech or developed start-ups for financial education (Choi 2020; Shim

2020). Meanwhile, Robert Kiyosaki's *Rich Dad, Poor Dad*, a book that topped South Korea's best-selling list in 2000 (see chapter 3), became a top seller again in 2019 (Park and Choi 2020).

Ten in Ten Academy was renamed the "Academy of Financial Freedom" in the late 2010s, and Café Ten in Ten is still very much alive, albeit less active, with more than 720,000 users as of 2023. When I met Bum Young that same year, he said that the Academy's enrollment was down to 12 to 15 in each cohort, a nosedive from 50 to 60 during the mid-2010s. This might be related to the fact that Daum Café is an old community platform and has given way to younger competitors; moreover, investing advice exploded after the pandemic on a variety of platforms such as YouTube and KakaoTalk. During the height of the Donghak Ants Movement, a national newspaper published a long interview with Bum Young in which he was asked to reflect and comment on the "twenty years of South Korea's asset tech storm" (Jang HJ 2020). On an explicitly bitter note, he described the investing boom as deplorable. He was regretful about Café Ten in Ten's possible involvement in its dire development. "Twenty years ago," he said in the interview, "this community [Café Ten in Ten] intended to study, save, and grow together to accomplish financial freedom, but it has all boiled down to a nasty fight." Bum Young was lamenting that many users of the Café, and Korean lay investors more broadly, were only going after ruthless speculation rather than pursuing financial freedom.

When I began my research in the early 2010s, global populism was not as palpable, which perhaps helped me frame Ten in Ten and its derivatives as agents of critical capitalism, not mere instances of economic populism. However, it seems that the distinction between critical capitalism and the dominant culture of financial neoliberalism has become increasingly blurry in the 2020s. Previous chapters have emphasized the need to understand vernacular and popular critiques enacted by ordinary people navigating the asset market; but critical capitalism is *capitalist* after all, with its growing pitfalls. I will return to a discussion of some of the pitfalls of critical capitalism below; but, before doing so, I will first situate critical capitalism within its global context.

Outside of South Korea, lay investors became a sensation when the FIRE movement grabbed media attention in the US through a series of articles published by the *New York Times*, the *Washington Post*, and the *Wall Street Journal* between 2018 and 2019 (Kurutz 2018; Singletary 2018; Smith 2019; Tergesen and Dagher 2018). Not long after, in 2021, a group of Reddit users (r/wallstreetbets) picked up the fight against Wall Street hedge funds to disrupt the shorting of GameStop stocks (see Hasso et al., 2022; Lee SC 2022b). The protagonist in the global resistance to financial capitalism seems to have shifted from the Occupy Wall Street movement to lay investors.

The heightened visibility of lay people who are gaming the system has attracted ample scholarly attention. Participants in the FIRE movement are seen as engaging in "resistance" or even in "anti-capitalism" in the sense that they are critical of consumerism (Taylor and Davies 2021). The GameStop short squeeze is seen as an instance of democratization based on information pluralism (Duterme 2023). Other scholars see it as an instance in which retail investors were transformed into a public who negotiated access and input into digital infrastructures (Yang and Adamczyk 2023). It seems that anti-capitalism is now being widely disseminated at the center of the contemporary capitalist economy (Fisher 2009), as instantiated by the global success of South Korea's "anti-capitalist entertainment," including the movie *Parasite* (2019, directed by Bong Joon-ho) and the TV series *Squid Game* (2021, directed by Hwang Dong-hyuk) (Pitcher 2021). After all, some scholars seem to have come to terms with financial capitalism or, at least, with the disruptive potential of speculation. Michel Feher, for instance, writes:

> [W]hat is politically meaningful in the GameStop frenzy is neither the populist story of the little guys beating the fat cats at their own game [...] nor the reminder that Wall Street is out of whack [...]. The important message conveyed by the Redditors is that [...] *another speculation is possible.*
>
> (2021; emphasis added)

I wonder, in fact, if the populist narrative of the little guys versus the big guy is reproduced both in critical capitalism and in scholarly critiques of the asset economy. Conceptualizing speculation as a new mode of imagination, Komporozos-Athanasious (2022) discusses the emergence of "speculative" publics who actively embrace contemporary capitalism's radical uncertainty. He describes the speculative public as "enthusiastically embrac[ing] finance's speculative imagination" (106) and sharing "an acceptance [...] of the growing volatility of their lives as inevitable in the face of broader uncertainties" (111). To him, it is this active endorsement of uncertainty, inspired by modern finance, that opens up the political possibility of what he calls counter-speculation. But what do Feher's "another speculation" and Komporozos-Athanasious' "counter-speculation" exactly mean and who gets to enact such new forms of resistance?[3] Wouldn't this call for (another/counter-)speculation crystalize what Mark Fisher (2009, 2) calls "capitalist realism"—that is, "the widespread sense that not only is capitalism the only viable political and economic system, but also that it is now impossible to even imagine a coherent alternative to it"?

The idea that the premises and technologies of modern finance can and should be deployed by the public surprisingly resembles what my research participants have put into practice. In the same way that the asset owners and asset seekers I observed set themselves as the little guys resisting the ambiguous "capitalist class" or the state, the call for another/counter-speculation effectively reaffirms the financial elites-versus-retail investors duality at the expense of more finely tuned understandings of the differences within individual investors and non-investors. A point worth emphasizing here is that many of the recent popular financial movements were led by those with high disposable incomes and a great deal of financial literacy; many of the FIRE participants were in high-tech industries and finance (Taylor and Davies 2021, 700). Likewise, "the demographics of the GameStop frenzy skewed profoundly towards men and the already well-heeled: according to one study, 88% of participants were men and had an average income almost twice the American median" (quoted in Haiven, Kingsmith, and Komporozos-Athanasious 2022, 106). So, who belongs to the "publics" that bear "a shared yearning for uncertainty" (Komporozos-Athanasious 2022, 10)?

Despite the fact "that speculation is now available to a vastly wider population [...] not just [to] banks, mutual funds, pension funds, and hedge funds" (Feher 2021), retail investors are not on a level playing field and, more crucially, they are predominantly middle class. A 2020 poll shows that "active investors" in the Donghak Ants Movement were mostly those in the (upper-)middle class or those in a higher-income group (those earning above 4 million won or about US$3,389 every month) (Choi, Kim, and Park 2020). The poll also shows that those in the (upper-)middle class used a variety of sources for investment including wages, parental support, and credit, which likely allowed them to manage risks more effectively. Likewise, most of my research participants had stable jobs and/or higher incomes, had the time to take a class after work, could afford the seminar fee, and had the capital and access to credit for investment. Here lie the pitfalls of critical capitalism as an inter-class phenomenon. Critique, emotion, and community become an alibi for continuous speculation for the so-called "retail investors" who are poised to mobilize higher capital and are seen as fighting against financial elites, while the affective community of critique operates as cruel optimism (Berlant 2011) for those without capital for investment.

When Sihoon, the 40-year-old man who lived below the poverty line most of his life, felt that there might be some hope in stocks and real estate (see chapter 4), his newly found optimism may have been an obstacle to his flourishing. Similar to Sihoon, Jina (45, F) was one of the few I met who grew up in a poor family and did not have a college degree. As a single woman living alone in one of Seoul's low-income neighborhoods, she moved through a variety of blue- and pink-collar jobs after high school, across the factory, telemarketing, car wash, and restaurant sectors. She also floated around the informal economy for a long time, including managing the clients of sex workers, among many other activities. When I met her in the Ten in Ten Academy in the mid-2010s, she was often in a happy and excited mood because the stock market was a bull market. It was not just the Ten in Ten Academy she attended in order to learn about asset tech. She had also taken another investing class, which I guessed to be a predatory scheme and for which she had paid 800,000 won (about US$759). Quickly reading the doubt overshadowing my face, Jina tried to reassure me: "It's expensive if you think of it as course tuition. But if you think of it as paying for networking, I don't think it's expensive."

The thresholds for access to the asset markets and popular investing are especially high for low-income precariats such as Sihoon and Jina. People who are marginalized in the labor market are likely marginalized or excluded from the financial and asset markets as well (Song 2014; see also McClanahan 2017). Although popular finance is not necessarily about ownership in direct shares but has to do with the wages and salaries of workers being managed in the capital market through various investment and savings schemes, low-income precariats may be involved in the capital market only through loan sharks. Despite the ascent of platforms for knowledge sharing and easy investing that gave us Ten in Ten and r/wallstreetbets, the poor and less-educated population still has far less access to this shared knowledge, and they pay a higher price to participate in the "resistance," as seen in Jina's case. Critical capitalism veils this reality. After all, the capitalism that is justified by the spirit of critical capitalism is the economy where the free market and deregulation are called for and public welfare is greatly reduced.

It would have been absurd to ask wage workers during industrial capitalism why they contributed to capitalism by participating in the labor market; it would be equally unreasonable to castigate asset seekers for participating in capitalism today. We seem to be arriving at a point where the conditions for such post-work aspirations have been amplified. A new path of intellectual critique might be found through the close examination of how non-academic forms of critique reconstruct the broken legitimacy of capitalist modernity, and how its simultaneous condemnation and acceptance take place at the ordinary level of acting, thinking, and feeling.

# Methodological Appendix

In the Appendix, I discuss aspects of my research process and a reflection of my experience as an ethnographer in order to elucidate in what conditions my ethnographic account was produced. I began by attending Ten in Ten Academy during the summers of 2012 and 2013 in order to negotiate access and to find an initial group of informants. When I moved to Seoul for fully fledged fieldwork in 2014, I contacted Bum Young to get his consent to observe the Academy. My prior two enrollments in the Academy were central to obtaining his permission. I attended the program four more times, meaning that I observed four more cohorts between 2014 and 2015.

In addition to participant observation, I conducted in-depth interviews with 64 people over the course of my fieldwork, some of whom I interviewed multiple times. Among the 38 interviewees who had attended Ten in Ten Academy, the youngest was a 24-year-old female radiographer and the oldest was a 61-year-old male retiree. The demographic makeup of my interviewees reflected the larger composition of the broader community of lay investors in the 2010s, which skewed toward college-educated individuals with secure jobs. I met, for instance, a number of civil servants who were envied for their job security and good benefits while also recognized for their low salaries. At the same time, however, I also interviewed housewives, job seekers, self-employed individuals, and those in the service industry. The material gathered from these interviews were supplementary to participant observation (see Chong 2018, 24), but chapter 6 drew upon interviews more heavily than other chapters did.

Although I focused on Café Ten in Ten and the Academy in the initial stage of my research, Alumnigroup and Singlesgroup emerged as independent sites of observation. Among the four cohorts that I joined in 2014–2015, three of the cohorts each formed an alumni group for further networking. All three of these groups began by creating social media groups and soon organized study meetings. Two of them quickly disbanded, but the participants of Alumnigroup communicated actively online and met regularly in person as well for more than a year. I carried out participant observation both on- and offline. My engagement with this group was highly participatory from the beginning, as I took on a clerical role (총무) that included tasks such as handling the group's finances and updating schedules online. This responsibility organically fell to me because, first, I was the second-youngest among the members, and, second, I was there for my own research. It was not unusual for a younger person to be expected to do such chores, and participants seemed to want me to reciprocate for their help in my study by taking on an organizing role in the group.

I learned about Singlesgroup while interviewing Dongsoo, who was attending Ten in Ten Academy. I was able to join its closed online group thanks to his invitation. I approached Singlesgroup with the intention of recruiting more interviewees, but came to the realization that the group itself need to be treated as another field. Because I joined Singlesgroup for just four months before wrapping up my 2014–2015 fieldwork, my interactions with its participants were more limited than those I had with Alumnigroup. Still, I was able to participate in a few study meetings and social gatherings. In addition, because they remained active in their social media group, I continued online observations for an additional year after I left Seoul. Within Singlesgroup, I conducted eight interviews in-person in Seoul and three phone interviews after I came back to the US; these became the core data for chapter 6.

I would like to add some notes on how my positionality and relationship with participants may have shaped my research. I was a latecomer to Singlesgroup and did not quite acquire the full "insider" status that I felt I had within Alumnigroup. Most of all, I was distinctly marked as a *young woman* within Singlesgroup. Because I was among the youngest within the group, I felt particularly welcomed by the men. Outside Singlesgroup, it was harder for me to recruit male interviewees than women interviewees. In contrast, it was more convenient for me to contact the men within Singlesgroup because they were hospitable and showed interest in my presence. Perhaps, this dynamic allowed me to focus on the simultaneous reproduction of heterosexual singlehood and investor subjectivity in chapter 6.

In Alumnigroup, due to the highly participatory nature of my engagement, I was quickly able to establish strong rapport with its participants. Many of them were eager to help with my research and felt close enough to me that they wanted me to participate fully in the group conversations at afterparties;

and, although I wanted to take notes rather than using a recorder at pubs and restaurants to make sure that no one would feel uncomfortable in such informal settings after group study, they asked me to use a recorder so that I could participate in their chats instead of focusing on notetaking. I also often hung out with Alumnigroup's participants (especially with the women in the group) through meals, coffee dates, and casual gatherings.

My status of being a doctoral student in a US university was sometimes pitied from a financial point of view, but was held in esteem in general. However, it is worth noting that my financial status undercut the authority that ethnographers are often assumed to have over the population they observe. As a penniless graduate student, I did not have a say about investing, while the most experienced and knowledgeable participant gained authority in the asset tech community. My research participants were often slightly patronizing to me, suggesting that the information I was gathering about asset tech would help me financially in the future, not just in my research.

Fridman (2016, 188–9) notes the predicaments involved in observing financial self-help groups, many of whose ideas he personally rejected. Similarly, I was often jealous of other ethnographers who studied a group of people they could sympathize with. This was not the case for me. Like Fridman, I personally reject many of the ideas embraced by asset tech adherents. Also, although I became good friends with several of my research participants during my time in Seoul, I was often exhausted and drained by the endless money talk. Furthermore, I sometimes had to endure sexual harassment; for example, one male participant compared me to an overvalued stock and another woman to an undervalued stock. For a variety of reasons, I often dreaded going to the field.

I had reservations about much part of the asset tech discourses not only because I was firmly positioned in cultural studies and its critiques of capitalism, but, perhaps, because I was also affected by the culture of development. If my research participants could sense my reservations, it is because our shared culture of development had made them sensitive to how their interests and pursuits were seen by others. This book is an outcome of an encounter and a collision between two different worlds—the world of a cultural studies scholar and the world of lay investors—shaped by a shared culture.

# Notes

## ONE

1. In this book, I convert Korean won to US dollars based on the annual average exchange rate of KRW to USD of the year under discussion (Statista 2024).

2. Daum Dictionary, s.v. "재테크," https://dic.daum.net/word/view.do?wordid=kkw000221322&q=%EC%9E%AC%ED%85%8C%ED%81%AC&supid=kku000279541.

While very few English writings, scholarly or journalistic, have covered *jaetekeu*, Jesook Song (2014) has touched upon it, translating the term as "financial know-how" and "financial techniques." An article from *The Wall Street Journal* once translated it as "personal financial planning" (Woo 2011). As these translations are too narrow to include the broad range of practices included in the original word, following Minseok Choi (2011), I initially translated *jaetekeu* as "wealth tech" to emphasize the term's connotation that finance can make you rich (Kim B 2017, 2020, 2022). Hoping to better reflect the original word, and to better capture the different activities carried out under its name, I have chosen "asset tech" as its new translation. Jin-Ho Jang (2011, 57) has also translated *jaetekeu* (transliterated as "jae-tech") into "asset-tech."

The neologism *jaetekeu* (translated as "asset tech" in this book) first appeared in a national newspaper in 1986 when it was used by journalists who imported the term *jaetekeu* directly from its Japanese equivalent *zaiteku* (Kim G 1986). Referring to financial technology, *zaiteku* was an important buzzword within Japan's business circles in the second half of the 1980s when many Japanese corporations turned to equity financing in place of their previous reliance upon banks (Kikkawa 2012). The neologism *zaiteku* disappeared quickly in Japan whereas *jaetekeu* became a widely used word in South Korea.

The meanings and connotations of asset tech were much more indeterminate when the term first emerged. Particularly in the early 1990s, most news coverage of *jaetekeu* used the term to refer to the speculative activities of big conglomerates or *chaebol*. In the early 1990s, the media attributed Korea's staggering economic growth to the *chaebols' jaetekeu* activities instead of focusing on production and exports. The corporate activities of financial and real estate speculation were deemed harmful to the national economy because they distorted the flow of capital, prevented technological innovation, and precipitated declines in industrial competitiveness; *jaetekeu*, understood in this way, was declared immoral and ineffective, and many media accounts described corporate *jaetekeu* as pernicious to the country. It was not until the mid-1990s that the current meanings of *jaetekeu* were introduced.

3. The "tech" in "asset tech" works like a suffix that connotes a Foucauldian notion of self-managing techniques. South Korea's neoliberalization involved the promotion of new forms of self-managing practices that asset tech was part of. As in the term "asset tech," the English word "tech" (*tekeu*) has been used to coin other self-managing practices as well; this is exemplified by "time tech" (*sitekeu*; 시테크), which was seen as one of the most important self-management technologies in the early 1990s (see Seo 2011, 95). While "time tech" did not gain as much traction and never entered the popular lexicon, other words have been derived from asset tech including "app tech" (앱테크), "thrift tech" (짠테크), and "marriage tech" (혼테크). Similar to each other, "app tech" and "thrift tech" refer to the practices of using smartphone apps and devising various ideas of extreme frugality in order to cut back on spending, save money, and build capital (Kim B 2022; Kim, Choi, and Shin 2020). The discourse of "marriage tech" encouraged women to approach marriage strategically from an investment point of view, and surfaced in the mid-2000s as part of women's self-management discourses (Yum 2016). Importantly, the suffix "tech" in all of these words is a shorthand for "asset tech," not just an abbreviation of "technique," which is indicative of the popular currency of "asset tech" as a term.

4. In this book, I use "financial capitalism" and "asset capitalism" interchangeably to characterize the contemporary capitalist economy legitimized by critical capitalism. These are all contested terms (see Adkins, Cooper, and Konings 2020) and the contemporary capitalist economy has been defined in many different ways including, but not limited to, "the debt economy" (Lazzarato 2012) and "rentier capitalism" (Standing 2017). The capitalist economy that is reaffirmed and legitimized by the spirit of critical capitalism is capitalism itself as opposed to its outside. Financial capitalism and asset capitalism capture capitalism's most recent and identifiable aspects such as the centrality of financial markets in the economy and the generation of profits by trading or owning assets.

5. With the exception of the names of the Ten in Ten brand and its creator, I have used pseudonyms to protect the identities of my interlocutors.

6. *Eok* (억) means one hundred million, and 10 *eok* won means 1 billion won. The value of 10 *eok* won in US dollars fluctuated. For instance, it was approximately US$775,193 in 2001, but it amounted to about US$1,076,426 in 2007. On a symbolic level, 10 *eok* won would be what US$1 million is to the average American (see chapter 1).

7. Guy Standing (2017) defines a rentier as someone "living off income gained from property and other assets" (xx) and "someone who gains income from possession of assets, rather than from labor" (5).

8. Williams defines the emergent as "new meanings and values, new practices, new relationships and kinds of relationships [that] are continually being created" (1978, 123).

9. Williams (1978) states that things that eventually turn out to be new elements of the dominant culture are not emergent in a strict sense. He views new meanings and practices that are alternative or oppositional to the dominant culture as the emergent. I refer to critical capitalism as emergent, not to position it as an alternative or in

opposition to the dominant but to emphasize the present-ness of critical capitalism that is indeterminate and inchoate. In doing so, my use of Williams' theory stresses that history is neither linear nor progressive (see Lee N 2022).

10. A residual culture does not simply refer to things of the past. Rather, it means something that "has been effectively formed in the past, but … is still active in the cultural process, not only and often not at all as an element of the past, but as an effective element of the present" (Williams 1978, 122).

11. According to Nark-Koo Sohn (2008, 26–7), the first phase in the history of South Korea's real estate speculation was between 1965 and 1969. During the time, sale prices for land rose by 34.9 percent and those for homes by 38.2 percent Myungji Yang also writes that "many of the first generation of the Korean middle class acquired their wealth by purchasing homes and gaining hefty benefits from skyrocketing real estate prices" (2018, 7). According to her, "at the height of a real estate boom in the 1970s and 1980s, flipping apartments and moving frequently from one apartment unit to another were popular entrepreneurial investment strategies that many relatively affluent families adopted" (140).

12. The condemnation of investing activities was imbricated with gender as Yang (2019) has pointed out. Middle-class housewives contributed to social mobility through real estate investing in the 1970s and afterwards, but the derogatory term "Mrs Speculator" (*bokbuin*, 복부인) was coined to disparage them. The typical images of *bokbuin* were "of women with several checkbooks in their purses, driving their luxurious cars to apartment lotteries" (Chung E 1978; quoted in Yang 2019, 52).

13. According to a report by the Korea Labour & Society Institute, nonregular workers account for 41.6 percent of the entire workforce as of 2019, while the government estimates the ratio of nonregular workers to be 36.4 percent, significantly lower than the Institute's figure (Kim Y-S 2019). The government and the Institute use the same dataset but define nonregular workers differently.

14. The IMF asked for full liberalization and deregulation of the financial system and, as Ji (2013, 39) writes, much of the IMF's prescriptions represented "Wall Street-led global financial capital's interests in profitable investment opportunities." The Kim Dae-jung government, backed by pro-market and anti-*chaebol* intellectuals and a foreign capital-oriented neoliberal faction within economic bureaucrats, "faithfully embraced the IMF's neoliberal prescription for financial liberalization and deregulation to liberate banking and finance from state control as well as to attract foreign capital" (Ji 2013, 39). Although gradual efforts for the transition to financial capitalism were made in and after the 1980s, the IMF crisis heralded South Korea's turn to a new regime of accumulation. The Kim Dae-jung administration embraced "the combination of shareholder-oriented corporate governance, a stock market-centered financial system and a flexible labor market" as the "global standards" (Jang 2011, 48–9) and the Roh Moo-hyun administration hailed the financial sector as a new growth industry (Jang 2011, 51–2).

15. During the time—while the aftermath of the IMF crisis was still painfully felt throughout society—the dot-com bubble was landing in South Korea. At the turn of the century, the media was filled with the stories of those making fortunes overnight in the stock market, while numerous workers lost jobs and real wages declined. At the same time, South Korea was rapidly becoming one of the world's most wired countries and stock trading became just a click away thanks to the development of the home trading

system. As a result, the number of stockholders skyrocketed by 57 percent between 1998 and 1999 (Korea Financial Investment Association 2015, 90) whereas the unemployment rate jumped from around 2.5 percent pre-crisis to 7–8 percent in the years of 1998 and 1999 (Choi M 2011, 45; Song 2007, 333). The dot-com bubble came to an end at the end of 2000 and so did the IMF crisis. The Kosdaq Composite Index, which had spiked 263.4 percent between 1997 and 1999, nosedived from 256.1 to 52.55 points between 1999 and 2000 (Shin and Chang 2003, 110–11). The government announced the official end to the IMF crisis around the same time.

16. See Kyung-Sup Chang (2012) for a discussion of the social and economic policies of the Lee Myung-bak administration.

17. In 2013, 47.5 percent of the entire workforce earned 20 million won (about US$18,264) or less yearly (Hankook Ilbo 2015).

18. According to these sources, in 2014, South Korea's average number of work hours (2,124) was 1.2 times more than the average for the thirty-four OECD countries. In 2015, South Korean workers logged 2,113 working hours, which was 54 percent more than workers in Germany and 18 percent more than workers in the US.

19. See Cho et al. (2017) and Lee Minyoung (2019) for scholarly discussions of transnational movements of South Korean youth in relation to the Hell Joseon discourses.

20. This also concurs with cultural studies' long incitement to see those outside the academy as producers of economic knowledge (Grossberg 2010; Ruccio 2008)

21. It also shares commonalities with what Fraser and Jaeggi (2018, 120) call "moral critique," which contends that capitalism "withholds from people the fruits of their labor in an unfair or unjust way, and it makes them subservient to a system that ... cheats them out of what they are due."

22. Varnelis (2008) and boyd (2014) developed the account of networked publics. See Baym (2000), Cho (2020), Jenkins (2006), Jin (2010), Kendall (2002), and Rheingold (2000) for empirical research on what can be seen as networked publics, including the examples of fans and hobbyists. See Elder-Vass (2016) for the practice of digital gifting and Jiyeon Kang (2016) for political mobilizations of networked publics.

23. Feher discusses the notion of self-appreciation based on the ways corporate governance is concerned with "capital growth or appreciation rather than income, stock value rather than commercial profit" (2009, 27). Observing that the same logic is applied to the regime of human capital, he writes that the practice of self-appreciation is "appreciating, that is, increasing the stock value of, the capital to which he or she is identified" (2009, 27).

24. See Hartelius (2020) for a discussion of how expertise in the digital commons is constructed in large part by giving.

25. My point here is in line with other scholars who have noted that the logic of economic rationality, or of entrepreneurial self-interest, has changed under neoliberalism (Chakravartty and Sarkar 2013; Foucault 2008; Fridman 2016; Irani 2019; Lee SC 2018; Martin 2002). For a discussion of the more complex relationships between capitalism, communities, and the commons, see Arvidsson (2020) and Arvidsson and Peitersen (2013).

26. Chouliaraki (2021, 12) emphasizes the need to distinguish victimhood and vulnerability. While the latter is "an embodied and social condition of openness to violence," the former is an act of "attach[ing] the moral value accrued to the vulnerable to everyone who claims it."

27. As Eunjung Kim (2017, 19) has observed, South Korea's public culture was occupied with psychological discourses in the late 2000s and afterwards. The English word "healing" (*hilling*) emerged as a key word in popular and consumer culture, along with "cure" (*chiyu*) and "therapy" (*terapi*).

28. Nancy Fraser's account represents this expansive view of social reproduction: "Variously called 'care,' 'affective labor,' or 'subjectivation,' this activity forms capitalism's human subjects, sustaining them as embodied, natural beings, while also constituting them as social beings, forming their habitus and the socio-ethical substance (*Sittlichkeit*) in which they move. Central here is the work of socializing the young, building communities, and producing and reproducing the shared meanings, affective dispositions, and horizons of value that underpin social cooperation, including the forms of cooperation-cum-domination that characterize commodity production" (Fraser and Jaeggi 2018, 31).

29. In the 1980s and 1990s, it was mostly market institutions (e.g., securities firms, media corporations, the publishing industry, department stores, various continuing education programs) that offered financial education to socialize Koreans into new economic logics and dispositions suitable for the shifting economy. For instance, the Korea Securities Dealers Association began to offer a seminar called "Securities for Ladies (여성전용증권교실)" in 1987 (Jeong S, May 16, 1987). In 1989, the Maeil Business Newspaper company, which was the most crucial proponent of asset tech in the 1980s and 1990s, launched an instructional program, sponsored by the Daehan Investment Trust, for lay investors ("the College for Stock Investors"; 증권대학강좌) (Jeong G, May 10, 1989).

30. In line with many other scholars who stress the integration of research across online and offline spaces (Hine 2015; Lingel 2017a; Marwick, 2013; Miller et al. 2016; Pink et al. 2016), my attention to offline practices and sites was explicit and intentional from the outset rather than opportunistic. In retrospect, my attention to going beyond what was online was also in tune with the practices of my research participants, who consider offline activities and interactions (e.g., talking to people, going on field trips) crucial to their financial projects. Asset tech learners are advised to value first-hand experience and attend to their physical surroundings, not just seek information online, in order to capture where investing opportunities lie. They were advised, for example, to observe which snacks sell out in grocery stores as a way to decide which corporation to invest in or observe how many passengers pass by the corner of a commercial district to judge the investing potential of the location. The way learners travel across on- and offline as well as across multiple online forums is not just due to technological affordances but signals that such movement itself is crucial to their goal.

## TWO

1. Bum Young might have been inspired by a Korean translation of Michael LeBoeuf's *The Perfect Business: How to Make a Million From Home With No Payroll, No Debts, No Employee Headaches, No Sleepless Nights!* Published in 1996, its Korean edition translated the title into *Making 10 eok won in 10 Years.*

2. One of the news reports that covered the ten *eok* won fervor estimated that ten *eok* won in assets would generate a yearly interest of 70 million won (US$55,955), which would allow one to rise into the top 10 percent income group through interest earnings alone (Yu 2002).

3. Miyazaki (2013) observed professional derivative traders in Japan and one of his interlocuters also used a very similar activity to compute his own market value.

4. In this regard, he shared with participants of the FIRE movement of the US a commitment to a lifestyle in which one tries to achieve financial freedom through extreme frugality and the detailed logging of income and expenditure (Taylor and Davies 2021; Tergesen and Dagher 2018).

5. The collaborative relation between Café Ten in Ten and *Maeil Business Newspaper* has been ongoing. Most importantly, a year-long subscription to a weekly business magazine published by the same company is offered at a lower price to users of Café Ten in Ten. Also, the same magazine is freely circulated to participants of the Ten in Ten Academy. This collaboration helped the financial media company widen their readership while helping Café Ten in Ten establish its legitimacy. Other newspaper companies, securities firms, and banks, as well as financial services companies also offered asset tech lectures to Café Ten in Ten participants in the early 2000s for free or at a discounted rate.

6. Divisions existed within each group of stock investors and real estate investors. For example, devoted stock investors were broadly divided by two noticeable strategies: those who had faith in fundamental analysis (aka value investing, 가치투자) and those who believed in technical analysis (기술적 분석; aka chartism). Bum Young firmly believed in the former, promoting it in the Ten in Ten Academy but never imposing it upon users of Café Ten in Ten. See Bryan and Rafferty (2013) and Bjerg (2014) for scholarly discussions of different stock investing strategies. See Souleles and Hansen (2019) for a discussion of another stock investing strategy called the contrarian approach.

7. Two of his favorite books were *The 7 Habits of Highly Effective People* (Stephen R. Covey 1989; translated into Korean in 1994) and *Awaken The Giant Within* (Anthony Robbins 1991; translated into Korean in 2002). He was also a big fan of Osho-Rajneesh, a guru of countercultural spirituality. According to historian of religions Hugh B. Urban (2015), Osho-Rajneesh was well known to Americans of the 1980s as the "Guru of the Rich," and his movement was "perhaps the first to explicitly unite spirituality and capitalism, wedding the ideal of otherworldly transcendence to the unapologetic pursuit of material wealth" (3).

8. Fridman (2016, 103) also points out that accurate bookkeeping is seen in personal finance as an important skill for the self-discipline vital to one's financial success.

9. Initially, Café Ten in Ten had only three discussion boards. One was to be an archive of financial news articles. Another was where users exchanged asset tech strategies by sharing their financial status, goals, and investing plans. The other was the socially oriented discussion board. The original make-up of discussion boards set the tone of Café Ten in Ten, showing Bum Young's concern for community from the beginning. Meanwhile, the addition of a non-topical discussion board—where users could talk about virtually anything—was a widely shared feature of many online communities. Observing a Korean online bitcoin community, for instance, Seung Cheol Lee (2022a, 101) writes that it "has mainly focused on exchanging cryptocurrency news and sharing investment know-how. The community, however, is also famous for its diverse and active bulletin boards on which members share their everyday experiences, post funny memes, and discuss various topics including cryptocurrencies." See also Younghan Cho (2020) for similar practices in the case of an online community for baseball fans.

10. The program fee has changed over time, from 100,000 won (US$88) in 2012 to 120,000 won (US $113) in 2014, 200,000 won (US $181) in 2018, and 160,000 won (US $122) in 2023. The Academy consists of four days, one day down from five, as of 2023.

11. In this sense, he exemplifies what Foucault calls an entrepreneur of himself: "being for himself his own capital, being for himself his own producer, being for himself the source of [his] earnings" (2008, 226). My discussion of self-assetization is also in line with Kylie Jarrett's (2022) discussion of digital labor as assetization. Observing new forms of digital labor, she writes that "the logics of commodification which involve the complete domination of exchange-value that produces absolute alienation does not really capture the persistence of the ineffable and inalienable in evidence in digital labor" (158).

12. I borrow the notion of *socializers* from Brennan, Monroy-Hernández, and Resnick (2010) where they discuss the different modes of participation of young people in an online community for programming. They describe the different modes of participation in terms of a spectrum from socializing to creating. The socializers, they observed, are "participants who are predominantly motivated by socializing, the group dynamics, and interactions with others" (78).

13. In their study of "lifestyle gurus," Baker and Rojek write that while the term "guru" traditionally referred to a spiritual master, it is used more liberally now to refer to "those with native experience, knowledge and skills associated with the domestic sphere and everyday life" (2020, 4). Being accessible and collegial are two important characteristics shared by contemporary lifestyle gurus. Baker and Rojek (2020, 4) indicate that "the old distinction of hierarchy between the master and the follower, which was reproduced in most guru relationships, has been replaced by a more approachable and sustainable alternative." The emergence of investing "gurus" in South Korea is illustrative of the incorporation of spirituality into asset tech discourses (on the surface), to signal that the pursuit of assets can be more than merely material. Although investing gurus share approachability with the "lifestyle gurus" prominent in the realm of wellness and health, they are positioned on the more traditional side of the spectrum as they exercise authority in a persisting relationship between a master and their followers.

14. The point I am making is in line with the observation that "gifting," in addition to "knowing," is essential to "expertising" in the digital commons (Hartelius 2020).

15. This particular plan was part of Seoul's ongoing urban redevelopment project called "New Town (뉴타운)." Whereas the New Town Project (2002–2012) was intended to help provide housing for low-income residents and create better living conditions for them, it generated massive evictions and an investment boom. Overall, South Korea's urban redevelopment has been profit-driven and has provided developers and investors with speculative benefits (see Shin 2021; Shin and Kim 2016; Yang 2018).

16. This posting (2008) reflected on his 2005 transaction, and the KRW to USD conversion is based on the average exchange rate in 2005.

17. Chapter 5 develops an account of South Korea's unique rental system, which allows a homebuyer to use the deposit given by the property's tenant as part of the buyer's home-purchasing capital.

18. Bum Young once jokingly said that divorced users also requested a separate social board but he refused to make one for them.

## THREE

1. Note that the Korean term *noye* (노예) does not necessarily evoke racialized labor or chattel slavery.

2. In this regard, I agree with Fassin and Harcourt's (2019, 2) argument that we need to pay attention to "what sort of critique people produce in critical situations." In the same volume, Fassin (2022) explores the possibility that populist discourses (conspiracy theories in particular) play a role in producing a critique of official authorities (see also Fassin and Harcourt 2022). At the same time, I also credit Holm (2020) for his insight that vernacular critiques have increasingly become a mode of cultural consumption in service of class distinctions.

3. Kiyosaki has published more than 30 books that have been translated into dozens of languages (Fridman 2016).

4. Bum Young used the metaphor of "system robot (시스템 로봇)" to describe the notion of financial freedom. His core recommendation in Ten in Ten Academy was a three-step regimen consisting of extreme saving, stock investing, and creating a system robot. The system robot refers to a set of assets that generate investment income sufficient for one to live off (e.g., interest, dividends, rental incomes, capital gains). The system robot should automatically generate income with no labor put into it; this reproduces Kiyosaki's notion of freedom as "making a living through 'passive income'" (Fridman 2016, 36). Importantly, Garboden (2021, 9) indicates that "the notion of passive income itself is an example of the enormous influence Kiyosaki has exercised on amateur investors" in the US. According to him, "although it is technically defined by the IRS [Internal Revenue Service], the way amateur investors mention it is primarily inspired by Kiyosaki" (Garboden 2021). In South Korea, the metaphor of the system robot repeatedly emerged in the larger world of asset tech, albeit under different names. For instance, one writer and Café Ten in Ten's lay expert called it "a means of production" (*saengsan sudan*) (Cheongullim 2018) and another named it "a profit robot" (*suik robot*). (Apateia 2012).

5. Historically, male workers were expected "to spend more time drunk with colleagues than sober with their families" (Harkness 2013, 22). Bum Young condemned this ritualized corporate culture, especially after-work socials (*hoesik*, 회식) that encouraged excessive drinking. Although the younger generation has become resistant to the corporate culture of after-work drinking, it is still a significant part of corporate Korea that continues in the name of boosting collective morale and unity. Bum Young lamented that many Koreans simply conformed to the convention, even though many tended to make inappropriate mistakes under the influence. This criticism of *hoesik* has been commonly found among cultural critics and left-leaning intellectuals. For instance, Kang Jun-man describes the necessity of going to *hoesik* as a kind of structural violence. He goes so far as to call it "a kind of mafia culture (*jopokmunhwa*)," meaning that it is part of the efforts to increase absolute loyalty to the corporation (Prentice 2022, 139).

6. He named what are commonly seen as the top three colleges in South Korea.

7. Bum Young ultimately changed his program's name from the "Ten in Ten Academy" to the "Financial Freedom Academy" in the late 2010s.

8. Kiyosaki revised this book after the 2008 global economic crisis and published a new edition in 2012. In the new edition, he revised B as "big business" and S as "small business or self-employed." The new edition was immediately translated into Korean, in

which B (big business) was translated as *saeopga* and S (small business or self-employed) was translated as "small business owners (자영업자) or working professionals (전문직 종사자)."

9. Sunam Joung (2011) points out that advice literature offered accounts that required readers to change their existing negative perspectives on rich people. Some literature distinguished "good riches" and "bad riches." Bad riches were described as selfish and vulgar while Protestant asceticism and frugality were required for good riches.

10. In this passage, we learn that Bum Young did not entirely dismiss real estate investing; but when it came to authenticity he placed higher value on stock investing than on real estate investing. Although his perspective changed over time as he later came to engage more deeply in real estate, he remained contradictorily consistent about the superior morality of stock investing compared to real estate investing.

11. Similar to what I observed about Ten in Ten Academy, however, Fridman (2016) also indicates that Kiyosaki's diagnosis of contemporary capitalism includes elements similar to a Marxist diagnosis: "The notion of class structure based on ownership of the means of production instead of level of income; a hint at Marx's idea of alienated labor; the idea of social reproduction based on education, which resembles Marxist philosopher Louis Althusser's analysis of the school system; and the certainty that the state contributes to the reproduction of the conditions for capitalism and the advantages of the capitalist class" (47).

12. Bum Young used "large corporation" (*daegieop*, 대기업) and "*chaebol*" interchangeably, which is common in South Korea.

13. As indicated in chapter 1, notoriously long working hours were among the common complaints in the Hell Joseon discourse. According to Lie (1992), the average number of work hours in South Korea topped the International Labor Organization charts in the 1980s (quoted in Nelson 2000, 16). In 2016, South Korean workers worked 2,069 hours on average, which was the second most among members of the OECD countries (Bak 2017). It was not until 2018 that South Korea lowered its maximum number of working hours from 68 hours a week to 52 hours (Moulite 2018).

14. Nelson (2000) points out that, ever since the end of the Korean War, real estate has been one of the investments with the highest returns in the South Korean economy. Between 1970 and 1985, while consumer prices increased by 635 percent and wages and salaries increased by 1,248 percent, land prices increased by an astonishing 1,585 percent over their original value (Korea Housing Bank 1988; quoted in Nelson 2000, 52).

15. Campaign participants were expected to receive the dollar value (in Korean won) of the gold items they gave (Park S 1997).

16. As the next section will show in more detail, this comment is also similar to the postcolonial critique that "those already in a subaltern position […] have paid for fixing or keeping the system intact, while those who have profited from the inequality/vulnerability of debtors have been rescued either by a particular government or a multilateral juridico-economic body" (Chakravartty and Silva 2012, 373).

17. The Bretton Woods system "put in place national political capital controls that by regulating the segregation of foreign and domestic money markets enabled a nation's central bank to adjust interest and currency rates based on domestic economic objectives" (LiPuma and Lee 2004, 70). John Maynard Keynes and Harry Dexter White, the two architects of Bretton Woods, "were in near complete accord that capital controls were necessary to allow governments to set interest rates to advance their domestic aims

(such as full employment) and to prevent short-term speculative movements and flights of currency" (LiPuma and Lee 2004, 71).

18. My discussion here is not limited to the moniker of poststructuralism.

19. Ironically, even though anti-communism was the most virulent mechanism that suppressed freedom, the transcendent valence of anti-communist freedom was so strong that it was shared by many political dissent groups. For example, in calling for resistance against the Rhee Syngman regime, a 1959 editorial published in *Sasanggye* (1953–1970), a major intellectual journal that operated as "a vocal critic of authoritarian rule" (Kim M 2007, 363), included a proverb that was evoked in the following decades by pro-democracy groups: "The tree of freedom grows through blood" (see Kwon 2008, 141). This was basically a reproduction of Thomas Jefferson's famous saying, "The tree of liberty must be refreshed from time to time with the blood of patriots and tyrants," which worked to justify Westward expansion by military force (Chakravartty 2018, 128). This is one of many historical instances in which the imperial and anti-communist root of freedom overshadowed the freedom of anti-dictatorship. See Song (2009) and Abelmann, Park, and Kim (2009) for a discussion of individual freedom in post-authoritarian South Korea. See Kwang-Yeong Shin (2017), Namhee Lee (2007), and Jaewon Joo (2017) for a discussion of anti-communism.

20. Dong-Choon Kim (2018) argues that South Korea's neoliberal market economy should be understood as economic anti-communism. See also Dong-Choon Kim (2014).

## FOUR

1. Stephen Covey's *The 7 Habits of Highly Effective People*, one of Bum Young's two favorite books, argues that successful people have creative, passionate, and positive attitudes. Financial self-help gurus such as Suze Orman (2006) and Robert Kiyosaki also suggest that people should overcome inner fears and anxieties to attain financial freedom (Joung 2011, 286).

2. Illouz (2007, 52) writes that "the very therapeutic narrative of self-realization can function only by identifying the complication in the story—what prevents me from being happy, intimate, successful—and make sense of it in reference to an event in one's past."

3. Anthropologist Nikolas Harkness observes that South Korea's mundane drinking occasions are a "social space of emotional intensity" (2010, 302).

4. https://www.landmarkworldwide.com/about.

5. *Hyeonmo* (현모) originally refers to a wise mother—where "*hyeon*" means being wise. However, Mina sarcastically used the word as a homonym to mean a mother who goes crazy about her children's field trip. In this context, "*hyeon*" meant "field trip" (현장 학습).

6. I credit Patricia Stuelke's (2021) *The Ruse of Repair* for this idea of "flight from critique to repair."

7. Jin Kyu Park (2016), who studies communication of religion in South Korea, points out how healing discourses in South Korea focused on socioeconomic issues, not just issues of mental health. According to him, "whereas the Western therapeutic generally deals with pathological disorders, such as alcoholism, gambling, depression,

addiction or violence, its Korean counterpart is not necessarily associated with mental illness" (383). The healing discourse brought attention to the social aspect of suffering/wounds caused by issues "such as cruel job market, competition, insecure employment, low income and social inequality" (383).

## FIVE

1. According to a 1995 article from the *Maeil Business Newspaper*, several colleges that had a real estate major—including Konkuk University, Kangnam University, and Jeonju University—noted that the major had the highest ratio of alums who found employment immediately after graduation (Kang H 1995, 21).

2. Kangnam University began to offer an undergraduate course called "Theory of Asset Tech" in Spring 1998, for which more than 300 students wanted to enroll (Kang H 1998, 31). In 2004, Seoul Women's University began to offer a course called "Affluent Studies" (*bujahak*) to teach students "everything about rich people—from the definition of being rich to analyses of their characteristics," and, ultimately, to instruct them on how ordinary people could get rich (Park M 2011).

3. Over time, during the years that I attended the Ten in Ten Academy from 2013 to 2016, Bum Young himself showed a growing interest in real estate.

4. Civil servant jobs, including the lowest grade (grade 9), became one of the most sought-after jobs among young people after the IMF crisis due to the employment security and retirement pensions. Three civil servants in Alumnigroup were all young women and all of them had left their previous jobs for these highly competitive civil service positions.

5. Over the span of just three years between 2017 and 2020, for instance, Seoul's average apartment price escalated more than 50 percent to 925 million won (US$774,000) (Lee J and Kim S 2020).

6. Another study reports that real estate prices "skyrocketed in tandem with condominium development in urban areas, rising more than 300 percent in Seoul between 1986 and 2002" (Song 2014, 47).

7. As a result, housing prices rose well ahead of incomes, and South Korea witnessed the rise of house flippers and rentiers instead of mass homeownership (Ronald and Kyung 2013). Seoul's homeownership rate of 42.1 percent (as of 2015; 56.8 percent for the country) is significantly lower than in other East Asian countries and OECD countries (Japan at 80.5 percent and Singapore at 91 percent as of 2018; and the US at 67.4 percent as of 2020). For South Korea, see http://www.index.go.kr/potal/main/EachDtlPageDetail.do?idx_cd=1239. For the US, see https://www.census.gov/housing/hvs/index.html. For Singapore, see https://tradingeconomics.com/singapore/home-ownership-rate (all accessed in November 2020).

8. A 1986 poll showed a similar result in which 50 percent chose savings, 25 percent chose real estate investments, and 9.3 percent chose stock investments (*Maeil Business Newspaper*, March 24, 1986).

9. Jesook Song (2014) calls the bustling informal financial markets that were developed since the end of the Korean War "sedimented financialization" (e.g., rotating credit associations or *kye*, private loans, rental housing practices, and money gift exchanges), in order to distinguish them from the process of global financialization that South Korea increasingly became part of after the IMF crisis.

10. The foreclosure auction had not been feasible for amateur investors for several other reasons. Most of all, listings were difficult to access, and gangsters often appeared in the courthouse to overwhelm other bidders. The bidding process changed in 1993 from verbal to silent, allowing it to take place in secret. Also, with the development of the Internet, listings were made accessible and searchable to the public (Moon and Lee 2013).

11. Garboden (2021, 11) adds that amateur investors in the US believed that "stocks represent an alien and elitist form of investment, to which things happen for no apparent reason, whereas real estate is something you can touch and control."

12. Before 2004, South Korea had had some limited housing loan programs (주택 담보대출) that may be seen as a kind of mortgage. However, unlike US-style mortgage loans that can be lent up to 95 percent of the purchase price, Korean banks before the IMF crisis lent up to 70 percent of the purchase price of the property only after the sale had been closed. Not only was it rare to get the maximum of 70 percent, but only those who worked full-time for large corporations (less than 20 percent of the labor force) had access to credit through their employers as a benefit (Song 2014). In 2004, the Korea Housing Finance Corporation was established to introduce North American-style mortgage loans (Kim D 2018a, 200–5). In addition, the real estate sector witnessed broad-ranging deregulation during the post-IMF era. Between 1996 and 1998 alone, for instance, the Kim Dae-jung administration lifted 17 anti-speculation measures (Sohn 2008).

13. A 2004 newspaper article reported that many of these programs cost 300,000–500,000 won (US$262–437) (Heo and Jo 2004).

14. Whereas the aggregate total mortgage debt measured 7.81 trillion won (US$10.99 billion) in 1990, it increased to 66.9 trillion won in 2006 (US$70.05 bn) and to 73 trillion won (US$78.56 bn) in 2007 (Ronald and Lee 2012, 124).

15. According to Jesook Song's (2014, 46) succinct example, if a property is "worth 300 million won (approximately $300,000), it is annually or biannually leased through a lump-sum security deposit of 200 million won (about $200,000)." Earlier research indicates that the amount of a *jeonse* deposit ranged from 30 percent to 70 percent of the purchase value of the housing unit (Nelson 2000, 53; Kim S-H 2011, 184)."

16. For a long time, *jeonse* deposits comprised the largest source of home-purchasing capital to many homebuyers. Kim Soo-Hyun (2011, 185) notes that "of all capital used for purchasing homes, long-term mortgages make up only about 5 percent, and, even including short-term loans, the proportion of bank loans in home-purchase capital remains at around 34 percent on average. The largest sources of such capital are lease deposits [*jeonse*], savings and familial support." Therefore, the *jeonse* system made real estate a crucial part of the informal financial market and created "a profound infrastructure for household economy" (Song 2014, 41).

17. Paying the deposit upfront and acquiring tenancy do not automatically make a tenant a secured creditor. It is the tenant's responsibility to check the ownership and credit status of the property and to go through multiple processes to create a security lien on the property in the amount of their deposit. It is important to complete this process as quickly as possible because preexisting creditors receive priority for recovering their money in the event of foreclosure. Those with less economic and social capital might be unable to read through complex title documents before signing a lease and creating a security lien. Many of these tenants neither check the credit status

of the property nor go through the process of creating a security lien. More importantly, even if one completes all the processes on time and secures the deposit money, it is difficult to recover one's money if the foreclosed home has been underwater with preexisting creditors.

18. It has been noted that lay investors in the US often shared a sense of entitlement to the asset market and that they also conceived of investing as a duty. American amateur stock investors, for example, seemed to share a genuine sense of "belief in limitless possibilities for expansion" (Harrington 2008, 16) and "a collective duty to seize those opportunities" (Garboden 2021, 5). In the realm of real estate, amateur investors tied their speculative activity to "putting land into what they view as productive use" (Garboden 2021, 5).

19. The average exchange rate of KRW to USD was 953.19 in 1997 and 1,400.40 in 1998 according to https://www.govinfo.gov/content/pkg/ERP-2011/pdf/ERP-2011-table110.pdf.

20. In an ethnography of group Bible study, Bielo (2009, 12) concludes that it "is a site where individuals are able to critically and reflexively articulate the categories of meaning and action that are central to their spiritual and social life." Meanwhile, Harrington (2008) conducted an ethnography of seven investment clubs in the San Francisco Bay area in the late 1990s to observe the mass movement of Americans into investing during that period. According to her, investment clubs were more similar to small businesses than to hobbyist groups. Participants "must submit to a degree of formalization, legal stricture, and hierarchy that, while common in work organizations, is not commonly associated with voluntary associations" (22). She observes that "investment clubs (typically) meet every month for about two hours to decide which stocks to buy or sell using the money amassed from each member's contribution, averaging $35 per person per month. The groups have hierarchical leadership structures, elect officers, make decisions jointly, and own assets (stocks) in common; new members pay an initiation fee, must sign a contract to join the club, and provide their Social Security numbers for the club's federal and state tax filings" (22).

In Alumnigroup, what Hongkoo (51, M, small business owner) imagined was akin to Harrington's model. He hoped that Alumnigroup would develop as an investor club in which everyone would try investing in the same stocks picked collectively and report on their returns. In so doing, he believed that members would be more engaged and Alumnigroup would be sustained longer. He never brought up this idea, though, because he was afraid that it would place high pressure on others, especially on women participants who he knew had small amounts of capital and were less confident about investing. Instead, Hongkoo suggested that a couple of participants would give a "five-minute speech" during the monthly meeting in which each would share her own asset tech interests and strategies. This idea was realized and everyone took a turn speaking.

21. Although participants agreed in the beginning that members would take turns, we ended up having only four participants, all of whom were male, rotate in leading meetings. This gendered pattern was observed in Singlesgroup as well, which will be discussed in more detail in chapter 6.

22. The amount of money differs according to region. In Seoul, for instance, tenants with a deposit of 100 million won (US$86,206) or less can recover up to 34 million won (US$29,310) as of 2016. In most other metropolitan cities, tenants with a deposit of 60 million won (US$51,724) or less are entitled to recover up to 20 million

won (US$17,241). In the "overpopulated constraint districts," tenants with a deposit of 80 million (US$68,965) or less can recover up to 27 million won (US$23,275). For the rest of the country, tenants with a deposit of 50 million won (US$43,103) can recover up to 17 million won (US$14,655) (Ministry of Government Legislation 2016).

## SIX

1. The percentage of unmarried men in the 30–34 age group skyrocketed from 19 percent to 56 percent between 1995 and 2015. The percentage in the 25–29 age group soared from 64 percent to 90 percent, the 35–39 age group increased from 7 percent to 33 percent, and the 40–44 age group changed from 3 percent to 23 percent during the same period. For women, the changes during the same period are: 30 percent to 77 percent (ages 20–29), 7 percent to 38 percent (ages 30–34), 3 percent to 19 percent (ages 35–39) and 2 percent to 11 percent (ages 40–44) (Lee H 2019).

2. All names are pseudonyms (for both screen names and real names). Members of Singlesgroup addressed each other by their screen names, which most participants had created for Café Ten in Ten. Some did not know each other's real names.

3. According to a study that used nationwide time-diary data, single women appear to socialize far more than single men (Lee and Lee 2014).

4. Koreans are encouraged to keep a savings account specifically for housing (주택 청약예금), which allows them to bid on new apartments. Although individuals can bid to purchase a new apartment unit if they have had a savings account for long enough, single-person households are given the lowest priority in the bidding process (Song 2014, 43).

5. Each participant paid US$6 every time they attended a monthly meeting: US$5 for the rental of a seminar room and US$1 for a membership fee.

6. Dividend stocks are a type of stock through which a company makes regular distributions to its shareholders, usually in the form of cash payments (Hall 2022).

7. Here, Joong-Ki emphasized that inflows of a great number of lay investors to Café Ten in Ten ultimately resulted in the weakening of information quality. In addition, he also pointed out that malicious comments and personal attacks against big names made them stop sharing information. His observation holds true in many respects. Some lay experts in Café Ten in Ten stopped posting due to pushback, and Bum Young expressed concerns about such phenomena. Yongmi also emphasized that even the Beautiful Singles board became increasingly less amicable and more antagonistic.

8. See Note 6 of Chapter 2 for the difference between value investing and chartism.

## EPILOGUE

1. According to *The Wall Street Journal*, South Korea became "a hotbed for global bitcoin trading" in 2017 as "roughly 4.5% of all global bitcoin transactions used the Korean won" during the same year, "making it the fourth most widely used national currency in bitcoin trading after the U.S. dollar, the Japanese yen and the euro" (Eun-Young Jeong 2018).

2. According to a 2020 poll of 1,000 adults between the ages of 20 and 34 years old, 49.1 percent of respondents had bought shares in the stock market; 42.8 percent said investment was necessary, not optional (Choi and Kim 2020).

3. By "another speculation," Feher (2018) primarily means the capacity of investees to participate in the politics involved in allocating credit. For Komporozos-Athanasious (2022), counter-speculation is the public's mobilization of finance-inspired imagination and technologies for political visibility and obfuscation.

# References

Abelmann, Nancy. 2003. *The Melodrama of Mobility*. Honolulu: University of Hawai'i Press.

Abelmann, Nancy, So Jin Park, and Hyunhee Kim. 2009. "College Rank and Neo-Liberal Subjectivity in South Korea." *Inter-Asia Cultural Studies* 10 (2): 229–47.

Adkins, Lisa, Melinda Cooper, and Martijn Konings. 2020. *The Asset Economy: Property Ownership and the New Logic of Inequality*. Cambridge, UK: Polity Press.

Ahmed, Sara. 2004. "Affective Economies." *Social Text* 22 (2): 117–39.

Allon, Fiona. 2015. "Everyday Leverage, or Leveraging the Everyday." *Cultural Studies* 29 (5–6): 687–706.

Anderson, Ben. 2007. "Hope for Nanotechnology: Anticipatory Knowledge and the Governance of Affect." *Area* 39 (2): 156–65.

Andrejevic, Mark. 2012. "Estranged Free Labor." In *Digital Labor: The Internet as Playground and Factory*, edited by Trebor Scholz, 149–64. New York: Routledge.

Ang, Ien. 2006. "From Cultural Studies to Cultural Research: Engaged Scholarship in the Twenty-First Century." *Cultural Studies Review* 12 (2): 183–97.

Apateia 2012. 마흔살, 행복한 부자 아빠. Seoul: Gilbut.

Arvidsson, Adam. 2020. "Capitalism and the Commons." *Theory, Culture & Society*, 37 (2): 3–30. https://doi.org/10.1177/0263276419868838.

Arvidsson, Adam, and Nicolai Peitersen. 2013. *The Ethical Economy: Rebuilding Value after the Crisis*. New York: Columbia University Press.

Bahng, Aimee. 2018. *Migrant Futures: Decolonizing Speculation in Financial Times*. Durham, NC: Duke University Press.

Bak, Se-hwan. 2017. "South Koreans Work Second-Longest Hours in OECD for Below Average Pay." *The Korea Herald*, Aug 16. https://www.koreaherald.com/view.php?ud=20170816000716.

Baker, Stephanie A., and Chris Rojek. 2020. *Lifestyle Guru: Constructing Authority and Influence Online*. Malden: Polity Press.

Banet-Weiser, Sarah. 2012. *Authentic™: The Politics of Ambivalence in a Brand Culture*. New York: New York University Press.

Banner, Stuart. 2017. *Speculation: A History of the Fine Line between Gambling and Investing*. New York: Oxford University Press.

Baym, Nancy. 2000. *Tune In, Log On: Soaps, Fandom, and Online Community*. Thousand Oaks, CA: Sage.

Belk, Russel W. 2013. "Extended Self in a Digital World." *Journal of Consumer Research* 40 (3): 477–500.

Berlant, Lauren. 2011. *Cruel Optimism*. Durham, NC: Duke University Press.

Bhattacharya, Tithi, ed. 2017. *Social Reproduction Theory: Remapping Class, Recentering Oppression*. London: Pluto Press.

Bielo, James S. 2009. *Words Upon the Word: An Ethnography of Evangelical Group Bible Study*. New York: New York University Press.

Binkley, Sam. 2014. *Happiness as Enterprise*. Albany: State University of New York Press.

Binkley, Sam. 2009. "The Work of Neoliberal Governmentality: Temporality and Ethical Substance in The Tale of Two Dads." *Foucault Studies* 6: 60–78.

Bjerg, Ole. 2014. *Making Money: The Philosophy of Crisis Capitalism*. New York: Verso.

Boellstorff, Tom, Bonnie Nardi, Celia Pearce, and T. L. Taylor, eds. 2012. *Ethnography and Virtual Worlds: A Handbook of Method*. Princeton, NJ: Princeton University Press.

Boltanski, Luc. 2011. *On Critique: A Sociology of Emancipation*. Malden: Polity.

Boltanski, Luc, and Eve Chiapello. 2005a. *The New Spirit of Capitalism*. New York: Verso.

Boltanski, Luc, and Eve Chiapello. 2005b. "The New Spirit of Capitalism." *International Journal of Politics, Culture, and Society* 18 (3–4): 161–88.

boyd, danah. 2015. "Making Sense of Teen Life: Strategies for Capturing Ethnographic Data in a Networked Era." In *Digital Research Confidential: The Secrets of Studying Behavior Online*, edited by E. Hargittai and C. Sandvig, 79–102. Cambridge, MA: MIT Press.

boyd, danah. 2014. *It's Complicated: The Social Lives of Networked Teens*. New Haven, CT: Yale University Press.

Brennan, Karen, Andrés Monroy-Hernández, and Mitchel Resnick. 2010. "Making Projects, Making Friends: Online Community as Catalyst for Interactive Media Creation." *New Directions for Youth Development* 128: 75–83.

Bröckling, Ulrich. 2015. *The Entrepreneurial Self: Fabricating a New Type of Subject*. Translated by Steven Black. Thousand Oaks, CA: Sage.

Bryan, Dick, and Michael Rafferty. 2018. *Risking Together: How Finance is Dominating Everyday Life in Australia*. Sydney: Sydney University Press.

Bryan, Dick, and Michael Rafferty. 2013. "Fundamental Value: A Category in Transformation." *Economy and Society* 42 (1): 130–53.

Burrell, Jenna. 2009. "The Field Site as a Network: A Strategy for Locating Ethnographic Research." *Field Methods* 21 (2): 181–99.

Callon, Michel. 2007. "What Does It Mean to Say That Economics Is Performative?" In *Do Economists Make Markets?*, edited by D. MacKenzie, F. Muniesa, and L. Siu, 311–57. Princeton, NJ: Princeton University Press.

Campbell, John, Gordon Fletcher, and Anita Greenhill. 2009. "Conflict and Identity Shape Shifting in an Online Financial Community." *Information Systems Journal* 19 (5): 461–78.

Cha, Byeongjun. 2002. "여론조사 부자 기준 최소 10억원." *SBS*, March 9. https://news.sbs.co.kr/news/endPage.do?news_id=N0311203365.

Chakravartty, Paula. 2018. "US Media Power and the Empire of Liberty." *Media Theory* 2 (2): 127–37.

Chakravartty, Paula, and Denise Ferreira da Silva. 2012. "Accumulation, Dispossession, and Debt: The Racial Logic of Global Capitalism—An Introduction." *American Quarterly* 64 (3): 361–85.

Chakravartty, Paula, and Sreela Sarkar. 2013. "Entrepreneurial Justice: The New Spirit of Capitalism in Emergent India." *Popular Communication* 11 (1): 58–75.

Chang, Kyung-Sup. 2019. *Developmental Liberalism in South Korea: Formation, Degeneration, and Transnationalization.* Switzerland: Palgrave MacMillan.

Chang, Kyung-Sup. 2012. "Economic Development, Democracy and Citizenship Politics in South Korea: The Predicament of Developmental Citizenship." *Citizenship Studies*, 16 (1): 29–47. DOI: 10.1080/13621025.2012.651401.

Chen, Carolyn 2022. *Work Pray Code: When Work Becomes Religion in Silicon Valley.* Princeton, NJ: Princeton University Press.

Chen, Yu-Hsiang. 2013. "Stock Trading and Daily Life: Lay Stock Investors in Taiwan." PhD diss., The University of Edinburgh.

Cheon, Hyejung 2017. "IMF 외환위기 기억의 사회적 구성: 조선일보의 금 모으기 운동 기사를 중심으로.'" 사회과학연구논총 29 (1): 359–95.

Cheongullim 2018. 나는 오늘도 경제적 자유를 꿈꾼다. Seoul: RH Korea.

Cho, Hae-Jeong. 2015. "The Spec Generation Who Can't Say 'No': Overeducated and Underemployed Youth in Contemporary South Korea." *positions: asia critique* 23 (3): 437–62.

Cho, Han Hae-joang. 2007. "'You Are Entrapped in an Imaginary Well': The Formation of Subjectivity within Compressed Development. A Feminist Critique of Modernity and Korean Culture." In *The Inter-Asia Cultural Studies Reader*, edited by Kuan-Hsing Chen and Chua Beng Huat, 291–310. Abingdon: Routledge.

Cho, Mun Young et al. 2017. 헬 조선 인 앤 아웃. Seoul: Nulmin.

Cho, Younghan. 2020. *Global Sports Fandom in South Korea: American Major League Baseball and Its Fans in the Online Community.* Singapore: Palgrave MacMillan.

Choi, Hayan, and Seo Eori. 2013. "나만 안 하면 바보되나… 재테크 하다 피 본 사람들." *Pressian*, November 12. https://www.pressian.com/pages/articles/109704.

Choi, Jang Jip. 1993. "Political Cleavages in South Korea." In *State and Society in Contemporary Korea*, edited by Hagen Koo, 13–50. Ithaca, NY: Cornell University Press.

Choi, Jungwook. 2006. "부동산 경매 큰 인기… 감정가 규모 85조 전년비 24% 증가." *Kookmin Ilbo*, January 3. https://n.news.naver.com/mnews/article/005/0000231014?sid=101.

Choi, Minseok. 2011. "1997년 경제위기 이후 일상생활의 금융화와 투자자 주체의 형성." MA thesis, Seoul National University.

Choi, Mirang. 2020. "88년생 돈알못의 파산 후기." *Kyunghyang Shinmun*, October 6. https://www.khan.co.kr/national/national-general/article/202010060600011.

Choi, Mirang, and Yujin Kim. 2020. "청년투자자 22% "투자에 빚은 필수." *Kyunghyang Shinmun*, October 13. http://biz.khan.co.kr/khan_art_view.html?artid=202010130600025&code=940100#csidx9bab3c771af3859808d2a2662536377.

Choi, Mirang, Yujun Kim, and Gwangyeon Park. 2020. "계층 소득이 높을수록 '주식 부동산 투자, 부모가 권해요.'" *Kyunghyang Shinmun*, October 13. http://biz.khan.co.kr/khan_art_view.html?artid=202010130600045&code=940100#csidx73f09cc9550bcdbbdf832f677637076.

Choi, Sihyun. 2021. 부동산은 어떻게 여성의 일이 되었나. Paju: Changbi.

Chong, Kimberly. 2018. *Best Practice: Management Consulting and the Ethics of Financialization in China*. Durham: Duke University Press.

Choo, Hae Yeon. 2022. "'Layoffs Are Murder, But They Are Also Everyday Life: A Critique of Labor and Living in the Era of Ghost Capital." In *Crisis under Critique: How People Assess, Transform, and Respond to Critical Situations*, edited by Didier Fassin and Axel Honneth, 76–96. New York: Columbia University Press.

Choo, Hae Yeon. 2021. "Speculative Homemaking: Women's Labor, Class Mobility and the Affect of Homeownership in South Korea." *Urban Studies* 58 (1): 148–63.

Chouliaraki, Lilie. 2021. "Victimhood: The Affective Politics of Vulnerability." *European Journal of Cultural Studies* 24 (1): 10–27.

Chouliaraki, Lilie, and Sarah Banet-Weiser. 2021. "Introduction to Special Issue: The Logic of Victimhood." *European Journal of Cultural Studies* 24 (1): 3–9.

Clark, Gordon L., Nigel Thrift, and Adam Tickell. 2004. "Performing Finance: The Industry, the Media and Its Image." *Review of International Political Economy* 11 (2): 289–310.

Comaroff, Jean, and John Comaroff. 2000. "Privatizing the Millennium: New Protestant Ethics and the Spirits of Capitalism in Africa, and Elsewhere." *Africa Spectrum* 35 (3): 293–312.

Covey, Stephen R. 1989. *The 7 Habits of Highly Effective People*. New York: Simon and Schuster.

Daum Dictionary Online, s.v. "재테크," accessed April 26, 2024, https://dic.daum.net/word/view.do?wordid=kkw000221322&q=%EC%9E%AC%ED%85%8C%ED%81%AC&supid=kku000279541.

Davidson, Roei. 2012. "The Emergence of Popular Personal Finance Magazines and the Risk Shift in American Society." *Media, Culture & Society* 34 (1): 3–20.

Davies, William. 2012. "The Emerging Neocommunitarianism." *The Political Quarterly* 83 (4): 767–76.

Dean, Jodi. 2009. *Democracy and Other Neoliberal Fantasies*. Durham, NC: Duke University Press.

de Goede, Marieke. 2005. *Virtue, Fortune, And Faith*. Minneapolis: University of Minnesota Press.

Deville, Joe, and Gregory Seigworth. 2015. "Everyday Debt and Credit." *Cultural Studies* 29 (5–6): 615–29.

Doucette, Jamie. 2015. "Debating Economic Democracy in South Korea: The Costs of Commensurability." *Critical Asian Studies* 47 (3): 388–413. doi.org/10.1080/14672715.2015.1057025.

Duffy, Brooke Erin, and Urszula Pruchniewska. 2017. "Gender and Self-Enterprise in the Social Media Age: A Digital Double Bind." *Information, Communication & Society* 20 (6): 843–59.

Dunford, Michael, and Godfrey Yeung. 2011. "Towards Global Convergence: Emerging Economies, the Rise of China and Western Sunset?" *European Urban and Regional Studies* 18 (1): 22–46.

Duterme, Tom. 2023. "Bloomberg and the GameStop Saga: The Fear of Stock Market Democracy." *Economy and Society* 52 (3): 373–98. doi.org/10.1080/03085147.2023.2189819.

Eckert, Carter J. 1991. *Offspring of Empire: The Koch'ang Kims and the Colonial Origins of Korean Capitalism, 1876–1945*. Seattle: University of Washington Press.

The Economist. 2014. "Lumping It: South Korea's Housing Market." *The Economist*, February 15. http://www.economist.com/news/finance-and-economics/21596566-landlords-are-having-ditch-century-old-rental-system-lumping-it.

Edwards, Amy. 2022. *Are We Rich Yet? The Rise of Mass Investment Culture in Contemporary Britain*. Oakland: University of California Press.

Elder-Vass, Dave. 2016. *Profit and Gift in the Digital Economy*. Cambridge: Cambridge University Press.

Fackler, Martin. 2011. "Lessons Learned, South Korea Makes Quick Economic Recovery." *New York Times*, January 6. https://www.nytimes.com/2011/01/07/world/asia/07seoul.html?searchResultPosition=1.

Falzon, Mark-Anthony, ed. 2009. *Multi-sited Ethnography: Theory, Praxis and Locality in Contemporary Research*. Farnham: Ashgate.

Fassin, Didier. 2022. "Conspiracy Theories as Ambiguous Critique of Crisis." In *Crisis under Critique: How People Assess, Transform, and Respond to Critical Situations*, edited by Didier Fassin and Axel Honneth, 403–419. New York: Columbia University Press.

Fassin, Didier, and Bernard Harcourt, eds. 2019. *A Time for Critique*. New York: Columbia University Press.

Fassin, Didier, and Axel Honneth. 2022. "Introduction. The Heuristic of Crisis: Reclaiming Critical Voices." In *Crisis under Critique: How People Assess, Transform, and Respond to Critical Situations*, edited by Didier Fassin and Axel Honneth, 1–8. New York: Columbia University Press.

Feher, Michel. 2021. "Another Speculation is Possible: The Political Lesson of R/WallStreetBets." *Progress in Political Economy*, February 5. https://www.ppesydney.net/another-speculation-is-possible-the-political-lesson-of-r-wallstreetbets/.

Feher, Michel. 2018. *Rated Agency: Investee Politics in a Speculative Age*. Brooklyn: Zone Books.

Feher, Michel. 2009. "Self-Appreciation; or, the Aspirations of Human Capital." *Public Culture* 21 (1): 21–41.

Felski, Rita. 2015. *The Limits of Critique*. Chicago: The University of Chicago Press.

Ferguson S., Genevieve LeBaron, Angeliki Dimitrakaki et al. 2016. "Special Issue on Social Reproduction." *Historical Materialism* 24 (2): 25–37.

Fifield, Anna. 2016. "Young South Koreans Call Their Country 'Hell' and Look for Ways Out." *The Washington Post*, January 31. https://www.washingtonpost.com/world/asia_pacific/young-south-koreans-call-their-country-hell-and-look-for-ways-out/2016/01/30/34737c06-b967-11e5-85cd-5ad59bc19432_story.html.

Fisher, Mark. 2009. *Capitalist Realism: Is There No Alternative?* Alresford, UK: Zero Books.

Fortunati, Leopoldina. 2007. "Immaterial Labor and Its Machinization." *ephemera* 7 (1): 139–57.

Foucault, Michel 2008. *The Birth of Biopolitics: Lectures at the Lectures at the Collège De France, 1978–79*. New York: Palgrave MacMillan.

Fraser, Nancy. 2016. "Contradictions of Capital and Care." *New Left Review* 100: 99–117.

Fraser, Nancy, and Rahel Jaeggi. 2018. *Capitalism: A Conversation in Critical Theory*. Cambridge, UK: Polity.

French, Shaun, and James Kneale. 2009. "Excessive Financialisation: Insuring Lifestyles, Enlivening Subjects, and Everyday Spaces of Biosocial Excess." *Environment and Planning D: Society and Space* 27:1030–53.

Fridman, Daniel. 2016. *Freedom from Work: Embracing Financial Self-Help in The United States and Argentina*. Stanford, CA: Stanford University Press.

Gago, Verónica. 2017. *Neoliberalism from Below: Popular Pragmatics and Baroque Economies*. Durham, NC: Duke University Press.

Garboden, Philip ME. 2021. "Amateur Real Estate Investing." *Journal of Urban Affairs*. https://doi.org/10.1080/07352166.2021.1904781.

Gibson-Graham, J. K. 2006. *A Postcapitalist Politics*. Minneapolis: University of Minnesota Press.

Go, Duhyeon. 2000. "돈 버는 것보다 관리가 중요." *The Korea Economic Daily*, May 20. https://www.hankyung.com/article/2000051906571.

Grandin, Greg. 2011. *The Last Colonial Massacre: Latin America in the Cold War*. Chicago: The University of Chicago Press.

Greenfield, Cathy, and Peter Williams. 2007. "Financialization, Finance Rationality and the Role of Media in Australia." *Media, Culture & Society* 29 (3): 415–33.

Grossberg, Lawrence. 2012. "Modernity and Commensuration: A Reading of a Contemporary (Economic) Crisis." In *Cultural Studies and Finance Capitalism: The Economic Crisis and After*, edited by Mark Hayward, 13–50. New York: Routledge.

Grossberg, Lawrence. 2010. *Cultural Studies in the Future Tense*. Durham, NC: Duke University Press.

Grynberg, Noah, and Tyler Anderson. 2018. "Flippers are Using an End-Around to Kick Tenants out of Affordable Housing. They Need to be Stopped." *Los Angeles Times*, October 2. https://www.latimes.com/opinion/livable-city/la-oe-grynberg-eviction-loophole-california-20181002-story.html.

Haiven, Max. 2014. *Cultures of Financialization: Fictitious Capital in Popular Culture and Everyday Life*. New York: Palgrave Macmillan.

Haiven, Max, A. T. Kingsmith, and Aris Komporozos-Athanasiou. 2022. "Dangerous Play in an Age of Technofinance: From the GameStop Hunger Games to the Capital Hill Jamboree." *TOPIA: Canadian Journal of Cultural Studies* 45: 102–32.

Hall, Jason. 2022. "Investing in Dividend Stocks." *The Motley Fool*. December 18. https://www.fool.com/investing/stock-market/types-of-stocks/dividend-stocks/.

Hall, Sarah. 2011. "Geographies of Money and Finance 2: Financialization and Financial Subjects." *Progress in Human Geography* 36 (3): 403–11.

Hall, Stuart. 1996. "The Problem of Ideology: Marxism without Guarantees." In *Stuart Hall: Critical Dialogues in Cultural Studies*, edited by David Morley and Kuan-Hsing Chen, 25–46. London: Routledge.

Han, Didi K. 2019. "Weaving the Common in the Financialized City: A Case of Urban Cohousing Experience in South Korea." In *Neoliberal Urbanism, Contested Cities and Housing in Asia*, edited by Yi-Ling Chen and Hyun Bang Shin, 171–92. New York: Palgrave MacMillan.

Han, Hyung-Sung. 2017. "1970년대 박정희 체제에서의 가계부적기 운동." 경영사학 32 (2): 203–30.

Han, Jeong Hui. 2004. "재테크 커뮤니티 CEO 박범영씨." *Economy* 21, May 21. http://www.economy21.co.kr/news/articleView.html?idxno=52735.

Han, Ju Hui Judy. 2011. "'If You Don't Work, You Don't Eat' Evangelizing Development in Africa." In *New Millennium South Korea: Neoliberal Capitalism and Transnational Movements*, edited by Jesook Song, 142–58. London and New York: Routledge.

Hankook Ilbo. 2015. "우리들의 일그러진 월급통장." May 11. https://interview.hankookilbo.com/v/ad198673cbd34caa8f4ab930007d8153/.

Harkness, Nicholas. 2013. "Softer Soju in South Korea." *Anthropological Theory* 13 (1–2): 12–30.

Harkness, Nicholas. 2010. "The Voices of Seoul: Sound, Body, and Christianity in South Korea." PhD diss., The University of Chicago.

Harrington, Brooke. 2008. *Pop Finance: Investment Clubs and the New Investor Populism*. Princeton: Princeton University Press.

Hartelius, Jonhanna. 2020. *The Gifting Logos: Expertise in the Digital Commons*. Oakland: University of California Press.

Hasso, Tim, Daniel Müller, Matthias Pelster, and Sonja Warkulat. 2022. "Who Participated in the GameStop Frenzy? Evidence from Brokerage Accounts." *Finance Research Letters*, 45: 1–11.

Hayward, Mark, ed. 2012. *Cultural Studies and Finance Capitalism: The Economic Crisis and After*. New York: Routledge.

Heo, Jinseok, and Jo Injik. 2004. "경매재테크 낙찰가는 시세75-80%가 적당." *Donga Ilbo*. November 2. https://n.news.naver.com/mnews/article/020/0000268292?sid=101.

Hine, Christine. 2015. *Ethnography for the Internet: Embedded, Embodied and Everyday*. London: Bloomsbury.

Ho, Karen. 2017. "Finance, Crisis, and Hollywood: Critique and Recuperation of Wall Street in Films about the Great Recession." In *Global Finance on Screen: From Wall Street to Side Street*, edited by Constantin Parvulescue, 89–104. New York: Routledge.

Holm, Nicholas. 2020. "Critical Capital: Cultural Studies, the Critical Disposition and Critical Reading as Elite Practice." *Cultural Studies* 34 (1): 143–66.

Holmes, Frank. 2016. "How Gold Rode to The Rescue of South Korea." Forbes, Sep 27. https://www.forbes.com/sites/greatspeculations/2016/09/27/how-gold-rode-to-the-rescue-of-south-korea/?sh=b1daeb233d33.

Illouz, Eva. 2007. *Cold Intimacies: The Making of Emotional Capitalism*. Malden: Polity Press.

Im, Sanggyun. 1999. "김대통령 투자펀드 배 이상 수익." *Maeil Business Newspaper*, August 4, p. 21.

Irani, Lilly. 2019. *Chasing Innovation: Making Entrepreneurial Citizens in Modern India*. Princeton, NJ: Princeton University Press.

Ito, Mizuko, Sonja Baumer, Matteo Bittanti, danah boyd, and Rachel Cody. 2010. *Hanging Out, Messing Around and Geeking Out*. Cambridge, MA: MIT Press.

Jackson, Sarah, Moya Bailey, and Brooke Foucault Welles. 2017. "#GirlsLikeUs: Trans Advocacy and Community Building Online." *New Media & Society* 20 (5): 1868–88.

Janelli, Roger L., and Dawnhee Yim. 1988. "Interest Rates and Rationality: Rotating Credit Associations among Seoul Women." *Journal of Korean Studies* 6 (1): 165–91. https://doi.org/10.1353/jks.1988.0001.

Jang, Hasung. 2014. 한국자본주의: 경제민주화를 넘어 정의로운 경제로. Seongnam: Hey Books.

Jang, Hui Jeong, 2020. "재테크 커뮤니티 텐인텐 운영자 박범영씨가 돌아본 대한민국 재테크 열풍 20년." *Kyunghyang Shinmun*, August 14. https://m.khan.co.kr/national/national-general/article/202008141607005.

Jang, Jin-Ho, 2011. "Neoliberalism in South Korea: The Dynamics of Financialization." In *New Millennium South Korea: Neoliberal Capitalism and Transnational Movements*, edited by Jesook Song, 46–59. New York: Routledge.

Jang, Kang-myung. 2015. 한국이 싫어서. Seoul: Minumsa.

Jarrett, Kylie. 2022. *Digital Labor*. Cambridge, UK: Polity Press.

Jarrett, Kylie. 2016. *Feminism, Labor and Digital Media: The Digital Housewife*. New York: Routledge.

Jarrett, Kylie. 2014. "The Relevance of 'Women's Work': Social Reproduction and Immaterial Labor in Digital Media." *Television & New Media* 15 (1): 14–29.

Jenkins, Henry. 2006. *Convergence Culture*. New York: New York University Press.

Jenkins, Henry, Sam Ford, and Joshua Green. 2013. *Spreadable Media: Creating Value and Meaning in a Networked Culture*. New York: New York University Press.

Jeon, Changhyeop, Namgeun Gwon, and Eunjeong Kim. 2003. "'자녀, 연금 못 믿겠다' 노후 돈에 의지." *The Herald Business*, November 10.

Jeong, Eun-Young. 2018. "Uproar as South Korea Plans Cryptocurrency Crackdown." *The Wall Street Journal*. January 15. https://www.wsj.com/articles/uproar-as-south-korea-plans-cryptocurrency-crackdown-1516010494.

Jeong, Ganghyeon. 1989. "주식 대중화로 국민 복지 실현." *Maeil Business Newspaper*, May 10. p. 11.

Jeong, Seonghee. 1987. "돈도 벌고 자아도 개발하고. 주부 이재 강좌 붐." *Donga Ilbo*, May 16, p. 11.

Ji, Joo-Hyoung. 2013. "The Neoliberalization of South Korea after the 1997 Economic Crisis: A Cultural Political Economy of Crisis Discourse and Management." *Korean Political Science Review* 47 (3): 1–27.

Jin, Dal Yong. 2010. *Korea's Online Gaming Empire*. Cambridge, MA: MIT Press.

Jo, Yubin. 2016. "네이버 카페 매매 의혹. 광고수익 노렸나." *Sisa Journal*, October 15. http://www.sisajournal.com/news/articleView.html?idxno=158999.

Joo, Jaewon. 2017. "민주화 이후 한국 언론의 반공 담론 연대기." 언론과 사회 25 (3): 158–220.

Joseph, Miranda. 2013. "Gender, Entrepreneurial Subjectivity, and Pathologies of Personal Finance." *Social Politics: International Studies in Gender, State & Society* 20 (2): 242–73. http://doi.org/10.1093/sp/jxt009.

Joseph, Miranda. 2002. *Against the Romance of Community*. Minneapolis: University of Minnesota Press.

Joung, Seung Hwa. 2010. "감정 자본주의와 치유 문화." In 친밀한 적: 신자유주의는 어떻게 일상이 되었나, edited by Kim Hyun Mee, 163–86. Seoul: Ihoo.

Joung, Sunam. 2011. "부자되기 열풍의 감정동학과 생애프로젝트의 재구축." 사회와 역사 89: 271–303.

Jung, Heon-mok. 2017. 가치 있는 아파트 만들기. Seoul: Banbi.

Jung, Jin-Heon. 2015. *Migration and Religion in East Asia: North Korean Migrants' Evangelical Encounters*. London: Palgrave.

Kang, Areum. 2018. "똑똑한 한 채 집착은 그만! 현금 파이프 4개 만들어라!" *Hankook Ilbo*, April 3. http://m1.hankookilbo.com/News/Read/201804030389097712.

Kang, Hyungkoo. 1998. "강남대, 재테크론 개설 인기강좌 부상." *Maeil Business Newspaper*, April 2, p. 31.

Kang, Hyungkoo. 1995. "건국, 강남, 전주대 부동산학과 취업률 100%… 상한가 행진." *Maeil Business Newspaper*, June 3, p. 21.

Kang, Jiyeon. 2017. "Internet Activism Transforming Street Politics: South Korea's 2008 'Mad Cow' Protests and New Democratic Sensibilities." *Media, Culture & Society* 39 (5): 750–61.

Kang, Jiyeon. 2016. *Igniting the Internet: Youth and Activism in Postauthoritarian South Korea*. Honolulu: University of Hawai'i Press.

Kang Jun-man. 2011. 룸살롱 공화국. Seoul: Inmul.

Kang, Laura Hyun Yi. 2012. "The Uses of Asianization: Figuring Crises, 1997–98 and 2007–?" *American Quarterly* 64 (3): 411–36.

Kendall, Laurel. 2009. *Shamans, Nostalgias, and the IMF: South Korean Popular Religion in Motion*. Honolulu: University of Hawai'i Press.

Kendall, Lori. 2002. *Hanging Out in the Virtual Pub. Masculinities and Relationships Online*. Berkeley: University of California Press.

Kikkawa, Takeo. 2006. "Beyond the 'Lost Decade': Problems Confronting Japanese Companies, and Solutions." *Japanese Research in Business History* 23: 107–26.

Kim, Bohyeong. 2022. "Thrift Television in South Korea: The Long Recession and the Financial Makeover of Female Consumers in *Homo Economicus* (EBS)." *Television & New Media* 23 (3): 257–75.

Kim, Bohyeong. 2020. "The Ecosystem of a 'Wealth-Tech' Culture: The Birth of Networked Financial Subjects in South Korea." *Media, Culture & Society* 42 (2): 207–24.

Kim, Bohyeong. 2017. "Think Rich, Feel Hurt: The Critique of Capitalism and the Production of Affect in the Making of Financial Subjects in South Korea." *Cultural Studies* 31 (5): 611–33.

Kim, Byoung Kweon. 2012. "18대 대통령 선거와 경제민주화의 주요 쟁점." 황해문화 76: 114–32.

Kim, Cynthia. 2020. "South Korea's Stocks Go Marching as Ants Load Up." *Reuters*, June 17. https://www.reuters.com/article/southkorea-markets-stocks/rpt-south-kor eas-stocks-go-marching-as-ants-load-up-idINL4N2DT4PK?edition-redirect=uk.

Kim, Daejung. 2003. 나의 꿈 10억 만들기. Seoul: One and One Books.

Kim, Dokyun. 2018a. "한국의 자산기반 생활보장체계의 형성과 변형에 관한 연구: 개발국가의 저축동원과 조세정치를 중심으로." PhD diss., Seoul National University.

Kim, Dokyun. 2018b. 한국 복지자본주의의 역사: 자산 기반 복지의 형성과 변화. Seoul: Seoul National University Press.

Kim, Dong-Choon. 2018. "한국형 신자유주의 기원으로서 반공자유주의." 경제와 사회 118: 240–76.

Kim, Dong-Choon. 2014. "How the National Division and the Korean War Affected South Korean Politics: The Notions of Liberty, Democracy, and Welfare." In *Contemporary Korean Political Thought in Search of a Post-Eurocentric Approach*, edited by Jung In Kang, 45–64. Lanham, MD: Lexington Books.

Kim, Eleana. 2022. *Making Peace with Nature: Ecological Encounters Along the Korean DMZ*. Durham and London: Duke University Press.

Kim, Eunjung. 2017. *Curative Violence: Rehabilitating Disability, Gender, and Sexuality in Modern Korea*. Durham, NC: Duke University Press.

Kim, Eunjune. 2015. "초기 힐링담론의 자기통치프레임과 담론효과." 한국언론정보학보 74: 38–71.

Kim, Gwanghui. 1986. "일본에 자산 늘리기 '재테크' 붐." *Donga Ilbo*, Nov 18, p. 9.

Kim, Gyu-sik, Woo-seok Kang, and Eun-joo Lee. 2020. "Korean Stock Market Ends Best-ever 2020 with KOSPI up 30% on Doubled Trade Volume." *Pulse*, December 31. https://pulsenews.co.kr/view.php?year=2020&no=1337905.

Kim, Hyun Mee, ed. 2010. 친밀한 적: 신자유주의는 어떻게 일상이 되었나. Seoul: Ihoo.

Kim, Jisup, Eunkyung Choi, and Jaehyun Shin. 2020. "코로나 청춘들의 눈물겨운 짠테크." *Chosun Biz*, March 13. https://biz.chosun.com/site/data/html_dir/2020/03/12/2020031200334.html.

Kim, Jodi. 2022. *Settler Garrison: Debt Imperialism, Militarism, and Transpacific Imaginaries*. Durham, NC: Duke University Press.

Kim, Joohee. 2020. 레이디 크레딧. Seoul: Hyunsil.

Kim, Jung Min. 2019. "누적회원 수 5억명, 게시물 42억개… 대한민국 '트렌드 제작소' 다음카페 스무살 됐다." *Joongang Ilbo*, June 7. https://news.joins.com/article/23490415.

Kim, Michael. 2007. "The Discursive Foundations of the South Korean Developmental State: *Sasanggye* and the Reception of Modernization Theory." *Korea Observer* 38 (3): 363–85.

Kim, Seung-kyung, and John Finch. 2002. "Living With Rhetoric, Living Against Rhetoric: Korean Families and the IMF Economic Crisis." *Korean Studies* 26 (1): 120–39.

Kim, Soo-Hyun. 2011. "Housing Policy Issues in South Korea since the Global Economic Crisis: Aspects of a Construction-Industry-Dependent Society." In *Housing Markets and the Global Financial Crisis*, edited by Ray Forrest and Ngai-Ming Yip, 179–93. Cheltenham, UK: Edward Elgar Publishing.

Kim, Soon-Young. 2011. 대출 권하는 사회. Seoul: Humanitas.

Kim, Sung-min. 2015. "경매 후끈. 감정가 90% 넘으면 매력 없다는데." *Chosun Ilbo*, June 29. https://biz.chosun.com/site/data/html_dir/2015/06/28/2015062802404.html.

Kim, Young-Nam. 2016. "Koreans' Hours Are Long, But Pay's Not So High." *Korea JoongAng Daily*, August 15. https://koreajoongangdaily.joins.com/2016/08/15/econ omy/Koreans-hours-are-long-but-pays-not-so-high/3022655.html.

Kim, Yu-Seon. 2019. "비정규직 규모와 실태: 통계청, '경제활동인구조사 부가조사' (2019.8) 결과." Korea Labour & Society Institute (KLSI) Issue Paper 118: 1–34. www.klsi.org/bbs/download.php?bo_table=B03&wr_id=2521&no=0&page=3.

Kirk, Donald. 2016. "What 'Korean Miracle'? 'Hell Joseon' is More Like It as Economy Flounders." *Forbes*, February 27. https://www.forbes.com/sites/donaldkirk/2016/02/ 27/what-korean-miracle-hell-joseon-is-more-like-it-as-economy-flounders/.

Kiyosaki, Robert T. 2000. 부자 아빠 가난한 아빠 (*Rich Dad Poor Dad. What the Rich Teach Their Kids About Money—That the Poor and Middle Class Do Not!*). Translated by Seonho Hyeong. Seoul: Mineumin.

Kiyosaki, Robert T. 2000. 부자 아빠 가난한 아빠 2 (*The Cashflow Quadrant! Rich Dad's Guide to Financial Freedom*). Translated by Seonho Hyeong. Seoul: Hwanggeum Gaji.

Klassen, Thomas R. 2010. "Korea: Extending Working Lives." *Global Brief*, April 29. http://globalbrief.ca/blog/2010/04/29/extending-working-lives/.

Komporozos-Athanasious, Aris. 2022. *Speculative Communities: Living with Uncertainty in a Financialized World*. Chicago: The University of Chicago Press.

Konings, Martijn. 2014. "Financial Affect." *Distinktion: Scandinavian Journal of Social Theory* 15 (1): 37–53.

Koo, Hagen. 2007 [2002]. "Engendering Civil Society: The Role of the Labor Movement." In *Korean Society: Civil Society, Democracy and the State*, 2nd edn, edited by Charles K. Armstrong, 73–94. New York: Routledge.

Koo, Hagen. 2001. *Korean Workers: The Culture and Politics of Class Formation*. Ithaca, NY: Cornell University Press.

Koo, Se-Woong. 2015. "Korea, Thy Name is Hell Joseon." *Korea Exposé*, September 22. https://koreaexpose.com/korea-thy-name-is-hell-joseon/.

Korea Financial Investment Association. 2015. "2015 금융투자 Fact Book." https://www. kofia.or.kr/brd/m_52/view.do?seq=221&srchFr=&srchTo=&srchWord=2015&src hTp=0&multi_itm_seq=0&itm_seq_1=0&itm_seq_2=0&company_cd=&company _nm=&page=1.

Korea Herald. 2016. "Korea's Income Inequality High in Asia: IMF Report." *Korea Herald*, March 16. https://www.koreaherald.com/view.php?ud=20160316000 905&ACE_SEARCH=1.

Kurutz, Steven. 2018. "How to Retire in Your 30s with $1 Million in the Bank." *New York Times*, September 1. https://www.nytimes.com/2018/09/01/style/fire-financial- independence-retire-early.html.

Kwon, Boduerae. 2008. "실존, 자유부인, 프래그머티즘: 1950년대의 두 가지 '자유' 개념과 문화." 한국문학연구 35:101–47.

Laclau, Ernesto, and Chantal Mouffe. 2001. *Hegemony and Socialist Strategy: Towards a Radical Democratic Politics*, 2nd edn. New York and London: Verso.

Lampel, Joseph, and Ajay Bhalla. 2007. "The Role of Status Seeking in Online Communities: Giving the Gift of Experience." *Journal of Computer-Mediated Communication* 12 (2): 434–55.

Langley, Paul. 2008. *The Everyday Life of Global Finance: Saving and Borrowing in Anglo-America*. New York: Oxford University Press.

Lapavitsas, Costas. 2013. *Profiting Without Producing: How Finance Exploits Us All*. London: Verso.

Lapavitsas, Costas. 2011. "Theorizing Financialization." *Work, Employment & Society* 25 (4): 611–26.

Lazzarato, Maurizio. 2012. *The Making of the Indebted Man: An Essay on the Neoliberal Condition*. Translated by Joshua David Jordan. Los Angeles: Semiotext.

Lazzarato, Maurizio. 2009. "Neoliberalism in Action: Inequality, Insecurity and the Reconstitution of the Social." *Theory, Culture & Society* 26 (6): 109–33.

LeBoeuf, Michael. 1999. 10년 안에 10억 벌기 (*The Perfect Business: How to Make a Million from Home with No Payroll, No Debts, No Employee Headaches, No Sleepless Nights!*). Translated by Seong Kim and Eunyeong Park. Seoul: Global Publisher.

Lee, Byoung-Hoon, and Eunae Kang. 2009. "임시직, 빈부격차 당연시. 시장만능의 포로, 한국인." *Kyunghyang Shinmun*, March 2. https://www.khan.co.kr/economy/economy-general/article/200903011756375.

Lee, Hyein. 2019. "34세 이하 미혼율, 한국이 일본 추월." *Kyunghyang Sinmun*, January 8. https://www.khan.co.kr/national/national-general/article/201901081557001.

Lee, JinSook, and Yun-Suk Lee. 2014. "비혼 1인가구의 사회적 관계: 여성과 남성의 교제활동 시간 비교를 중심으로." 한국인구학 37 (4): 1–24.

Lee, Jiyeun, and Sam Kim, 2020. "South Korea Unleashes New Property Curbs Amid Soaring Prices," *Bloomberg*, July 9. https://www.bloomberg.com/news/articles/2020-07-09/south-korea-tries-to-cool-home-prices-without-derailing-recovery.

Lee, Micky. 2014. "A Feminist Political Economic Critique of Women and Investment in the Popular Media." *Feminist Media Studies* 14 (2): 270–85.

Lee, Minyoung. 2019. "Escape from Hell-Joseon: A Study of Korean Long-term Travelers in India." *Korean Anthropology Review* 3 (February): 45–78.

Lee, Namhee. 2022. *Memory Construction and the Politics of Time in Neoliberal South Korea*. Durham. NC: Duke University Press.

Lee, Namhee. 2007. *The Making of Minjung: Democracy and the Politics of Representation in South Korea*. Ithaca and London: Cornell University Press.

Lee, Sangho. 2002. "재력가들." *Hankook Ilbo*, June 24.

Lee, Seung Cheol. 2022a. "Magical Capitalism, Gambler Subjects: South Korea's Bitcoin Investment Frenzy." *Cultural Studies* 36 (1): 96–119.

Lee, Seung Cheol. 2022b. "금융의 프랑스 혁명? 게임스탑 사태와 투자자 포퓰리즘의 등장." 문화연구 10 (1): 75–99.

Lee, Seung-Cheol. 2018. "The Social Life of Human Capital: The Rise of Social Economy, Entrepreneurial Subject, and Neosocial Government in South Korea." PhD diss., Columbia University.

Lee, Yoonkyung. 2011. *Militants or Partisans: Labor Unions and Democratic Politics in Korea and Taiwan*. Stanford: Stanford University Press.

Lingel, Jessa. 2017a. "Networked Field Studies: Comparative Inquiry and Online Communities." *Social Media + Society* October–December: 1–9.

Lingel, Jessa. 2017b. *Digital Countercultures and the Struggle for Community*. Cambridge, MA: The MIT Press.

LiPuma, Edward, and Benjamin Lee. 2004. *Financial Derivatives and the Globalization of Risk*. Durham, NC: Duke University Press.

Lukács, Gabriella. 2020. *Invisibility by Design: Women and Labor in Japan's Digital Economy*. Durham, NC: Duke University Press.

Maeil Business Newspaper. 2004. "10억 모으기 도와드립니다." March 31, https://www.mk.co.kr/news/all/3262962.

Maman, D., and Zeev Rosenhek. 2023. "Governing Individuals' Imaginaries and Conduct in Personal Finance: The Mobilization of Emotions in Financial Education." *Journal of Consumer Culture* 23 (1): 188–208.

Marcus, George. 2009. "Multi-sited Ethnography: Notes and Queries." In *Multi-Sited Ethnography: Theory, Praxis and Locality in Contemporary Research*, edited by Mark-Anthony Falzon, 181–96. Farnham, UK: Ashgate.

Marcus, George. 1998. *Ethnography Through Thick and Thin*. Princeton, NJ: Princeton University Press.

Martin, Chris. 2018. "Clever Odysseus: Narratives and Strategies of Rental Property Investor Subjectivity in Australia." *Housing Studies* 33 (7): 1060–84.

Martin, Randy. 2002. *Financialization of Daily Life*. Philadelphia: Temple University Press.

Marwick, Alice E. 2013. *Status Update: Celebrity, Publicity, and Branding in the Social Media Age*. New Haven, CT: Yale University Press.

McClanahan, Annie J. 2017. "Becoming Non-Economic: Human Capital Theory and Wendy Brown's *Undoing the Demos*." *Theory & Event* 20 (2): 510–19.

Miller, Daniel, Elisabetta Costa, Nell Haynes, Tom McDonald, Razvan Nicolescu, Jolynna Sinanan, Juliano Spyer, Shriram Venkatraman, and Xinyuan Wang. 2016. *How the World Changed Social Media*. London: UCL Press.

Ministry of Government Legislation. 2016. "소액보증금 우선변제." https://www.easylaw.go.kr/CSP/CnpClsMain.laf?popMenu=ov&csmSeq=629&ccfNo=5&cciNo=2&cnpClsNo=2.

Mitchell, Timothy. 1998. "Fixing the Economy." *Cultural Studies* 12 (1): 82–101.

Miyazaki, Hirokazu. 2013. *Arbitraging Japan*. Berkeley: University of California Press.

Moon, Hyejung, and Lee Hyunjin. 2013. "부동산 경매 온 국민의 리그: 꾼들, 먹을 게 없어졌다… 살림꾼들, 살 게 많아졌다." *The Korea Economic Daily*, October 18. https://www.hankyung.com/realestate/article/2013101832481.

Moulite, Maritza. 2018. "South Korea Cuts Its Work Limit from 68 Hours a Week to 52." *CNN*, July 2. https://www.cnn.com/2018/07/02/health/south-korea-work-hours/index.html.

Mulcahy, Niamh. 2017. "Entrepreneurial Subjectivity and the Political Economy of Daily Life in the Time of Finance." *European Journal of Social Theory* 20 (2): 216–35.

Nelson, Laura. 2022. "Single Women's Invisibility in South Korea's First Decades." In *Opting Out: Women Messing with Marriage around the World*, edited by J. Davidson and D. Hannaford, 74–86. Newark: Rutgers University Press.

Nelson, Laura. 2006. "South Korean Consumer Nationalism: Women, Children, Credit and Other Perils." In *The Ambivalent Consumer: Questioning Consumption in East Asia and the West*, edited by S. M. Garon and P. L. Maclachlan, 188–207. Ithaca, NY: Cornell University Press.

Nelson, Laura. 2000. *Measured Excess: Status, Gender, and Consumer Nationalism in South Korea*. New York: Columbia University Press.

Ock, Hyun-ju. 2015. "Koreans' Average Work Hours Still Second-longest in OECD." *Korea Herald*, November 2. http://www.koreaherald.com/view.php?ud=2015110 2001240.

Oh, Yunhyeon. 2003. "10억 만들기 왕도는 있다." *Sisa Journal*, August 26. http://www.sisajournal.com/news/articleView.html?idxno=77838.

Ono, Kent A., and John M. Sloop. 1995. "The Critique of Vernacular Discourse." *Communications Monographs* 62 (1): 19–46.

Orman, Suze. 2006. *The 9 Steps to Financial Freedom. Practical and Spiritual Steps So You Can Stop Working*. New York: Three Rivers Press.

Osburg, John. 2013. *Anxious Wealth: Money and Morality among China's New Rich*. Stanford: Stanford University Press.

Parish, Jessica. 2020. "Re-Wilding Parkdale? Environmental Gentrification, Settler Colonialism, and the Reconfiguration of Nature in 21st Century Toronto." *EPE: Nature and Space* 3 (1): 263–86.

Park, Daemin. 2014. "담론의 금융화: 서민주택담론으로 본 한국 금융통치성의 대두." PhD diss., Seoul National University.

Park, Gwangyeon, and Mirang Choi. 2020. "2020. 5%만 성공한다 해도… 노동보다 투자가 가성비 높다." *Kyunghyang Shinmun*, October 6. https://www.khan.co.kr/economy/economy-general/article/202010060600125.

Park, Ji Hyun, and Whang In Seong. 2018. "김제동의 톡투유, 걱정말아요 그대 (JTBC)에 드러난 힐링담론의 특성에 대한 비판적 고찰." 한국언론정보학보 89: 42–80.

Park, Jin Kyu. 2016. "'Healed to Imagine': Healing Discourse in Korean Popular Culture and Its Politics." *Culture and Religion* 17 (4): 375–91.

Park, Min-young. 2011. "Key to Wealth: Have You Tried Hard Enough?" *Korea Herald*, February 7. http://www.koreaherald.com/view.php?ud=20110131000793&mod=skb.

Park, Sanghyun. 1997. "(주)대우, 주택은행, 고려아연, 장롱 속 금 수집운동." *Yonhap News*, December 30. https://n.news.naver.com/mnews/article/001/0004212321?sid=101.

Park, So Jin. 2011. "Educational Manager Mothers as Neoliberal Maternal Subjects." In *New Millennium South Korea: Neoliberal Capitalism and Transnational Movements*, edited by Jesook Song, 101–14. New York: Routledge.

Peck, Janice. 1995. "TV Talk Shows as Therapeutic Discourse: The Ideological Labor of the Televised Talking Cure." *Communication Theory* 5 (1): 58–81.

Phillips, Matt. 2014. "It Takes $290,000 in Cash to Rent an Apartment in Seoul." *Quartz*, March 10. https://qz.com/183412/koreas-crazy-system-for-rentingapartments-is-driving-the-country-deeper-into-debt/.

Pink, Sarah, Heather Horst, John Postill, Larissa Hjorth, Tania Lewis, and Ja Tacchi, eds. 2016. *Digital Ethnography: Principles and Practices*. Thousand Oaks, CA: Sage.

Pitcher, Laura. 2021. "Squid Game & The Rise of Anti-Capitalist Entertainment." *Refinery29*, October 5. https://www.refinery29.com/en-us/squid-game-netflix-anticapitalist.

Preda, Alex 2009. *Framing Finance: The Boundaries of Markets and Modern Capitalism*. Chicago: The University of Chicago Press.

Prentice, Michael. 2022. *Supercorporate: Distinction and Participation in Post-Hierarchy South Korea*. Stanford: Stanford University Press.

Renninger, Bryce J. 2014. "'Where I Can Be Myself … Where I Can Speak My Mind': Networked Counterpublics in a Polymedia Environment." *New Media & Society* 17 (9): 1513–29.

Rheingold, Howard. 2000. *The Virtual Community: Homesteading on the Electronic Frontier*. Cambridge, MA: MIT Press.

Rimke, Heidi. 2017. "Self-Help Ideology." In *The SAGE Encyclopedia of Political Behavior*, edited by Fathali M. Moghaddam, 734–37. Thousand Oaks, CA: Sage.

Robbins, Anthony. 1991. *Awaken the Giant Within*. New York: Simon and Schuster.

Ronald, Richard, and S. Kyung. 2013. "Housing System Transformations in Japan and South Korea: Divergent Responses to Neo-Liberal Forces." *Journal of Contemporary Asia* 43 (3): 452–74.

Ronald, Richard, and Hyunjeong Lee. 2012. "Housing Policy Socialization and Decommodification in South Korea." *Journal of Housing and the Built Environment* 27 (2): 111–31.

Rose, Nikolas. 2004. *Powers of Freedom: Reframing Political Thought*. Cambridge: Cambridge University Press.

Rose, Nikolas. 1999. *Governing the Soul: Shaping of the Private Self*. London: Free Association Books.

Ruccio, David, ed. 2008. *Economic Representations: Academic and Everyday.* New York: Routledge.

Ryu, Hanso. 2012. "신자유주의적 위로, 치유문화." 문화과학 69: 206–13.

Santos, Mariana. 2021. "High Net-Worth Attachments: Emotional Labor, Relational Work, and Financial Subjectivities in Private Wealth Management." *Journal of Cultural Economy* 14 (6): 750–64.

Schaupp, Simon. 2016. "Measuring the Entrepreneur of Himself: Gendered Quantification in the Self-Tracking Discourse." In *Lifelogging. Digital Self-Tracking and Lifelogging: Between Disruptive Technology and Cultural Transformation*, edited by Stefan Selke, 249–66. Wiesbaden: Springer Fachmedien.

Seo, Donghan. 2016. "최근 주택경매시장 동향 및 주요 특징 분석." *KB Financial Group.* May 12. https://www.kbfg.com/kbresearch/report/reportView.do?reportId= 1003288.

Seo, Dongjin. 2011. "The Will to Self-Managing, The Will to Freedom: The Self-Managing Ethic and The Spirit of Flexible Capitalism in South Korea." In *New Millennium South Korea: Neoliberal Capitalism and Transnational Movements*, edited by Jesook Song, 84–100. New York: Routledge.

Seo, Dongjin. 2009. 자유의 의지, 자기계발의 의지. Paju: Dolbegae.

Shim, Bo-Seoun, 2013. "힐링이라는 이름의 권력." 문학과 사회 26 (2): 249–61.

Shim, Yeongcheol. 2003. 그냥 구질구질하게 살아라: 2030 샐러리맨의 10억 모으기. Seoul: Pampas.

Shim, Yunji. 2020. "나만 빼고 다 주식하나, 불안한 돈알못들에게." *Kyunghyang Shinmun*, October 21. https://www.khan.co.kr/national/national-general/article/ 202010210600001.

Shin, Hyun Bang. 2021. "Urban Transformation 'Korean Style': Lessons from Property-Based Urban Development." In *Exporting Urban Korea? Reconsidering the Korean Urban Development Experience*, edited by Se Hoon Park, Hyun Bang Shin, and Hyun Soo Kang, 58–80. New York: Routledge.

Shin, Hyun Bang. 2008. "Living on the Edge: Financing Post-Displacement Housing in Urban Redevelopment Projects in Seoul." *Environment and Urbanization* 20 (2): 411–26.

Shin, Hyun Bang, and Kim Soo-Hyun. 2016. "The Developmental State, Speculative Urbanization and the Politics of Displacement in Gentrifying Seoul." *Urban Studies* 53 (3): 540–59.

Shin, Jang-Sup, and Ha-Joon Chang, 2003. *Restructuring Korea Inc.* New York: Routledge.

Shin, Kwang-Yeong. 2017. "The Trajectory of Anti-Communism in South Korea." *Asian Journal of German and European Studies* 2 (1): 1–10. doi:10.1186/s40856-017-0015-4.

Singletary, Michelle. 2018. "3 Myths about This Early Retirement Movement." *Washington Post*, December 3. https://www.washingtonpost.com/business/2018/12/ 03/myths-about-this-early-retirement-movement/.

Skeggs, Beverley. 2009. "The Moral Economy of Person Production: The Class Relations of Self-Performance on 'Reality' Television." *Sociological Review* 57 (4): 626–44.

Smith, Kelly Anne. 2019. "The Forbes Guide to Fire." *Forbes*, July 24. https://www.forbes.com/advisor/retirement/the-forbes-guide-to-fire/.

Sohn, Nark-Koo. 2008. 부동산 계급 사회. Seoul: Humanitas.

Song, Hakjoo. 2013. "확정일자 받고도 7천만원 전세금 떼인 50대 남." *Money Today*, August 24. https://news.mt.co.kr/mtview.php?no=2013082113565099153.

Song, Jesook. 2014. *Living on Your Own: Single Women, Rental Housing, and Post-Revolutionary Affect in Contemporary South Korea*. Albany: State University of New York Press.

Song, Jesook, ed. 2011. *New Millennium South Korea: Neoliberal Capitalism and Transnational Movements*. New York: Routledge.

Song, Jesook. 2009. *South Koreans in the Debt Crisis: The Creation of a Neoliberal Welfare Society*. Durham, NC: Duke University Press.

Song, Jesook. 2007. "Venture Companies, Flexible Labor, and the New Intellectual: The Neoliberal Construction of Underemployed Youth in South Korea." *Journal of Youth Studies* 10 (3): 331–52.

Sosohagekeuge. 2020. "동학개미운동! 10조 매수, 개인투자자들의 혁명, 이번엔 다르다." *YouTube*, March 6. https://www.youtube.com/watch?v=p6HfV5020Tk&t=67s.

Souleles, Daniel, and Kristian Bondo Hansen. 2019. "Can They All Be 'Shit-Heads'? Learning to Be a Contrarian Investor." *Journal of Cultural Economy* 12 (6): 491–507.

Standing, Guy. 2017. *The Corruption of Capitalism: Why Rentiers Thrive and Work Does Not Pay*. London: Biteback Publishing.

Statista. 2024. "Annual Average Exchange Rate of the South Korean Won (KRW) to U.S. Dollar (USD) from 2000 to 2023." https://www.statista.com/statistics/647920/krw-usd-annual-exchange-rate/.

Stout, Noelle. 2016. "#Indebted: Disciplining the Moral Valence of Mortgage Debt Online." *Cultural Anthropology* 31 (1): 82–106.

Streeter, Thomas. 2015. "Steve Jobs, Romantic Individualism, and the Desire for Good Capitalism." *International Journal of Communication* 9 (December): 3106–24.

Stuelke, Patricia. 2021. *The Ruse of Repair: US Neoliberal Empire and the Turn from Critique*. Durham, NC: Duke University Press.

Taylor, Nick, and William Davies. 2021. "The Financialization of Anti-Capitalism? The Case of the 'Financial Independence Retire Early' Community." *Journal of Cultural Economy* 14 (6): 694–710.

Tergesen, Anne, and Veronica Dagher. 2018. "The New Retirement Plan: Save Almost Everything, Spend Virtually Nothing." *The Wall Street Journal*, November 3. https://www.wsj.com/articles/the-new-retirement-plan-save-almost-everything-spend-virtually-nothing-1541217688.

Terranova, Tiziana. 2000. "Free Labor: Producing Culture for the Digital Economy." *Social Text* 18 (2): 33–58.

Thompson, E. P. 1971. "The Moral Economy of the English Crowd in the Eighteenth Century." *Past & Present* 50: 76–136.

Thrift, Nigel. 2008. "The Material Practices of Glamor." *Journal of Cultural Economy* 1 (1): 9–23.

Urban, Hugh B. 2015. *Zorba the Buddha: Sex, Spirituality, and Capitalism in the Global Osho Movement.* Oakland: University of California Press.

Varnelis, Kazys, ed. 2008. *Networked Publics.* Cambridge, MA: MIT Press.

Van der Zwan, Natascha. 2014. "Making Sense of Financialization." *Socio-Economic Review* 12 (1): 99–129.

Velkova, Julia. 2016. "Open Cultural Production and the Online Gift Economy: The Case of Blender." *First Monday* 21 (10): DOI: 10.5210/fm.v21i10.6944.

Wilkis, Ariel. 2018. *The Moral Power of Money: Morality and Economy in the Life of the Poor.* Stanford: Stanford University Press.

Williams, Raymond. 1978. *Marxism and Literature.* Oxford: Oxford University Press.

Williams, Raymond. 1958[2014]. "Culture is Ordinary." In *Raymond Williams on Culture & Society: Essential Writings,* edited by Jim McGuigan, 1–18. London: Sage.

Woo, Jaeyeon. 2011. "Hot Tip in Korean Investing: Chanel." *The Wall Street Journal.* June 21. https://www.wsj.com/articles/BL-KRTB-1926.

Wosnitzer, Robert. 2014. "Desk, Firm, God, Country: Proprietary Trading and Speculative Ethos of Financialism." PhD diss., New York University.

Yang, Misti, and Christopher Lee Adamczyk. 2023. "Gamestop Investors as an Eng(r)aged Digital Public." *Javnost – The Public* 30 (3): 408–25. DOI: 10.1080/13183222.2023.2198935.

Yang, Myungji. 2019. "Shrewd Entrepreneurs or Immoral Speculators? Desires, Speculation, and Middle-class Housewives in South Korea, 1978–1996." In *Gender and Class in Contemporary South Korea: Intersectionality and Transnationality,* edited by Hae Yeon Choo, John Lie, and Laura C. Nelson, 37–61. Berkeley, CA: Institute of East Asian Studies, UC Berkeley.

Yang, Myungji. 2018. *From Miracle to Mirage: The Making and Unmaking of the Korean Middle Class, 1960–2015.* Ithaca, NY: Cornell University Press.

Yi, Jong-Hyun. 2015. *History of Korean Modern Retailing.* Leiden: Brill.

Yonhap News. 1998. "금모으기 운동 2백25t 수집… 외화 가득 18억 달러." *Yonhap News,* March 14. https://n.news.naver.com/mnews/article/001/0004374853?sid=102.

Yoon, Hyeong Jung. 2014. "인천 깡통 주택의 비극, 장애인 가장의 죽음." *Hankyoreh,* October 31. https://www.hani.co.kr/arti/economy/property/662437.html.

Yu, Byeong Lyul. 2002. "PB매니저들이 말하는 한국의 부자." *Hankook Ilbo,* September 16. https://www.hankookilbo.com/News/Read/200209160067817735.

Yum, Hae-Jin. 2016. "여성의 자기계발, 소명의 고안과 여성성의 잔여화." Issues in Feminism 16 (2): 215–65.

Zaloom, Caitlin. 2016. "The Evangelical Financial Ethic: Doubled Forms and The Search for God in The Economic World." *American Ethnologist* 43 (2): 325–38.

# Index